Henry Van Rensselaer S.J.

LIFE AND LETTERS

OF

HENRY VAN RENSSELAER

Priest of the Society of Jesus

BY THE

REV. EDWARD P. SPILLANE, S.J.

(Permissu Superiorum.)

FORDHAM UNIVERSITY PRESS
FORDHAM UNIVERSITY
NEW YORK
1908

To the Men
Followers, Penitents and Friends
of a Noble Priest
Who Spent his Life
In promoting their Spiritual Welfare
This Tribute
To Their Faithful " Father Van "
is
Respectfully Inscribed.

46141

Nihil Obstat:

REMIGIUS LAFORT, S.T.L.

Censor Deputatus.

Imprimatur:

JOANNES M. FARLEY

Archiepiscopus Neo-Eboracensis.

NEO-EBORACI,
   die 4 Octobris, 1908.

INTRODUCTORY.

A WORD of explanation as to the sources from which this life of Father Van Rensselaer has been drawn may not be amiss.

The story of the early history of the patroons is found in the Magazine of American History in an exhaustive paper on "The Van Rensselaer Manor," contributed by the editor, Martha J. Lamb. Further details have been gleaned from a carefully written article which appeared some years ago in the columns of the New York *Sun*.

The story of Father Van Rensselaer's conversion is told in an autobiographical sketch found among his papers after his death. This sketch is particularly valuable as revealing the inner workings of his soul, his habits of thought and temperament, the motives actuating his conduct, the long and arduous search for the truth, and the happiness with which his soul was filled when he found himself at last, as he says, "over the wall, and safe in the bosom of the One True Church."

It must not be forgotten, however, that the sketch was written a quarter of a century after most of the events recorded therein. It is unquestionably a faithful account of what happened at that time so far as memory served him. Due allowance, therefore, should be made for the disturbed condition of a mind at a period when it was going through most harrowing experiences; "for," to quote Cardinal Newman, "who can know himself, and the subtle influences which act upon him? and who can recollect, at the distance of twenty-five years, all that he once knew about his thoughts and his deeds, and that, during a portion of his life when even at the time his observation, whether of himself or of the external world, was less than before or after, by very reason of the perplexity and dismay which weighed upon him,—when, though it would be most unthankful to imply that he had not all-sufficient light amid his darkness, yet a darkness it emphatically was? " *

The autobiographical sketch was originally written in the first person and was reproduced verbatim in the pages of THE MESSENGER. As incorporated in this life, the form has been somewhat changed. Facts have been separated from opinions, the narration of events detached from the discussion of religion, in the belief that the logical processes which led to Father Van Rensselaer's conversion would stand out in bolder relief, and the sketch be more in keeping with the requirements of a biography. So the first person has been retained, as a rule, only when he describes his mental attitude. The letters from Oxford were an unexpected find. Father Van Rensselaer up to the day of his death never suspected their existence. The friend to whom they were written thought they had been destroyed, and discovered them only after a repeated and prolonged search. They will be found in almost every particular remarkably corroborative of the later narrative, and give very interesting information on the daily life of a student, and the character of the Dons at the University of Oxford. The portraits given of Dr. Liddon and Dr. King will be appreciated by those who are at all interested in the more recent history of Oxford. After the withdrawal of Newman from the classic halls of the University and from the historic pulpit

---

* Apologia, N. Y., 1865, p. 134.

of St. Mary's, Oxford might well be termed a City of Confusion, and these letters, though covering only the short period of a single year, give a very fair insight into the topsy-turvy condition of affairs prevailing there a generation later. In editing them, much had to be omitted, as it was of a character too personal for publication. Attention may well be called to the marvellous contrast prevailing between the letters from Oxford and those written after Father Van Rensselaer was received into the Church and enrolled among the members of the Society of Jesus. The same man speaks in both, but in the earlier ones he is harassed by doubt and misgivings, in the later his mind and heart are both at rest and in the possession of perfect peace.

The biographer has only a word to add. His work in piecing together the narrative has been a work of love. During twenty-eight years he knew Father Van Rensselaer intimately, and was associated with him as a student of philosophy and theology, as a professor in college, as a priest in the ministry. The reminiscences covering that period are for the most part personal, and on that account, it is hoped, will the better fill out the portrait of his friend, which is outlined in the autobiographical sketch and in the letters which appear in the volume. The writer makes grateful acknowledgement to the sister of Father Van Rensselaer, in religion Sister Dolores, for invaluable assistance by furnishing letters and biographical data; to Father Francis Mackall of Midland, Maryland, for the Oxford letters, and to Father Wynne and Father Campbell of THE MESSENGER staff.

EDWARD P. SPILLANE, S.J.

vii

CONTENTS.

LIST OF ILLUSTRATIONS.

CHAPTER I.

ANCESTRY AND FAMILY.

THE name of Van Rensselaer has always been a familiar one in the history of the Empire State. The family representative bore the ancient Dutch title of Patroon, and in the days of English ascendancy in America that of Lord of the Manor. Their titles fell into disuse during the Revolution, but their vast holdings in land remained until the middle of the nineteenth century, and their family and social distinction down to the present day.

The founder of the family in America was Kilian Van Rensselaer. He was born in 1595, and was a descendant of a long line of worthy citizens of Amsterdam. The manor from which the family took its name is still called Rensselaer, and is situated about three miles south-east of Nykerk in Holland. It was originally an estate the possession of which conferred nobility.

Kilian Van Rensselaer took an active part in the formation of the Dutch West India Company, furnishing the corporation with ships of his own and more than once advancing money to save its credit. He also sent an agent to trade with the Indians for land on the west side of the Hudson River from twelve miles south of Albany to Smacks Island, " stretching two days into the interior," and eventually effected the purchase of all the land on the east side of the river, both north and south of Fort Orange, and " far into the wilderness." This great feudal demesne, which, comprised the present counties of Albany, Columbia and Rens-

1

selaer, received the name of Rensselaerswyck. The estate was forty-eight miles long and twenty-four miles wide, while the Hudson divided it into two equal parts. It could not have been situated more advantageously, as the waters of the Hudson connected with the Atlantic and, through the Mohawk, with the great waterways of the North and West.

Van Rensselaer established his manor house at the confluence of the two rivers, a position which, at a time when the knowledge of the geography of America scarcely extended beyond its coastline, might have been justly looked upon as the key to the whole continent. Upon the territory once forming this great estate have since sprung up thriving towns and villages, and cities like Albany, Troy, Rensselaer and Schenectady.

Kilian Van Rensselaer sent over sturdy settlers with their families, servants and household goods. His colony grew and prospered, the soil was tilled, comfortable houses were built, schools and churches founded, and order and method established everywhere. He died in 1644. Strange to say, there is no record of his ever having visited America.

It would make interesting reading to follow the fortunes of the successive patroons who ruled over Rensselaerswyck. Few of them there were who did not leave an impression on the political, social or military history of their time.

Jan Baptist Van Rensselaer, the third patroon, was a half brother of his predecessor, Johannes. The latter had once or twice visited his great possessions in New York, but he, too, for the most part resided in Holland. In 1658 Jan Baptist also returned to Holland, where he ended his days.

Conspicuous in the family was a clergyman, the Rev. Nicholaus Van Rensselaer, the eighth child of the first patroon and brother of the second. He had been licensed by

2

Charles I to preach in the Dutch Church at Westminster, and, recommended by James, Duke of York, he came to New York to fill one of the Dutch pulpits in the Province. The dominie died in Albany, and his widow married Robert Livingston, the founder of the Livingston family in America.

Jeremias, the next Director of Rensselaerswyck, and brother to Jan Baptist, was deservedly popular for his prudent management of affairs during sixteen years. He acquired great influence among the Indians and won the respect of the French in Canada. His correspondence, which is still extant, evinces no little native talent as well as enormous industry. His autograph is remarkable for its beauty and is one of the most characteristic to be found in the records of the century. He was President of the Landtag, or Diet, which five months before the surrender of the province to the English had been summoned to New York to discuss the affairs of the colony. When the English came into possession of New York, he declined to cede to the new government the town of Albany, which he claimed as a part of Rensselaerswyck. After protracted negotiation, Governor Dongan in person visited the patroon, and obtained from him a formal concession of his feudal right over the miniature capital of the future State, along with sixteen miles of territory extending into the country westward. In the following year, 1686, Albany was incorporated as a city.

Jeremias' wife was a daughter of Oloff Stevenson Van Courtlandt, the first of the family of that name in New York; their daughter, Maria Van Rensselaer, married Peter Schuyler, the first Mayor of Albany.

Stephen Van Rensselaer III, the last of the patroons, and

3

perhaps the most distinguished in that long line of distinguished men, was destined to bridge the chasm which existed between two opposite political systems. Born in 1764, the subject of a King and the scion of a feudal aristocracy, with immense inherited estates and chartered baronial rights, he favored from the first the new political system in America, and was one of the staunchest upholders of popular sovereignty. His father having died, he was educated by his grandfather, Philip Livingston, who was one of the signers of the Declaration of Independence. In due course he was graduated from Harvard with high honors. Before he was of age, he married Margaret, the daughter of General Philip Schuyler, thus transmitting to his posterity the blood of five of the great Colonial families, Schuyler, Livingston, Van Courtlandt, Ten Broek, and Van Rensselaer. After his graduation, he kept up his studies and personally managed his large estates. In the period succeeding the Revolutionary War, no man in the State carried with him greater personal influence. He was a friend of Washington, and was successively a member of the Assembly and of the State Senate, as well as twice Lieutenant Governor of the State, when John Jay was Governor. In the war of 1812, when Governor Tompkins summoned the State Militia into immediate service, Van Rensselaer was appointed to take chief command; nor did he hesitate to leave his luxurious home and march to the frontier with the utmost dispatch. Among his officers were many of his kinsmen, notably Colonel Solomon Van Rensselaer, who was wounded at the battle of Queenstown Heights.

After the war Stephen Van Rensselaer entered heart and soul into every project which he considered advantageous to the State. He declared his willingness to construct, at his own expense, the whole of the Erie Canal, so confident was he of the feasibility of the enterprise. He was a member of Congress from 1822 to 1829, and cast the deciding vote in the election of John Quincy Adams to the Presidency of the Republic. During all these years he was Regent of the University of the State, and subsequently became its Chancellor.

His wife dying, he married again, his second wife being Cornelia Paterson, daughter of Judge William Paterson, of the Supreme Court, who was also Governor of New Jersey.

In 1824 he established, and in 1826 incorporated, the first scientific school in the New World, and he defrayed fully one-half its current expenses. His own words, which he put in the charter, show how far he was ahead of the times: " A school to qualify teachers to instruct in the application of experimental chemistry, philosophy and natural history, to agriculture, domestic economy and to the arts and manufactures." This school, now known as the Rensselaer Polytechnic Institute of Troy, will always be a memorial to the philanthropy, far-sightedness, and statesmanship of its founder. In 1825, Yale conferred upon him the degree of LL.D.

Stephen Van Rensselaer III left twelve children, three by his first and nine by his second wife. Of these, Stephen Van Rensselaer IV, usually referred to as the Young Patroon, was the eldest. To him had descended the bulk of the great Van Rensselaer estate or plantation, and by him, through political causes, it was dissipated forever. Although his father was legally the last of the patroons, yet the people of his time, by common consent, gave him that title, and as such he will go down to history.

The father of the future Rev. Henry Van Rensselaer was General Henry Van Rensselaer, brother of Stephen IV, and fifth son of Stephen III. He, too, holds a distinguished place in the civil and military history of his time. A graduate of West Point in 1827, he served later as lieutenant in the United States Army. In 1841 he was sent to Congress, and during the Civil War he held the rank of Colonel while Chief of Staff to General Scott, upon whose retirement, in November, 1861, he was made Inspector General of the United States Army. He died of typhoid fever just before the close of the war. The following sketch appeared in a New York paper shortly after his death:—

" Colonel Henry Van Rensselaer, Inspector General of the United States Army, died on Wednesday, March 23d, of typhoid fever, at Cincinnati, where he was stationed.

" Colonel Van Rensselaer was graduated from the Military Academy at West Point in 1831, having passed through the four years' discipline of that school without incurring a single demerit. This fact indicates the character of the man—an ever-present sense of duty, which would not permit the neglect of an obligation once assumed. Though young when entering the Academy, he formed and held resolutely to the purpose of complying in all respects, as far as possible, with its requirements. The writer dwells the more upon this rare trait of character, for that he had a son at the Military Academy at the time, whose good fortune it was to become the room-mate of Colonel Van Rensselaer, and who there acquired from his example that love of order, that diligence of application, that fidelity to the most minute as well as the more important details of duty, which go so far to make up the character of a useful and trustworthy man, whether soldier or citizen. Mr. Van Rensselaer did not remain long in the Army, and having married in 1833, a daughter of Hon. J. A. King, of Jamaica, L. I., he went to take possession of a patrimonial landed estate in St. Lawrence County, where he spent many years in the active pursuits of agriculture, and dispensing a liberal and elegant hospitality.

" In 1841 he was elected a member of the House of Representatives from his district, and served with his accustomed punctuality and diligence through the three sessions of the 27th Congress. Political life, however, had few attractions for him, and he returned willingly to his home and his accustomed occupations.

" For some years past, however, and as his family grew up, Mr. Van Rensselaer had been an inhabitant of this city, where the outbreak of the Rebellion found him in quiet and retired private life. But when the Rebel cannon against Fort Sumter aroused our Northern blood and national fidelity, true to his early training as a soldier, and to his instincts as a patriot, he at once wrote to General Scott, then in command of our forces, to ask for an opportunity, as a soldier educated by the Nation, to strike a blow for the national cause. The General immediately sent for him to Washington, took him into his military family, and with the rank of Brigadier-General, made him chief of his staff.

" Of this position he faithfully and intelligently discharged the duties until the relinquishment by General Scott, under the pressure of physical infirmities, of his high command. Upon the recommendation of his General, however, the commission of Inspector-General in the regular Army, with the rank of Colonel, was at once conferred by the President upon Colonel Van Rensselaer. In the duties of that

7

post he has ever since been assiduously engaged, and to them he, in fact, yielded up his life—refusing, though laboring under illness, to ask for a furlough—while the official calls upon him were urgent.

"The insidious disease made rapid progress. Informed of his serious illness—yet not apprehending imminent danger, his wife and daughter hurried to Cincinnati, but only had the consolation of ministering by his dying bed.

"He was aware of his approaching death, and prepared for it as a Christian soldier. In his last delirious moments his mind still ran upon his public duties—upon the condition of the troops—upon the progress of the war—and he died in the cause of his country, an earnest and unblemished soldier."

A summary of his life and services, in Father Van Rensselaer's handwriting, is preserved among the family papers. It reads like a page taken from the records of the Military Academy at West Point.

U. S. MILITARY ACADEMY.

NUMBER   CLASS RANK

648. Born N. Y. Henry Van Rensselaer. Ap'd N. Y. 20

Military History.—Cadet at the U. S. Military Academy, from July 1, 1827, to July 1, 1831, when he was graduated and promoted in the Army to

Bvt. Second Lieut., 5th Infantry, July 1, 1831. On leave of absence July 1, 1831, to Jan. 27, 1832.

Resigned Jan. 27, 1832.

Civil History.—Farmer, near Ogdensburg, N. Y., 1834-55. Aide-de-Camp with the rank of Colonel to Governor Seward, of New York, 1839-40.

COL. HENRY VAN RENSSELAER

Member of the U. S. House of Representatives, from the State of New York, 1841-43.

President of the American Mineral Company—of the Port Henry Iron Ore Company—and of the Consolidated Franklinite Company, 1855-60.

Military History.—Served during the Rebellion of the Seceding States, 1861-64: as Volunteer Aide-de-Camp, with the rank of Colonel, April 29 to Aug. 5, 1861, and as Regular Aide-de-Camp, Aug. 5, 1861, to Nov. 1, 1861.

(Col. Staff—Aide-de-Camp to the General-in-Chief, Aug. 5, 1861.)

Bvt. Lieut., General Scott, General-in-Chief, at the Headquarters of the Army, Washington, D. C.; on leave of absence and awaiting orders, Nov. 12.

(Colonel Staff—Inspector General, Nov. 12, 1861.)

1861, to Mar. 20, 1862—as Inspector General, 1st Army Corps.

Mar. 20 to Apl. 4, 1862—Department of the Rappahannock.

Apl. 4, to Aug. 12, 1862—3d Army Corps, Aug. 12 to Sept. 6, 1862, and Department of the Ohio, Sept. 17, 1862, to Mar. 23, 1864.

Died Mar. 23, 1864, at Cincinnati, O. Aged 54.

Among the family treasures is an autograph letter addressed by General Scott on his retirement from the Army to his Chief of Staff. It reads as follows:

" Adieu, my dear Colonel Van Rensselaer. No General has ever had greater cause to be proud of his staff than I have had in you and my other dear friends, Colonels Townsend, Hamilton, Cullen and Wright—all dear friends.

" Nov. 9, 1861. WINFIELD SCOTT."

9.

If he was beholden to his father for his name, and for the prestige which, even in America, despite the open profession of democracy, attaches to descent from one of the great Colonial families, Father Van Rensselaer was under still greater indebtedness to his mother, Elizabeth King Van Rensselaer, for the kindly traits which were so characteristic of him from his earliest years, and which became more manifest in his apostolic work as a priest when he was brought into contact with the poverty-stricken and the unfortunate.

The founder of the King family in America, John King, came from Kent, England, and settled in Boston in 1700. Later the family moved to Scarborough, Maine, where Father Van Rensselaer's great grandfather was born in 1755. Graduating from Harvard in 1777, he studied law and was admitted to the bar in 1784. He was elected to the Continental Congress and took a prominent part in the convention which in 1787 framed the Constitution of the United States. While in New York he married Mary Alsop, the only daughter of a prominent New York merchant, and for his wife's sake determined to live near her father.

He became a Senator of the United States in 1789, the first Senator elected from the State of New York, was re-elected in 1795, and in the following year was by President Washington appointed Minister Plenipotentiary to Great Britain.

Besides the distinction of being three times elected to the Senate of the United States, and being twice appointed as Minister to England, he was at various times the candidate of his party for the Governorship of New York, as well as for the Vice-Presidency and Presidency of the Nation; and although he failed of election to these high offices he was always regarded as one of the ablest statesmen and diplomats of his time.

John Alsop King, eldest son of Rufus, and grandfather of Henry Van Rensselaer, was a native of New York City, where he was born in 1788. During his youth he accompanied his father to England when the latter was Minister to the Court of St. James, and while there attended school at Harrow. Among his schoolmates were his brother Charles, afterwards president of Columbia College, New York, Lord Byron, Sir Robert Peel and other men of prominence.

He held the rank of Lieutenant during the war of 1812, and in 1825 was Secretary of Legation at London under his father. He was several times elected to the State Legislature, was a member of Congress in 1849-51, and Governor of the State in 1857-59. At the expiration of his term, he returned to his home, in the village of Jamaica, Long Island, where he died July 8, 1867, in his 80th year. John King filled these many official positions with credit to himself and honor to his country, and during his long career never failed to present to his fellow citizens, alike in his public and private life, a rare example of benevolence and manly virtue.

CHAPTER II.

Boyhood and Early Life.

HENRY VAN RENSSELAER, the future Jesuit, youngest but one of ten children, was born at Woodford, near Ogdensburg, October 21, 1851. His mother, Elizabeth Ray King, was the daughter of the Governor King mentioned in the last chapter. His father, General Van Rensselaer, was the fifth son of the last patroon, Stephen III, who by his will divided the vast estate among his children, bequeathing to the eldest, Stephen IV, the manor on the Albany side of the Hudson, and to the fifth the wild lands in St. Lawrence County on the river of that name.

In this remote domain were valuable farm lands in the townships of Lisbon, Canton, etc., and the county seat, Woodford, which was on high ground overlooking the river. There was a large old-fashioned garden, with greenhouses, graperies and an extensive farm. The old colonial house had been enlarged shortly before Henry's birth, and a billiard room and a ballroom were added for the entertainment of summer guests and of the townspeople, who were always welcome visitors to the Van Rensselaer homestead. It was an ideal home, and above all a Christian home, where each day was opened with family prayers, and Sunday was honored with the strictest observance. Mrs. Van Rensselaer was the Lady Bountiful of the neighborhood, ever ready to listen to and relieve the wants of the poor. Indeed, during her entire life, even when it was no longer in her power to give generously, she never permitted a poor person to be sent unaided from her door. This tender love for God's poor, inherited from her, was a most striking trait in the priestly career of her Jesuit son.

Mrs. Van Rensselaer's responsibility in rearing her large family was lightened by the devoted assistance of a nurse who entered her service in 1843 and remained a valued member of the household until her death in 1899. Monica Chapman was an Englishwoman of great native refinement. A devout Catholic, she never, by any attempt to influence the faith of her children, betrayed the perfect trust reposed in her by her Protestant mistress. She held each in her arms when they were presented for baptism in the Protestant Episcopal Church, and was faithful in seeing that they recited morning and evening the little prayers taught them by their mother. In after years, when he had found the true faith and was enrolled as a member of the Society of Jesus, Father Van Rensselaer, in conversation with intimate friends, would frequently speak of Monica, her piety, her devout recital of the Rosary and the religious influence she exercised, albeit unwittingly, in the family. He had no hesitation in ascribing to her prayers and to her example the special grace which led him eventually to seek refuge in the true fold.

When the family moved to New York City, Monica became a member of St. Francis Xavier's parish, where, forty-four years later, her Requiem Mass was sung by the one of her charges who had been most dear to her, and for whose conversion many Masses and prayers had been offered in that church. Before giving the absolution, Father Van Rensselaer paid a touching tribute to the virtue and fidelity of his beloved nurse.

13

When he was four years old, the family came to New York City to pass the winter months. Shortly after their departure from Woodford their country home was destroyed by fire, and was never rebuilt. His childhood was uneventful, except that in addition to the usual diseases of children, he had an attack of scarlet fever which threatened his life and left him of a rather nervous temperament and delicate constitution.

When he was twelve years old his father died. To this calamity were added serious financial reverses owing to mismanagement or dishonesty on the part of a trusted agent, and it became incumbent upon the boys of the family to provide for their own temporal welfare as well as for that of those dependent upon them. Henry had received his early education at the Charlier Institute, and entered Columbia College in 1867; he did not remain to graduate, but took a clerical position in the Bank of Commerce in 1869.

He was of a religious turn of mind, and from his tenderest years felt an attraction for church services.

"As a boy," he says, "I attended Grace Church, then, as now, very fashionable. But in those days it was of the extremely Low Church type. The service was dull, except for the singing by a celebrated quartet. The minister, arrayed in black silk gown and Geneva bands, preached, in an almost unintelligible voice, ponderous and somnolent sermons, duly read from a manuscript. In my teens I longed for a more active part in the service, and was attracted to the Church of the Holy Communion, founded by Dr. Muhlenberg, where there was a choir of men and boys to lead the singing, in which the whole congregation took part. It had the name, in consequence, of being ' High,' but there was not much advance in doctrine. True, there was an early

HENRY VAN RENSSELAER IN BOYHOOD

Communion service, but it was rather for convenience than for high teaching. However, I was on the rise and began the practice of bowing the head at the *Gloria Patri,* and then of kneeling in the Nicene Creed at the *Incarnatus.* I remember distinctly that those who did so were publicly rebuked one Christmas morning by Dr. Muhlenberg for bowing at the doxology, and we were bidden not to bend like bulrushes, but to hold our heads erect. My first notice of candles on an altar was in this church. They were used for light at the early morning celebration, and once a year, on the feast of the Epiphany, at the evening missionary service, there were thirty-nine candles lighted in honor of the thirty-nine articles of religion, which the ritualists slightingly called the forty stripes save one mentioned by St. Paul. In this church I was confirmed, and of it I was a member for over ten years. Then I began to feel the need of something more Catholic. The doctrines preached in Trinity parish, especially at Trinity Church and Trinity Chapel, were in those days considered high. The Rector, at that time a celibate, was an advocate of celibacy and virginity. The music was from Catholic sources, and Masses by celebrated composers were adapted to the Communion service. Great stress was laid on the teaching of the undivided Church and of the four Ecumenical Councils.

" The first ritualistic church in New York was St. Alban's. The naming of it was significant. It was meant to insinuate the continuity with the ancient British Church, of which St. Alban was the first martyr. Moreover its namesake in London had been the leader in ritualism and the storm-centre of opposition of the officials of the State Church.

" St. Alban's on this side of the water was an exact imitation of a Catholic Church. The minister dubbed himself

15

' father ' and donned the habiliments of a priest. It was a novelty, and sightseers frequented the services. The Church of St. Mary the Virgin was the next to follow suit, and offered all the attractions of Rome without being Roman. St. Ignatius' was the next in the field, with rival novelties from Rome. These were full-blown ritualistic churches. There were others tending upward—an unintentional tribute to the true Church, any tendency to which is truly described as *becoming high*.

" But ritualism had as yet no charm for me, and I recall my disgust at a visit to the Oratory of the Blessed Sacrament, which had been opened by an English clergyman of the advanced type, who later became a convert and a priest. Nor had St. Alban's any attractive power, and attendance at one service sufficed for me; neither could I abide St. Mary the Virgin's."

CHAPTER III.

General Theological Seminary, New York.

I T had always been the wish of his family that Henry should be clergyman, but, as we have said, the family circumstances had to be considered. So, on leaving college, he went into business. This was not his calling, though he persevered in it for several years. After this, however, he announced his intention of going to the seminary. It was in the autumn of 1873 that he took up his residence in one of the old granite buildings in the grounds of the General Theological Seminary at Chelsea Square. Here he found a wide divergence of views and practices among the professors and students alike. The following is his account of the conditions then existing in the seminary:—

"There were at that time seventy seminarians, and, I think, six professors. Both professors and seminarians represented every shade of belief tolerated by that most elastic of sects. The Dean, who was professor of Ecclesiastical *Seymour* History, passed for a very advanced churchman. The professor of Dogmatic Theology was high and dry. The professor of New Testament Exegesis was safely high. The professor of Hebrew hobnobbed with Ritualists. The professor of Canon Law was a moderate churchman of the dry *Seabury* type, while the professor of Pastoral Theology was an old-*Eigenbrodt* fashioned low churchman, dry as dust. Could a more composite set of churchmen be imagined? A truly 'happy family' collection."

The seminarians presented the same pleasing variety of

religious opinions. No two agreed exactly, and why should they agree when their instructors set the example of disagreeing? After all, was it not the logical Protestant position, the exercise of the claimed inherent right of private judgment? Naturally he was at once called upon to declare his own views; and he was ranked among the very high churchmen. "But," he says, "I could not go all the lengths to which a few went. Excessive bowing of the head, crooking of the knees, and signs of the cross, extravagant in size, seemed to me too conspicuous. The ultra-high churchmen affected the wearing of a clerical vest with neither opening or buttons down the front, which was yclept the 'mark of the Beast,' and was supposed to be intensely Roman. Strange to say, no 'Roman' priest was ever known to wear a waistcoat so constructed. Another very Romanizing sign was to pronounce amen, 'ahmen,' though such a pronunciation is unknown to the real Roman except in Latin."

He narrates with some detail the daily life in the Seminary:—

"As I had a rather large room with two smaller ones off it, I took one of the smaller rooms for an oratory. The other small one was a bedroom and the large one a study. The oratory was simplicity itself, for its furniture was a priedieu before a statuette of the Good Shepherd, on either side of which was a candlestick, holding candles to be lighted for devotions. To this oratory a few choice spirits resorted occasionally after class and at night. I had not yet advanced sufficiently to have a crucifix.

"The students took their meals in common, and I shall never forget the day when, at dinner, the news was circulated that the Rector of Trinity Church, the advocate and model of celibacy, was engaged to be married. And what made it worse was that the lady was a Presbyterian! Imagine the shock to the admirers of celibacy! It was said that a religious congregation of women, of which he had been the confessor and a great friend, had, in their indignation, turned his portrait with its face to the wall. The idol was found to be only flesh and blood. The effect of the defection of the leader was diverse. Some students changed their minds like him, and declared that they had given up the intention of being celibates. Others said, 'I told you so'; while still others, of whom I was one, remained faithful to their conviction that the unmarried clergyman, having no family to divide his attention, could give an undivided service to God and the flock committed to his care. Perhaps, with a view of encouraging matrimony among the seminarians, there were soirées at the Dean's house, where susceptible and unwary youths might lose their hearts, and where, in fact, the fate of several was thus settled in favor of the married state."

If so much latitude in doctrine is allowed to the various divisions that make up the Episcopalian body without imperiling their orthodoxy, it will be interesting to know what questions are asked and what answers must be given that a student may acquit himself with credit before an examining board. Van Rensselaer lets the cat out of the bag.

"Examinations were a curious thing at the seminary. The examiners adapted themselves marvelously to the examined. Every candidate's grade of churchmanship was pretty well known to the examiners, who dexterously put questions suitable to the religious convictions of those examined. No matter how unorthodox a man might be, the very obliging examiners were careful to avoid the crucial questions and to elicit only statements that would not shock

19

the broad sensibilities of the examining board and students present."

One of the events of seminary life he recalls was the occasional visit of a Cowley Father from Boston to hear confessions; and Van Rensselaer was one of the confessed. The acquaintance thus made with the mysterious visitor, who came in cassock, cloak and broad hat, had an important influence on his after life.

Though a pronounced high churchman himself, his particular friends were taken from all grades of churchmanship. "One of them was really a rationalist, but a charming man. One, now a bishop, was low church, while another, also a bishop, was broad. Two others were very high, while still another was evangelical." Yet withal, in spite of theological differences of opinion, they were very good friends.

During the summer vacation in his first year he made a trip to Europe, which tended to broaden his views considerably. "According to the theory generally accepted by us," he says, "it was positively wrong for Anglicans to attend 'Roman' services in English-speaking countries, so in England I visited only churches of the Established Religion. As this rule did not hold for the continent, I felt no compunction in going to the celebrated Catholic churches, although I was particular in being present at service in the American chapels, however bald and cold that service was, and baldness and coldness were the prevalent qualities."

Although only a seminarian, he had very decided ideas about the propriety of clergymen going to the opera and theatre, and as he had assumed the clerical collar, he considered himself a cleric. His principle in this regard was put to a severe test at Munich. A monster Wagner festival was being held, and he loved music. His inclination was in favor of going, he was urged by fellow-travellers to go, but he made the sacrifice and did not go. In Paris he had met several of the seminarians who were " doing " the sights, as they told him they had just been " doing " London. He expostulated. They defended themselves on the plea of gaining experience for future use in the ministry. " Pitch," he said, " would leave its mark and what was unbecoming in New York could not be becoming in Paris and London. They went their way, and I went mine."

He could not help contrasting the cathedrals, still sacred to Catholic worship on the continent, with those shorn of their ancient glory in England and Scotland. " Notre Dame of Paris and the Dom of Cologne," he writes, " were instinct with devotion, and the most inspiring music I ever heard was that of a vast congregation at Mass one Sunday in the Cologne Cathedral. My blood boiled at the desecration of the historic Cathedral at Basle and its tenure by Calvinists, just as it had boiled in poor St. Giles' in Edinburgh, divided in two for two Protestant sects—Presbyterian and Episcopalian."

The extensive trip through Europe enabled him to cultivate his taste for the fine arts by studying the world's masterpieces, stored in the great museums and galleries. He journeyed all the way to Dresden, solely to gaze upon Raphael's chef-d'œuvre, the Sistine Madonna, and he felt that, even had there been no other treasures of art in that wonderful collection, it was well worth the journey. What impressed him in all the great collections was the preponderance of subjects taken from the lives of Christ, His mother, and the saints. " What a superb testimony," he mused, " to the faith of the Catholic world before the great

21

revolt of the sixteenth century, which cast a blight for so long on Christian art, from which it has only in the last century partially recovered!"

In spite of warnings not to venture further south in Italy than Venice and Florence in early September, he decided to risk it. He made a hurried trip to Rome and even to Naples. *"Multum in parvo,"* he says, " would describe the amount of sightseeing I accomplished in a minimum of time. I realized that it was dangerous to rush about *à l'americaine,* but then it might be my only chance, though I did not neglect to throw a coin in the famous fountain of Trevi, which is supposed to ensure a return to the Eternal City, which in my case proved true. I recall perfectly one night, when I had that day dared Providence by going from the heat of the streets to the chill of buildings for hours, that I felt in danger of the fever, and for the first time made the sign of the cross with a prayer for safety. With that start the holy sign of our salvation became a familiar action. I can honestly say, however, that I had not the least attraction to Catholicism, as such, at that time. But undoubtedly the leaven was working. I know that I was disgusted with a cicerone who, to ingratiate himself, spoke slightingly of his religion."

" The motive of my European trip," he admits, " was rather artistic than religious, and so the art galleries claimed my chief attention, though, as I have already said, the world's most famous pictures portray the great mysteries of our faith and insensibly awaken our religious emotions."

While at Florence he had failed to visit the convent of San Marco, where Fra Angelico had exercised his matchless art in limning on the walls of the cells those ethereal spirits of another world in their ministry to the Incarnate Word and

His mother. He resolved at Naples to make good this omission, and returned to Florence via Leghorn and Pisa on a flying visit. He considered himself well repaid by the sight of the angelic brother's exquisite productions.

He was much annoyed at Turin to find the banks closed on a weekday that was not on the Protestant Episcopal calendar as a feast-day. It was the 8th of September, the Nativity of the Blessed Virgin Mary, and a holy day of obligation at that time in Italy. His funds were low, and he had expected to draw on his letter of credit at the bank. His time was very limited, as he had to return to America towards the end of the month. Fortunately there were at the hotel some very genial English officers, returning from India, who, on hearing of his plight, volunteered to advance him, though he was a perfect stranger to them, all the money he needed. When he reached London he failed to meet these true friends in need, but acquitted himself of his obligation to them.

All good things come to an end, and so did the trip to Europe. Seminary life was resumed. Henry's ideas had broadened, but he was not conscious of any trend Romeward. The second year was uneventful. " The various professors," he says, " still taught their varied doctrines, and the students still drew their own conclusions. The professor of ecclesiastical history enlightened us on St. Patrick's day with a lengthy disquisition to prove that St. Patrick, besides being a gentleman, was a Protestant and—an Anglican ! "

CHAPTER IV.

Germany and Oxford.

AT the close of the second year, our young seminarian grew tired of the very prosaic life at the seminary and resolved to spend the third year of preparation for holy orders in the University City of Oxford. For this he had to obtain leave from the Bishop, the Right Rev. Horatio Potter. Although he was an old personal friend of the Van Rensselaer family, he did not favor the project, but for lack of authority could not forbid it. Henry speaks amusingly of his visit to the Bishop on this occasion, though it ended rather awkwardly for the visitor. "The Bishop," he says, "was extremely tall, very thin and rather severe looking. According to my advanced schooling, the correct thing on taking leave of your Bishop was to kneel and ask his blessing, since there was no ring to kiss. The Bishop lived in an English basement house, and he received me on the second floor. My leave-taking was at the head of the staircase, and I narrowly escaped being helped down the flight when I knelt for the blessing. I then and there resolved to choose a safe place before again asking an episcopal blessing."

Henry carried out his intention and sailed in June, 1875, for Europe. One of his fellow-students, who had formed the same plan as himself, preceded him by a couple of weeks. Their rendezvous was to be in Hanover, where they were to study German during the vacation.

"My landing in Holland, the country of my forefathers, will never be forgotten. It is usual to uncover one's head

24

in token of respect. In this instance I was spared the act, as shortly before landing at Rotterdam my only hat disappeared from the cabin table, on which I had confidingly placed it. Perhaps it was taken as an American curio. The result was extremely embarrassing to me and entirely marred my first impression of the land of my forefathers. So disheartened was I, that I took the first train to Hanover, where my friend awaited me.

"He had secured board and lodging in the family of an ex-Hanoverian major, who, in consequence, was a cordial hater of the usurping king of Prussia and a most loyal adherent of the old blind ex-king. The household consisted of the major, his wife and daughter, a forward damsel of sixteen. We were really overpowered with their constant attention. And the German cooking! No disputing about tastes! We made progress in learning German, but at what costs! We were always *en famille*. We could not stir out of doors, unless accompanied, usually by the three. We had to resort to artifices. Sunday we declared exempt from company, as we had religious scruples on the subject. Then we discovered that there were two concert gardens, both highgrade. They recommended the Odeon and accompanied us there. In an unwary moment they disclosed the fact that the rival Tivoli was the resort of the hated Prussian garrison officers, and consequently was tabooed by all loyal Hanoverians. This threw the extra weight in the scale of Tivoli. We decided that the music at Tivoli was superior, and we forsook the Odeon and were freed from the company of the family on those evenings at least. The goodnatured, motherly, fat Frau Majorin Candau got us a terrible scolding from the Herr Major for once, in our simplicity. speaking of her to him as the Majorin without prefixing

Frau. I was a great lover of flowering plants. She had placed some flower-pots on our window-sill. Now the window was in the third story, and, though in Germany, it was a French window. One day, when the wind was high, we went out for a walk and left the window open. When we returned, our reception was frigid in the extreme. The chill was caused by the blowing down of a flower-pot, for which we were held guilty. When it occurred, shortly after, a second time, our guilt was so evident, and our malice so prepense, that for a while they would not speak to us. We went out and bought a beautiful china jardinière with lovely growing flowers. The peace-offering was accepted with profuse expressions of admiration for the gift and astonishment at our extravagance. However, we were tired of the uncertain temper of the toothless major, whose toothsome Hamburger steak was sometimes surreptitiously taken by us at table, instead of the tougher meat served on the same dish. We were tired of the pert Fräulein Mollie; tired even of the kind-hearted, but oppressive Majorin; but above all, tired of the irascible major. We decided that a trip to Berlin, Dresden, the Saxon Switzerland, Baden-Baden and other places of interest would be preferable to a longer sojourn in Hanover—the dullest of dull towns, although its inhabitants claim the purest pronunciation of German."

The summer on the Continent helped to moderate the decidedly puritanical views Van Rensselaer had entertained on the subject of Sunday observance. He had been brought up in the most rigid manner. As a child no toys, or playthings, or games, and no secular story books or music were ever allowed. The day was devoted to church-going, catechism, learning texts and chapters of the Bible, reading goody-goody books and singing hymns. It would have been considered an awful breach to sing a ballad or read a novel, however standard it might be. Amusements of all kinds were prohibited. Baseball or sports of athletic nature were under the ban. " Imagine," he says, " what a contrast to all this a ' Continental ' Sunday is! I was not converted to the latter, but an impression was made less antipathetic."

It so happened that during his stay in Germany the last of the conferences at Bonn on the Rhine was about to be held. It was a chance, and he embraced it. We cannot help being grateful for the interesting though brief account given by the observant American:

" There were present representatives of the Church of England, the Protestant Episcopal Church, the Lutherans, Old Catholics and Greeks—a motley collection. The language at the morning session was German; in the afternoon English was spoken. Dr. Döllinger, leader of the so-called old-Catholic schism, was the chief speaker. The supposed machinations of the Jesuits seemed to be his *pièce-de-resistance,* and on this he harped. The Greeks, though represented, held themselves aloof, and would not join in any religious exercise with the others. Of course, they soon discovered that many fundamental doctrines held by them were rejected by the Protestants. The result was—what might have been predicted—nothing. One novel bit of information was furnished by the Anglican Bishop of Gibraltar. He informed us that he had jurisdiction over all southern Europe, and that, consequently, Rome was in his rather extensive diocese. Was Pius IX his suffragan? He did not vouchsafe to tell us who had granted him jurisdiction. Did southern Europe belong to the Province of Canterbury? How about the time-honored triple branch

27

theory? But we must not look for consistency in such difficult questions."

For all that, Henry in a letter written at the time, and with the impression still vivid in his mind, declared that "Dr. Döllinger's closing address, in which he traced the rise and growth of the Papacy, was better than a course of lectures."

While at Bonn he made the acquaintance of the celebrated English preacher, Canon Liddon, of St. Paul's Cathedral, London, who was present at the conference. This was really fortunate, for it provided him with a friend to introduce him to the Dons at Oxford, of which university Dr. Liddon was a professor.

To Oxford, then, he went in the fall of 1875, his friend and fellow-student from the General Theological Seminary accompanying him. As they intended to spend only a year there, they thought it useless to attach themselves to any of the colleges, so they were what is known as unattached, or students-at-large, "a very suitable condition," he observes, "for young Americans."

They had charming rooms in a little house on the Iffley Road, in front of which was the broad level stretch of Christ Church Meadows. The Convent of the Cowley Fathers, as they are commonly called, was quite near. Thither Van Rensselaer went every morning and evening, mingled with the "Fathers," and was much impressed by their austerity. Indeed it is surprising that he was not at this time formally received into their community.

The Cowley Fathers are not unknown in America. They have at least two churches in the United States, the "Old" Advent in Boston and St. Clement's in Philadelphia. As Van Rensselaer saw so much of them at Oxford, a short account of this community from his pen, with characteristic comments, may be of interest:

" The Convent of the Cowley Fathers was founded by Father Benson, who was a fellow of Christ Church, I believe, and an Anglican minister. He was a man of large fortune, which he spent in building the monastery, in supporting the brethren, and in charitable works. Personally he was unprepossessing, carried his head always on one side, was usually unkempt and untidy. He was certainly pious in his own way, and self-sacrificing. He preached with great earnestness, but in a very nasal tone. The title of the community was Society of St. John Evangelist, and the Fathers were consequently S.S.J.E., not unlike the Jesuits, who are S.J. Moreover, they followed the exact rule of the Society of Jesus, but in an exaggerated way, and wore in different material the dress usually worn by the Jesuits in Europe: a cassock with girdle, a long cloak and broad-brimmed hat. They made themselves very conspicuous by appearing in public streets, in railway cars and on steam-ships, in full costume, to the astonishment of most behold-ers. As I have already hinted, they recite daily the Brevi-ary, but in English. The Jesuits make an annual eight-day retreat, and twice in their religious lives a thirty-day retreat preparatory to their first and last vows. Their imitators, like most imitators, overdo the originals by prescribing a yearly retreat of thirty days. In other matters the same spirit of exaggeration manifests itself. Although only a score or so in number, they scour the world, preaching, giving retreats and hearing confessions. From whom they get this universal mission and jurisdic-tion is so profound a mystery that not even they themselves pretend to give a solution. In fact, these two matters, mission and jurisdiction, are quietly ignored. If any explanation is insisted upon, these powers are claimed to be received in ordination. Now, supposing that Anglican Orders were valid, which we do not admit, they would only confer the powers of the priesthood radically, and for their exercise the further power of mission and jurisdiction are required. We might give an example from the army and navy. A man may receive the appointment of a captaincy. The appointing gives the rank, but the exercise of the duty requires the further designation of the regiment and the company. Furthermore, a captain assigned to a company in one regiment may not lawfully exercise authority as captain of a company in another. So a priest requires, besides the powers received in the sacrament of Holy Orders, faculties from his ordinary, the bishop of the diocese, for the exercise of those powers. The priest is appointed over a certain parish or mission by his bishop, and over it he has jurisdiction, but he cannot rove around outside of his own limits and perform priestly acts.

" So strict is the discipline of the Church that a priest in good standing in his own diocese, for instance, New York, could not pass over the ferry to New Jersey or Long Island and exercise his ministry without the permission and approbation of the Bishop of Newark or of Brooklyn. For universal ministry there must be a universal mission and jurisdiction, which belongs to the Apostolic See alone. Hence in the Catholic Church the Pope exercises this universal authority over the whole flock of Christ, and designates, or at least approves, the erection of dioceses, of vicariates apostolic and their incumbents. Compare the perfect order and discipline in the Church with the go-as-you-please methods among Protestant ministers."

While at the University of Oxford, Van Rensselaer's relations with some of the noted men there were of the friendliest kind. Chief among these were Canon Liddon and Dr. King, now Bishop of Lincoln.

"Canon Liddon," he says, "gave very profoundly critical views on the Epistle of St. Paul to the Romans. His exegesis of the Greek was admirable, though extremely technical. But it was an education in the art of studying the original text."

The Canon was undoubtedly one of the ablest of the passing generation of Anglican Churchmen, and a worthy successor of the giants of the Oxford movement. Most of his sermons have been published and show great erudition, particularly in Catholic theology. With him Van Rensselaer was on terms of easy familiarity, which was the occasion in later life of many pleasant reminiscences. The great man impressed him deeply and no doubt had a marked influence in shaping his career. He speaks of him always with respect and at times with a glow of enthusiastic admiration. Thus he tells us:—

"I used to see a great deal of Canon Liddon. It is strange how small incidents leave their impression. One day I was invited to lunch with him. To my horror the only dish provided was one of sweetbreads. Now I had never been able to school myself to eat them, as I had a repulsion for liver, kidneys and things of that ilk. I could not disgrace my breeding by refusing the only dish, so I conquered my antipathy then and there. He had proposed a long walk in the country for that day. I kept the appointment, although walking seemed out of the question, as it had poured down rain for several days, and the lowlands of Oxford were flooded. I never for a moment imagined the possibility of a walk under such conditions. But the Doctor remarked casually that he supposed I was prepared for the walk. 'Do you intend to go?' I asked. 'Certainly,' said he, 'I always carry out my plans. Will you go?' Was an Englishman to challenge an American and find him wanting?

"'Of course I shall go,' I replied, determined not to be outdone, though in my mind thinking it perfect folly. So the walk was taken, if it could be called a walk. It was rather a wade, and in several places we had to use rowboats as extemporized ferries where the roads were flooded. It was a life lesson for me to learn from this successful lecturer and preacher—the determination that overcomes all obstacles. Many pleasant and instructive rambles were taken in the company of that great man. I attended some of his Advent sermons under the dome of St. Paul's, where some five thousand persons assembled to hear him, as he ranked foremost among the preachers of the Establishment. He read his sermons, but so skilfully that one scarcely realized it. He had, however, an unpleasant habit of throwing up his head continually, as if to give greater resonance to his voice. And he made such efforts to be heard that, he told me, he was exhausted for three days after. He was very popular among the students, and was reputed to be the spiritual adviser of many of them."

There was an attempt on Van Rensselaer's part to become enrolled as a member of Dr. Pusey's class, but he met with discomfiture. He records the incident as follows:

"I rather plumed myself on my knowledge of Hebrew at that time, as I had studied it two years in the General Theological Seminary. So I paid a visit to Dr. Pusey, who enveloped me completely in a wet blanket. He inquired if

I were conversant with Aramaic, Chaldaic, Syriac, Arabic, and I do not recall how many other oriental tongues. On my answering in a very crestfallen way that they were all unknown to me, he said that his lectures on Daniel would be quite useless, as they presupposed such knowledge. Noticing my drooping spirits, he added encouragingly that I might acquire a sufficient acquaintance with them in two years to profit by his class, and that then I might attend. He little appreciated the spirit of rush that animates Americans. I was not altogether sorry, as I was not at all drawn to the great leader of the Oxford movement. He was not prepossessing in appearance or manner, and I wondered wherein his influence lay. Nor was I changed in my judgment when I afterwards heard him preach at St. Mary's, the University Church, in all the glory of a doctor's scarlet gown."

Another eminent Oxford Don whose kindness of heart always appealed to Van Rensselaer was Dr. King, the present Anglican Bishop of Lincoln. Contrasting him with Dr. Pusey, he says:—

"A very different type of man was Dr. King, Canon of Christ Church and Regius Professor of Pastoral Theology. He lived in Christ Church quadrangle with his mother, a dear old lady, and they formed the most charming couple. The Canon was gentleness and considerateness personified. He was not a learned man, but was well read, and had a heart overflowing with sympathy. He lectured familiarly on Liturgics, and endeavored to show that the Book of Common Prayer was in full accord with the primitive liturgies. He appeared, however, to best advantage when he gathered a select few of the theological students in a little oratory he had arranged in the quadrangle. Thither we resorted at night to hear a simple talk from his heart on the work of the ministry. He advised the leaving open of the clergyman's house-door at night, in order that poor Nicodemuses, fearful of being seen by day, might seek counsel unseen at night. The advice of the good Canon might be suitable in paradise, but rather risky in our state of civilization. We were great friends, and I used to go early mornings to assist him in a sort of mass which was celebrated in the quaintest little mediæval Gothic chapel, attached to an old convent then used by the Anglican Sisters of St. John Baptist as a reformatory for girls. Dr. King would array himself in colored silken vestments, and, at a very Catholic-looking altar, with my assistance, perform what was called a celebration of the Eucharist. In the early morning he was very ' high,' but at noon in the cathedral he was quite ' low,' wore the old-fashioned surplice down to the heels, and took the northward position at the communion table, of which the chief ornaments were two huge brass alms-basins stood up on edge. I never could exactly account for this Dr. Jekyll and Mr. Hyde conduct of the Canon. But he was otherwise so good and lovable."

The inconsistencies in religious worship at Oxford did not escape Van Rensselaer's notice and they had a share, no doubt, in undermining whatever belief he had in the Anglican position. As he observes in his narrative:

" Many a pre-Reformation custom has survived the change of religion, although they have become in most instances meaningless; for instance, the bidding prayers in the various chapels and in the university church for deceased founders and benefactors. Under the Protestant régime they are senseless, for the Established Church legislated Purgatory out of existence, and therefore she does not pray for the departed, for what would be the use? If they are in heaven or hell, they cannot be benefited by prayers. So the prayers are omitted, and only the names read out, probably for a perpetual memory of those whose benefactions have gone so far astray from the intention of the pious donors, and who, if they could return to life, would most certainly not recognize as their beneficiaries those who protest against the articles of the old faith so dear to their hearts. One cannot help being impressed by this act at every turn in the old university town. On all sides are the superb monuments of the ancient faith of England, proofs of the love of the founders for that faith, and of their desire to have it preserved and strengthened by a broad education. Many of the establishments were originally monastic. In other cases the professors were clerics, or if not, were at least celibates. Strangely enough, this last obligation holds to-day in some of the colleges, in which the fellows forfeit their fellowship upon marriage.

"One of the most striking cases in Oxford of the overturning of the intentions of the founders is that of All Souls' College. It was founded in the fourteenth century as a chantry for, I think, twenty fellows, whose duty was to offer Mass and pray for the souls of those who fell in the battles of Crécy and Agincourt. The present holders of the revenues are simply men of letters, like the late Max Müller, who are not obliged to believe anything and certainly cannot, if they would, do anything for the souls of those for whose sake the ample foundation was made. While we were in Oxford, some repairs being necessary in the chapel of that college, a superbly carved marble reredos was discovered. This the iconoclastic reformers of the sixteenth century had seriously damaged, and had destroyed the statues that once stood in the rich, Gothic, canopied niches. Not satisfied with partial destruction, they had plastered up the whole reredos so that it seemed only a plain wall. This was a common occurrence in England, and the substitute for the crucifix was the royal coat-of-arms, the lion and the dragon rampant, typical indeed of those who had banished the Lamb of God from His dwelling-place in the tabernacle of the altar."

As the Christmas vacation covered several weeks, Van Rensselaer proposed spending the time in a pilgrimage to the Holy Land, and made all the necessary arrangements. In an unlucky moment he informed the Cowley Fathers of his intention and they entreated him to forego it, on the plea that to pass the time in a sort of retreat in their house would be for his greater spiritual advantage, and a better preparation for the reception of Holy Orders. He allowed himself to be persuaded and abandoned the projected trip, and so lost his only chance of visiting the sacred places of Palestine. "I have always borne a grudge," he says, "to those who deprived me of this golden opportunity." The holidays were spent in great part in religious exercises in the private chapel of the "monastery." These began at 5 o'clock in the morning with the recital of the Divine Office, the Breviary in English. Then came a meditation and mass (?). The whole day was well filled with pious reading, meditation and reciting of the Office. He even took his meals with the community, and "very frugal ones they were and not over-appetizing."

CHAPTER V.

LETTERS FROM OXFORD.

DURING his stay at Oxford, Van Rensselaer wrote once a week with great fidelity to an intimate friend in America, who had been a fellow-student with him at the General Theological Seminary, and to whom he refers in the autobiographical sketch as having been received with him into the Catholic Church.

These letters, with proper omissions, are given here in the order in which they were written. Besides throwing light on his own narrative which was put together a generation later, they are descriptive of interesting phases of his religious life and its development.

" 31 IFFLEY ROAD, OXFORD,

" October 10, 1875.

" MY DEAR FRANCIS:

"   .   .   Wednesday we took a trip into the country. It was a perfect day, clear as possible and delightfully cool. We started off at eight o'clock for Warwick, as we were anxious to see the famous castle. The exterior is very impos-

37

ing, and the grounds beautiful, the Avon flowing through them. I was rather disgusted with the interior. Such a chapel! they certainly could not say: 'We have an altar.' And no ornament of any kind! We were led through several rooms where there was nothing unique or interesting except one or two pictures. One of Sir Philip Sidney, an original of Raphael, a Madonna and Child with Saints, among them your patron, St. Francis of Assisi, and a lovely face he had, too. I should like you to have seen it. We were also fortunate enough to have the privilege of seeing the bed in which her gracious majesty, Queen Anne, passed the night; also her travelling trunk. It was rather a bore, as we have seen so much of that sort of thing, but an Englishwoman who was also being led around, seemed much impressed; evidently she was green at it. I disgusted the major-domo by asking him if any one lived in the castle, being ignorant that there was still an 'Hearl' of Warwick. We rather enjoyed going up on the old walls, and up the tower, but the best thing was an old woman at the gate who had a small room full of mementos of Guy, 'Hearl' of Warwick, who lived about 900, and was a giant, being, as she said, 7 feet 11 inches, or, as she added for our instruction, 8 feet lacking one inch. There was a huge iron porringer belonging to the said 'Hearl,' and had been used at the last 'Hearl's' majority for a punch bowl. She said 'hit 'olds one 'undred gallons of brandy, one 'undred gallons of rum, one 'undred pounds of sugar, fifty gallons of water, hand horanges, hand lemons hin proportion.' The manner of jerking this out was the most absurd thing, and just think, on the eventful day this bowl was filled three times with punch. We nearly exploded with laughter at her manner and tried to beat a hasty retreat, but she begged us to wait for we hadn't had

38

the best thing yet, whereupon she seized an iron flesh hook and beat upon the porringer to show us that it was not cracked, till we thought our tympanums were, and so rushed out. Next we went in a carriage to Kenilworth, five miles off, having been enticed by a most 'insinivating' driver. . . . On the way we stopped at a place which he said we must see; we tried to refuse but he said, 'You misses a treat if you misses that,' and appeared so sorrowful that to please him we went over the house which was nine hundred years old, but nothing remarkable about it except some hideous pictures by a young gentleman of the family who, either in despair at his attempts, or from the melancholy at beholding them, *deceased* at the early age of twenty-two. Some of his subjects were Shylock, Lady Macbeth, and the Cave of Despair, representing two wretches starving to death. Can you imagine a more unhealthy brain?

" At length we reached Kenilworth, which is entirely in ruins, picturesque, but to me, who had only an indistinct remembrance of Amy Robsart and the Earl of Leicester, not particularly interesting. . . . Now we wanted to proceed to Stratford-on-Avon, and again the 'insinivating' coachy 'insinivated' himself and carriage, picturing to us the delights of driving in the country, the roads being, he said, as straight and level as a skittle ground. So, as it was pleasant, again we yielded, thereby spending some more money needlessly. We drove eight miles more and were landed on Charlecote Park, still in the Lucy family, and we walked across the Park where Shakespeare had been arrested for poaching, and which was full of such lovely deer, and then we were to walk about two miles and so reach Stratford, at least so said our 'insinivating' coachman, but alas, he was a fraud, or at least bad at figures, for he should have multiplied two by two and then would have been nearer the truth, for we walked and walked; at last, however, we reached our point, the church. The medallion did not seem to me at all like any picture of Will I had ever seen, and instead of being white, is painted *au naturel*. The church is now in Catholic hands, I am thankful to say.* We were intensely disappointed in Stratford itself, expecting a pretty little village and finding a commonplace town of ten thousand inhabitants. The old house had just been furbished up and looked very spick and span. We got back to Oxford at 9 P. M., after a very pleasant day's excursion.

"We had a treat to-day. Dr. Pusey preached this morning at the Cathedral. He is not nearly so ugly as his picture makes him. He is short and thick-set, rather stooping. bending under his weight of years and cares; he is seventy-five. As he preached, the sunlight streamed round his head, giving the appearance of a glory, and being raised above us, we did not see the skull-cap; he is a dear old man, with such a sweet expression and intellectual. He preached on prayer; a beautiful sermon, so simple and yet so true. . . .

"I am reading ahead, but I have a wretched memory. I don't see how anyone who has read Pusey on the Real Presence in the Church of England, and the Fathers, can help being convinced, unless he be possessed of invincible ignorance. I suppose the lectures will begin next week; the term is quite short, only a little more than six weeks. Won't it be delightful to go to the Holy Land or Italy?

"Yours affectionately,

"HENRY."

---

*Throughout these letters the word Catholic is invariably used for Anglican.

"31 Iffley Road, Oxford,   · ·

"October 17, 1875.

" My Dear Francis:

" .   .   .   Speaking about Absolution, I did not remember, if I ever knew, that our Protestant Episcopal
Church had left out that very useful little rubric in the Visitation Office about urging to a special confession, as also
the direct form of Absolution. It was brought to my attention by Dr. King's saying that he made great capital of it
in his lectures on the prayer book, whereupon I looked it
up, and alas, our dear P. E. C. had omitted it. I have not
had a chance to hear what remedy he can suggest consistent
with the rubrics; for in the Visitation of Prisoners we are
told to use the form of Absolution in the Communion Office.
I will see the dear soul to-morrow morning after Celebration
at this Sister's little chapel, where I go every Monday. He is
the most sympathetic and safe counsellor one could desire;
he has been exceedingly polite, and invited me to dinner on
Wednesday.   .   .   .

" Oxford is full now; all the graduates and fellows have
returned. I must say I am disappointed in their appearance;
they have not the style that *elegant* Americans possess so
eminently. We had a very excellent sermon this morning
at St. Mary the Virgin, before the University. It was by
the Dean of Rochester, Dr. Scott. Strange to say, his co-
lexicographer, Liddell, also discoursed this morning at the
Cathedral. The service consisted of enumerating all the
things for which one ought to be thankful and pray, a whole
Catalogue of the founders of Colleges, concluding with the
Lord's prayer, said by Dr. Scott, solo. The first was the

41

'bidding prayer,' so that the whole service consisted of the Lord's prayer and the Sermon, a beautiful one on 'To me to die,' etc., and very spiritual. He has a sweet voice and excellent delivery. For early celebration we went as usual to St. Cross. . . . Father Benson is always preaching on the same subject, the Eucharist, and one gets rather weary of hearing the same thing. This afternoon I went to the children's service at St. Barnabas', and was as much pleased as ever; lots of young men. This week is the dedication festival, and Dr. King preaches there to-morrow night.

"This week the lectures begin; Liddon three times a week, Monday, Wednesday and Friday, from 11 to 12. I believe he also has a Bible class Sunday evenings. Dr. King's are Tuesday, Thursday and Saturday, from 11 to 12. Dr. Bright, Monday, Wednesday and Friday, from 12 to 1, on the Extracts in Eusebius. As I have been reading Westcott on the Canon, I see the great importance of Eusebius and his testimony for establishing the authenticity of the Canonical Books, and so I am going to the lectures. He also lectures on the Canons of Chalcedon on Tuesdays at 12. Dr. Pusey lectures Tuesday, Thursday and Saturday at 9, on the Psalms after the 50th. I am in a quandary what to do. I fear he is too far advanced in Hebrew for me, but I should like to hear him occasionally, on the 51st for instance. The poor Evangelists [Father Benson's Order] have to write Hebrew prose compositions. . . . It is very hard to keep up to my good resolutions; sometimes I am almost discouraged, but am still struggling on. Of course one always finds it hard to break old habits, and then sometimes one's companions are a little aggravating. *Ora pro nobis.* There has been a Priests' Retreat here, seventy of them; it looked exactly like a large brotherhood as they passed here daily on their way to the church, all in their cassocks, a great many in priests' cloaks, some few with short Roman Catholic capes and birettas. Is the Catholic movement a failure, think you? All four of the Bishop's chaplains were present, and last week Father Benson gave a Retreat at the Bishop's *Palace*. Would that our Bishops would show themselves indeed Fathers in God! Speaking of them, I hear Father Horatio (Potter) spoke highly in Convention of my dear Sisters' German work. I regret to say that I have been suffering from rheumatism, owing to the damp weather and cold church of the Evangelist Fathers. I hope it will not be serious as my family would say it was a judgment on my coming here in spite of the Bishop. . . .

"Yours affectionately,

"HENRY."

"31 IFFLEY ROAD, OXFORD,

"October 24, 1875.

"MY DEAR FRANCIS:

" . . . This has been a week of weeks for me, since I have now made Dr. Liddon's acquaintance. Tuesday was the day for registering names for his lectures, so I went to his rooms. I mentioned my name to him, saying I had met him at Bonn, whereupon he appeared to remember me and said we must know each other, that he would be very busy for a day or two, but would I come and breakfast with him on Saturday? As you may readily imagine I did not decline. . . . Was it not a very kind and encouraging reception? He lectured twice last week, and very interestingly. The room is perfectly quiet; no one dreams of speaking or asking questions. He is now on the seventh chapter of Romans. He gave me an analysis of the preceding chapters, and I got him to write my name on it, as coming from him.

"It is very awkward getting from one lecture-room to another, for Dr. Liddon lectures in the Clarendon Building quite a distance from Christ Church, and we have to run and even then come in late. It is very unpleasant, as we are rather marked by being the only students not wearing caps and gowns. Apparently the same men do not go to Dr. Liddon's and Dr. Bright's lectures, which are on the same day. We go, however, and what is more, intend going.

"We were most favorably impressed by Dr. Bright. He is extremely interesting, has a very brisk and vivacious style and is full of humor. His subject is, 'The Fragments in Eusebius' History.' Last time it was upon the missionary labors, martyrdom, etc., of St. Thomas, St. Andrew, and the question of St. Peter's stay in Rome. I found it quite delightful, particularly as I have been reading about the testimonies of the Fathers, in Westcott. Dr. Bright, although intensely Catholic and poetical, attaches the proper value to apocryphal legends, as beautiful, sometimes, but not of course of historic importance. He lectures on Tuesdays on the Canons of Chalcedon, so that we shall have Canon Law.

44

" Thursday was my birthday, and I have now attained the venerable age of twenty-four, and am beginning to feel the weight of years. I celebrated the event by going to London to stay with an aunt and cousin who had just arrived from home, and it was a pleasure to see them. My mother sent me over by them a beautiful pair of sleeve buttons, black onyx, with my monogram engraved in white; no gold setting showing; they are exquisite, but too handsome for poor ' Brother Heinrich.' I went to a nice celebration at All Saints, Margaret Street. I was only a day and a night in London and then gladly returned to Oxford, although I had a very pleasant visit.

" I am sure you are anxious to hear about my breakfast with Dr. Liddon. It took place in a little cosy room opening into his large library. We were tête-a-tête. For love of him I ate sweetbreads. I think first we had fish, and he had to retire with a bone in his throat. Then came what he did not speak of by name, but I fear, were what I never could eat before, sweetbreads; but you would rather hear of him. Well, he is rather short, but not noticeably so; his head quite large, his complexion dark, his eyes dark, expressive and beautiful; his eyebrows nearly meet, his nose rather large and aquiline, his mouth quite large, his teeth white and regular without being handsome, his chin decided, his hair greyish and worn rather short, and small ultramontanes; his manner of speaking earnest, his laugh simple and hearty, his clothes not well cut, as if he did not trouble about them. He is rather quiet, so that I had to do most of the talking. These men never make one feel out of ease or palpably ignorant; anything they tell you they tell it as if very likely you knew it already. We talked chiefly about travelling and the Conference. The Cathedral service at ten gave me

45

warning when to make my exit. I said to him that he must let me walk with him sometimes (it is the custom here), and he said at once, ' When shall it be? A bird in the hand, etc. Will you come to-day at two and walk?' Of course I gladly accepted, being delighted to think that I had not bored him, and that he could stand any more of my society the same day. At two I presented myself. The weather was showery, and the walking shockingly muddy; the whole neighborhood is flooded, roads, fields, etc. I thought very likely the Doctor would not venture out, being delicate, but he never omits his walks, so off we started to see the progress of the floods. Having begun, nothing would stop him, so we walked in water up to our ankles, and in one place we had actually to get into a punt to go from one part of the road to the other; but he stuck to his purpose, although he was very polite and offered frequently to turn back if I wanted, but naturally where *he* could go, I was going too, and though it rained hard he minded it not a bit. He said he hated to be balked. Truly it was a grand sermon for me, who am too ready to turn back and give up. I think I shan't forget the lesson. We were gone three hours. He expressed great sorrow at having been the means of getting me such a wetting, and hoped we should have a pleasanter day the next time, which would be soon.

" Liddon never preaches here, and is not going to have his Bible class now; perhaps he may next term. You asked about his way of pronouncing. It does not strike me as being decidedly broad or flat, but I think inclined rather towards the latter. He has also rather a pretty stutter.

" On St. Luke's Day, in the evening, we went to St. Barnabas'. It was the week of Dedication Festival, and although a week day, a large congregation was present. The service was very nice, with incense at the Magnificat and during the procession. Canon King preached a beautiful sermon on 'Only Luke is with me,' deducing from it the lesson of *finishing* one's friendships. St. Luke having *written two books* for the perfecting of *one friend,* also from his constancy to St. Paul through thick and thin, he dilated on the *little* trouble we were willing to take for our friends. It came with great force. He alluded most affectingly to the late Bishop Forbes. Dr. Liddon told me the last time he had walked in the fields in which we were walking had been with Bishop Forbes.

"Dr. King preached to-day at the Cathedral on the Golden Rule—as usual, excellent. Dr. Liddon has not cut him out at all in my affections. This afternoon we heard Mr. Curteis at St. Mary the Virgin;—a very interesting sermon on Christ, the image of the invisible God, dealing with all the philosophic and scientific attempts of the day to find out God by the human intellect, and the utter futility of it. He is the author, you know, of 'Dissent and Church of England.' He is quite young and has a very good face and voice. I have abandoned the idea of attending Dr. Pusey's lectures. Liddon says the old Doctor devotes himself chiefly to the text, and to refuting objections which he takes for granted every one knows. I have bought Keil and Delitzsch and will study by myself. . . .

"Yours affectionately,

"HENRY."

" 31 IFFLEY ROAD, OXFORD,

" November 7, 1875.

" MY DEAR FRANCIS:

" . . . It is very refreshing to hear of a good class at the Seminary, and also that my friends are getting on well. I have really so much to write that I don't know where to begin; and so, as is often the way, I shall probably end by forgetting the half that I would say. I heard an interesting sermon last Sunday at the University Church, by Mr. Ffoulkes, on the evidences of Christianity. He brought forward a new one, the fact that all the records of antiquity, classics, history, everything, were due to Christian care. If, then, the classical authors are accepted as genuine—and who doubts them?—then, as certainly, must the writings of the Evangelists and Apostles receive the same treatment at the hands of the critics. It seems like sound reasoning, and the persons to whom I have spoken about it consider it so.

. . . " A great feature of the lecture room is the perfect quiet that reigns there; no one thinks of speaking either to the lecturer or to his neighbor. There does not seem to be much sociability among the men; as a rule, they do not know each other; of course I am speaking about University lectures, and not the College ones. Perhaps, too, the Theologs are more sober in their deportment, but I have never seen anything but the most dignified behavior in the streets or elsewhere. I did not expect to find so young a set of men; to be sure, at the schools one sees older men who are studying for their degree, but the generality are not older than the men at our colleges. The Divinity students, with whom I am most thrown, would

·compare favorably, I think, with our seminarians, though there are some scrubby looking fellows—one, who exasperates me by going regularly to Dr. Liddon's lectures, and as regularly *reading* books on Physical Geography, etc., all the time. I suppose he goes merely to have his name down as keeping so many terms.

"Dr. Bright continues to interest me very much, and as for Dr. King, he is perfect. There is not a single thing about him that I could wish changed; his lectures are very interesting, and he has a splendid way of stating good Catholic doctrine, so that people cannot take alarm or offense; not that he minces matters or is in the least underhand. He gives a meditation on some point of the priestly life every Friday evening, in a little oratory he has arranged with a prie-dieu and a large picture of The Light of the World. He has a little organ also and wears a surplice and stole. He opens with a hymn and prayer and closes in like manner; then he sits down between whiles, looking like the dear saint he is, and talks, oh so beautifully about the true priest's life. There are about fifty or sixty men who attend. It is entirely a labor of love, as, of course, it does not belong to the University course. Think of exerting such an influence on so many men! None but a devoted, unselfish man would do it, for of course it takes time, and he has a great many demands upon him. He never refuses to see anybody, however busy he may be, but gives a few minutes to every one.

"I hear there is a kind of conspiracy against the splendid Christ Church quartette, to try to break it up; at least it seems so. Dr. Liddon is spoken of as Bishop of Brechin, and Dr. King as Bishop of Bombay. Would it not be outrageous to take them away from the place where they wield so much power? I hope these are only unfounded rumors, or that, at any rate, they will not accept. Surely a State appointment could not be twisted into a call from above, so as to necessitate an acceptance.

"Have I ever abused the Cowley Fathers in my letters to you? If so, I retract; they are high in favor. I have just come back from Even-song at their church; it was crowded. I noticed some of our fellow theologs there, which augurs well. They have been keeping up a kind of a dedication festival ever since the 18th of October, and have a procession with cross and banners around the church every Sunday evening. The Father preached a good sermon, too.

"This morning I went to St. Barnabas'. They have an attractive service there always, and the singing is grand in its heartiness. They sing in unison, and use Gregorian tones. The vicar preached a sermon demonstrating from the Bible, especially from Revelations, the propriety of using incense. It was good enough, but rather trivial. They gave an illustration of the use of it which of course suited me very well. I saw lots of theologs there.

"I am struggling on and up, I hope. It is wonderful how, as the spiritual life deepens, one appreciates the beauty and use of things before unappreciated. Now, as one draws closer to the head, one learns the truth and meaning of the Communion of Saints, and realizes that one must make mention of those who have finished their course in faith and that the Blessed Saints have an interest in him as one of the elect whose consummation they are praying for and anxiously expecting.

"The epistle to Philemon was read this morning as a second lesson. I immediately thought of you, for surely it expresses our relationship; it was the coming to learn how to serve the Lord that threw us together; surely that same Blessed Lord will ever protect and cement the purest of all friendships—one begun, continued, and I trust it may be ended in Him. .   .   .

" Yours affectionately,

" HENRY."

" 31 IFFLEY ROAD, OXFORD,

" November 14, 1875.

" MY DEAR FRANCIS:

" .   .   . I have not so very much to tell you this week, still what little there is you shall have. I thought I ought to have another walk with Canon Liddon, so I stopped to speak to him before the lecture and asked him whether he was not going to give me another walk. He received me very kindly, and said he would that very day, Monday, so I went after him at lunch time, and then we started off. It was a lovely day, and we went up to the hills. He talks so pleasantly and kindly that one feels at perfect ease with him—at least I do. I asked him what he thought about taking vows of celibacy. We had quite a long talk about it. He seems to think it perfectly right to do so, of course, after very serious consideration. He naturally favors the single state, although not disparaging marriage before ordination, a canon of the undivided church, as you know, forbidding

51

marriage of priests. I thought Mr. Olmstead believed in the Church and *the* faith, which he used to emphasize, but when bishops set the example what can be expected? It is horrid about Bishop Hare. I would rather *die* at my post, and so would Liddon. He expressed himself so, apropos of Bishop Roger.

"I consulted my angelic Dr. King on the same subject some time ago. He is a celibate himself, you know, but has never actually taken any vow, I understood him to say. He does not disapprove of them, but said that circumstances, temptations and temperaments would decide as to their necessity. He advised me to consult Mr. Carter, but, as I told him, I considered *his* advice as good as any one's, in fact better, inasmuch as he is a practiser of all that he preaches. I have quite decided upon the step, the time only is uncertain. If I had gone to the Holy Land at Christmas time, as I had thought of doing, I think I should have taken the vow at the Holy Sepulchre or one of the sacred places; but now that I have nearly come to the conclusion that it would be more profitable to stay here quietly and study, I shall have to settle upon another time and place. But, to return to the Canon.

"We had a very pleasant walk. We talked at some length on the connection of the right belief in the Incarnation and the Eucharist. He is always willing to talk on any subject I introduce.

"Well, as you know, he invited me to dinner. I went expecting one or two persons, but found a large party, twelve in all. They have an awkward way here of not introducing people, so I thought it would have been very stupid, but it proved otherwise. Our places were not arranged, but I foolishly sat myself down at the end of the table from Liddon, but was next to Mr. Dodgson, the author of ' Alice in Wonderland.' He was exceedingly agreeable and amusing. Another of the party was Gladstone's youngest son, a refined, handsome fellow. I had a little conversation with him, and altogether we had a very enjoyable time.

" You cannot *conceive* how delightful it is to have some one to whom you can go for advice, such as my *angelic* Dr. King, though he is not my confessor. I was getting a little disheartened at the amount of work I ought to be doing, and the reality. He is always sympathetic and encouraging. I told him my great defect, the inability to analyze, so the dear soul, entering into my difficulty, took a sermon and analyzed it for me, and said I must write him an analysis of a sermon every week and he would criticize it; also he would try to systematize my studies more for me. Isn't he one among ten thousand? Would that we had such men at home! We had a pleasant Friday evening with him and discussed the subject of conducting services. As he does everything well himself, he is fitted to teach others. He is very impartial, giving occasionally a warning to the advanced as to the tendency of slurring over the pro-anaphoral service in this particular instance. He is not in the least afraid of speaking Catholic truth, but at the same time does it so as not to offend. There were more present than last week, in fact the oratory was crowded.

" I went to the Sisters' little chapel this morning and served for Liddon. He is a beautiful celebrant; every word seems to come from his heart, and he looks so well in the vestments. I had asked his permission to serve the other day but was not altogether sure he liked it, so I said after the service, that I hoped he did not mind having a server. He replied, ' Oh, no, it is a great delight to have you,' and called me ' dear friend,' and said we must have another walk soon. At the second service I heard Father Benson, and this afternoon Jowett. What a varied experience in one day, Liddon, Benson and Jowett! The latter is anything but attractive: a great, round, fat face, with hooked nose and retreating mouth. He wears a very low cut *waistcoat,* white choker and black gown. It is rather a good thing that he does not affect clerical attire. His sermon was long and utterly *commonplace,* nothing unorthodox really, but only a low conception. It was on the ' Temple of the Holy Ghost, which temple ye are.' He began with a long account of Solomon's and the second temple, which every one might have known, then the temple of Nature, then our souls. There was not a single original thought or expression, and on such a subject too! . . .

" The chapel of Balliol is handsome; the service, with its very old double Anglican chants, reminded me of the seminary. The prayers were said apparently for another congregation, for those present never made them theirs by responding. It is the only service I have been to in England where, in place of the Magnificat and Nunc Dimittis, they have sung the Cantate Domino and the Deus Misereatur. The change betrays the *Master's* hand of Jowett, who probably is unable to appreciate the Hymns of the Incarnation. Such a cold service I do not wish to attend again. . . . I am getting on very well and feel that I am making progress in the art of meditating and in meditation, and I realize as I never could before the great dogmas of our religion. . .

" Yours affectionately,

" HENRY."

54

" 31 IFFLEY ROAD, OXFORD,

" November 21, 1875.

" MY DEAR FRANCIS:

" . . . It is delightful to me to study this year like a responsible being, and not to be forced to recite verbatim what any received text-book contains. . . . I wish you could drop into some of Dr. King's lectures; the last was on Liturgies, some of which he deduced from the writings of Tertullian, Cyprian and Augustine. I was astonished to find them so exactly like, in most respects, our present advanced forms. It is splendid to have all these points *forced* upon the attention of men who could never dream of reading them for themselves, for when given by such men, in such a way, they are bound to make an impression. And strange to say, no one is offended. We had a beautiful meditation on the Eternal Word before the Incarnation; the next two are to be upon the Word Incarnate, and on earth; and then on Him, now in glory.

" I went to the Sisters' this morning to serve Liddon; he is such a reverent celebrant, though nothing of a ritualist. He called me ' dear friend ' again. Is it not strange to be writing about Canon Liddon in such a way?

" I had to break off here and go to my dinner at Pembroke. I had a charming time. It was in the large hall, but the men have small tables and kind of mess or club arrangement. . . . Well, after a pleasant dinner we adjourned to St. Barnabas', which, as usual, was crowded. The sermon was remarkable. It was an attack on Rome owing to the opening by that communion of a new church here as a kind of proselyting establishment. The building was intended for a Roman Catholic College, of which New-man was to have been the head, but it was squelched, and so they had the building on their hands. They have resorted to the expedient of starting a church, although they have no people here to fill it. Mr. Noel, the preacher, was exceed-ingly violent, and begged no one to be present at the opening of what he would not call a church, by a schismatical Bishop for the express purpose of poaching. Every one who went would be guilty of the sin of schism. I did think of going, as I wanted to hear Manning, but I think it would be wrong and so shall resist. . . .

"I may go to see Father Corbet of the Fathers of the Holy Ghost, also some of the Sisterhoods and London churches, and if possible some retreat. I have travelled much already, and have no excuse for being on the move for change of scene. I am perfectly well, so health is no plea. It is good for me, who have everything so propitious, to begin and make a little sacrifice. I am afraid sometimes when I think that ' to whom much is given from him,' etc., etc. . . .

God grant that we may work together some day as Brothers. Concentration is strength, and Religious Orders are a standing reminder to a worldly age, that true Christian self-abnegation is not a thing of the past nor antagonistic to culture. . . .

"Yours affectionately,

"HENRY."

" 31 IFFLEY ROAD, OXFORD,

" Advent Sunday, November 28, 1875.

" MY DEAR FRANCIS:

" . . . There has been great excitement in Oxford about the opening of the Roman Catholic *chapel,* as they call it. They place it on a footing with dissenting meeting-houses, and so will not call it *church*. Well, of course, all good Catholics stayed away, the Confraternity of the Blessed Sacrament, and the Brotherhood of the Holy Trinity of Oxford and Cambridge enjoining it, and the Warden of Keble and other colleges speaking very strongly against it. You cannot conceive how very intensely they feel about it, calling it schism and every other ugly name. Undoubtedly Roman Catholics stand on a very different footing here with us.

" I dined at Keble last Monday. It was quite imposing, as there are one hundred and twenty students; they all rose as the Dons passed by, my humble self among them. Rev. Mr. Mylne, my entertainer, is a very agreeable and genial man.

" Dr. King has been lecturing on the part of Hooker we studied last year and has made it exceedingly interesting. I can hardly believe it to be the same as what we had to re-cite to Dr. Buel. Dr. King throws *love* into very dogma, and life at the same time. I am quite encouraged at my ability to understand the Greek and Latin quotations from the Fathers.

" We had a most beautiful meditation on Friday on the Word Incarnate on earth, and Head of the Church Militant.

57

The room was full to overflowing. Dr. King inspires every listener, and he has the most wonderful faculty of bringing out of well-worn incidents in the Bible, new and unthought of lessons. Speaking of the demoniac in the country of the Gadarenes, he said there was a road made dangerous by the attacks of this man possessed, ' so that no one dared to go by that way.' That was the very road Our Lord chose. So must His priests choose the ways where they may be insulted, may be injured bodily; and they must make efforts to reclaim the men. Everything he says is so perfectly simple, yet so true, and so full of holy love. His own life is a sermon which everyone may read and copy. . . .

" Did I speak of Young, whom I met at Leary's? Well, he is a most fascinating little man, very attractive looking and very charming in conversation. He very politely invited me to breakfast with him at Pembroke. There were eight fellows there and it was exceedingly pleasant. It gave me an idea how delightful college life here must be. Is it not funny to be entertained by people who don't know your name or mention theirs when they give the invitation? We came to the conclusion that one of the most effective missionaries, was a church store where there was an attractive window and enticing little books lying about in people's way, the store being in the immediate neighborhood of the church, if possible, where people would be obliged to pass it going to the services. The talk began by speaking of a most enticing and gorgeous shop opened here in connection with the so-called Roman Schism.

" Dr. Pusey preached this morning, to a large congregation at the Cathedral, a beautiful sermon on ' Consider your ways.' They are going to ' restore ' the University

Church, St. Mary the Virgin, here. It is rather a pity, I think. It will, of course, improve the appearance of the church from an artistic point of view, but it will destroy its distinctiveness. The undergraduates' gallery will be pulled down, and the present arrangement, by which the pulpit is made the central point, around which are arranged the seats for the different grades of scholarship—D.D., M.A., B.A.—altered. If you want to see it as in the days when Newman and others entranced the University, you must come over very soon. I don't know when they begin operations; perhaps it may be deferred, as Burgon, who is Vicar, and very instrumental in the change, has been made Dean of Chichester. . . . I think, perhaps, I may run up to London for Sunday to hear Liddon in St. Paul's. . .

" Yours affectionately,

" HENRY."

" CHARING CROSS HOTEL, LONDON,

" December 5, 1875.

" MY DEAR FRANCIS:

" Here I am in London for the express purpose of Liddon, and I was more than satisfied this afternoon by his sermon. We went an hour and a quarter before the time, and got to St. Paul's just as the doors were opened, and so succeeded in getting excellent seats. In a few minutes the whole choir and the space under the dome were packed,

There must have been several thousand people, I should think. Well, we had Even-song very well sung, without any accompaniment, and then the sermon from the epistle for the day. 'Whatsoever things were written,' etc. The Bible was the theme, and grandly handled; his delivery was splendid, he was very distinct and very impressive. The sermon was written, but very flowingly delivered. He has a way of throwing up his head, as if to give out the words with greater distinctness and emphasis; he used very few gestures, but those were very effective; the use of the hands varied, sometimes using only the forefinger, at others the whole outspread. His a's are not broad. His face looked very handsome; he seemed much excited and was very hot. He stayed up in the pulpit and sang the hymn very heartily, and then gave the benediction. I was exceedingly interested and, fearing to be disappointed, was the more delighted. It lasted forty-five minutes, but seemed short. He is one of the *very few* preachers whose sermons I could wish to be longer; but I must travel backwards in my account.

"I went to early celebration at All Saints, and feeling quite at home there, enjoyed it very much. I then went to Mass at St. Anselm's Roman Catholic Church, to hear Manning. I cannot say I feel altogether easy about going to Roman Catholic Churches in England, for they are schismatic here. Still I went. The service was very good; they had a male quartette choir; the treble boy had a lovely voice, and so had the tenor, who sang a beautiful Ave Maria. Well, his Eminence preached. I had a splendid seat in the gallery directly opposite to him. He looks very old and is exceedingly thin. He wore a violet soutane, lace alb, violet cape; and kept his scarlet biretta on all the time, only touching it

HENRY VAN RENSSELAER AT OXFORD

when he remembered to do so at the Sacred Name. His text was, ' We must all appear before the judgment seat of Christ' etc. Strange to say, he never mentioned purgatory, but said the hour of death would be the hour of our judgment. He said one thing I didn't quite understand, in speaking of our relationship to Our Lord. He spoke of our having the same Eternal Father, and then added, the same Immaculate Mother, and concluded by begging everyone to say a ' Hail Mary ' for those who at that moment might be going to meet their Judge. Otherwise it was exactly what any one of our priests might have preached. Of course he preached without notes and without hesitation. It was very solemn and impressive, coming from such an old man. The church was not a large one, the congregation a poor-looking lot, very few nice people. On the stairs was a mite box inscribed ' For Masses for the souls in Purgatory.' It was singular the Cardinal should not have mentioned purgatory at all, wasn't it?

" Last Sunday night we went to Segur's rooms in Exeter College to Compline. There were about twenty or thirty men there, all Catholics, but a different set. They were all very manly fellows, quite old; many of them great boating men. It is so pleasant to see such men taking a lively interest in the church. A great many were candidates for Orders. They all belong to some church society and have Compline Sundays, Wednesdays and Fridays.

" Yours affectionately,

" HENRY."

61

"31 IFFLEY ROAD, OXFORD,

"December 13, 1875.

"MY DEAR FRANCIS:

" . . . I left London on Monday, at which time Bartholomew expected to sail during the week for home. What was my surprise to get a telegram from him the same evening saying that he had changed his plans and was going to the East, and asking me to accompany him, but I declined. It was a little tempting, for I wanted to go to the Holy Land, but I had made up my mind that one ought to practise a little self-denial and not do everything one wishes. Besides, I have a great deal to learn yet, so I was firm and telegraphed back, 'No.' Fancy me, if you can, so resolute. I, who last Spring needed so much bolstering. My whole life is so completely changed by being here, I can really feel now that I am alive; before, I was merely passively existing; before, I did not know what it was to think; now, my faculties are being developed. Father Benson gave me a shake mentally and set me vibrating, and Dr. King has kept me going so steadily that I hope to be so regulated when I leave them, that I shall be able to keep up to the mark.

"The Dr. gave us a beautiful meditation on the Vision of Isaiah, sixth chapter. The meetings are over for the nonce. Next term he will give a course in self-examination, and in Lent on the Seven Deadly Sins. The dear soul has to preach ten sermons this week, so you can see in what demand he is. It is a delight to hear him treat any dogma; he does it so reverently and lovingly and tenderly that one learns to appreciate what the Faith is. It makes me sad to think of the way the same great subjects are treated at the G. T. S.;

wrangling, bitterness, narrowness; love and **reverence en-** tirely eliminated. . . .

" I am trying to keep Advent Season very **care-** fully. I get up every morning at five, and go to Lauds at the Fathers' at six, followed by Prime and a celebration, and then we adjourn to the church for matins. I return home to breakfast at eight. During the day I read and take a walk. I keep all the canonical hours and am quite frugal in my fare. I find it very satisfactory. My meditations are improving, and altogether I am quite encouraged in my efforts for a deeper and more spiritual life. Although so entirely alone, I do not feel at all lonely, but am very happy. I am beginning to realize what it is to have one's life hid with Christ, and to feel that He is indeed the Life. Anything that holds us back from Him must be gladly thrown away, cheerfully given up.

" I have been reading a French book of the Abbé Perreyve ' Méditations sur les Saints Ordres.' My spirit is stirred that all Roman Catholic priests should count it all joy to give up all for Christ, and speak of that entire '*abandon*' and ' *dètachement*,' while the great mass of Anglican Catholics, not at all advanced, should be content to mix up the service of God and the world. Oh, what selfishness, what a low view of the priestly life! Let us give ourselves indeed to Him; not any half offering, which cannot be acceptable to Him. . . .

December 14.

". . . We had a fine sermon on the day of Intercession, from Dr. King, at the University Church. Although a week-night the church was crowded. The dear man has great power. Last week he gave a splendid lecture on the Eucharist, proving from the Fathers a real objective presence. I am sorry to say that we shall miss his last lecture to-morrow. His Friday meditation was beautiful. It was on the lessons to be learnt from Our Lord's life now in Heaven, as Intercessor. One point was, when priests grow too old to preach and do active work, they ought not to think they have nothing more to do; let them rejoice that young men should do their former active duties, leaving to them more time at the altar for their flock, and living a more hidden life with God. But I can't begin to do justice to the theme. The lecture was, as usual, very well attended. . . . "

Yours affectionately,

HENRY.

" 31 IFFLEY ROAD, OXFORD,

" December 19, 1875.

" MY DEAR FRANCIS:

" . . . This last week has gone very uneventfully, and the time seems to go very quickly. I do not seem to accomplish very much reading, but I certainly am beginning to grasp theology. I am very much interested in Wilberforce on the Incarnation. I like the tone; it is so reverential. I am getting to understand what the Incarnation really is. I think too many people believe in it as a thing of the past. I am sure that I for my part never until very lately began to realize it. I enjoy Forbes on the Creed and Articles, too, exceedingly. I go through Browne, as a matter of duty first, always feeling *protestant* to his statement, and then fall back on Forbes for support. I am trying to get a general idea of Ecclesiastical History, but find it very confusing, particularly the early and middle centuries; yet it is so very necessary when one appeals to antiquity to be able to give, as it were, chapter and verse.

I am becoming quite ascetic, more so than Mrs. Aldridge, my good landlady, thinks good for me, and I have taken her advice and moderated a little. My diet was the point in question, as I was confining myself pretty much to vegetable food. I really think it is good for one's mind; at least I found it so. Mrs. A. says I have been living too low, and that it is very wrong to do so in this climate, where one requires animal food and some kind of drink. I am rather convinced that there is some truth in it. She scared me by telling me that I should have boils and all kinds of troubles if I were not careful, so *verbum sap*. I have reformed a little as to food, but not as to drink. I must say, though, it does destroy one's spirituality a little, at least mine, but I am an odd case. I have been successful in waking up at the right time this last week, at about five, so that I have been able to go every morning to Lauds at six at the Mission House, staying through Prime and Celebration. I find it all a great help; then Matins at 7.30 and breakfast at 8. I am so monkish that I even read through mealtime, Baring-Gould's Lives of the Saints. I hope I am imbibing some of the martyr spirit. I was much struck by a passage where he is speaking about the monks in Egypt, and the effect they had in advancing, or at least in keeping alive, the spirit of Christianity. Contrasting it with the spirit of the present age, its unbelief, scepticism, Arianism and infidelity, he says, ' Such an age as this seems one meet for the revival of the hermit life as a witness for the truth and a protest against luxury. This, and this only, as far as we can judge, will meet the great want of the day. It is not preaching that will recover the multitude lapsed into religious indifference; it must be the *example* of men, believing with such fiery faith that they sacrifice everything the world holds precious for the sake of the truth, that Jesus Christ, the everlasting God, came into the flesh.'

" This is a long quotation to give you, but it almost exactly expresses my feelings on the subject. The more I see, the more absurd it seems to me for men to preach what they do not try or pretend to carry out. Take any of our clergy. In what are their lives better than those of unbelievers? What self-denial are they willing to practise? Absolutely none in reality, although perhaps much in their talk and sermons. As to the hermit part I would alter that a little. An example of a self-denying priest in a parish would undoubtedly have an immense influence for good, and it is astonishing how in small things example tells. I often remember an incident in Dr. Dix's former life; the warden of Bellevue Hospital, a plain Roman Catholic, went to see him on business, a Friday, at dinner time. He was shown into the dining-room and was at once impressed with the frugality of the meal, only a little fish. ' Why, Dr. Dix,' he said afterwards, ' must be a real Catholic.'

" Now, in reading about these Saints—I don't mean Dr. Dix, but to return—one is struck by their being in most cases men and women of no great or especial talents; and I find great comfort in the thought that no one is too small or insignificant to be able to witness to the truth. Some day, may God grant that I may, however feebly, do it; but

66

'l'union c'est la force.' Could we not band ourselves to-gether, living witnesses to a worldly generation, that the Christian spirit of self-denial and renunciation is not dead? At least we could try. I believe that I have a decided voca-tion, but shall take no steps for the present; only try and cultivate the spirit as much as possible. Don't think the Fathers have been influencing me. I have never spoken a word to them on the subject. I fully believe it is the call of a Higher Power; I feel it in all I do, wherever I go; nothing that is not connected with the higher life seems to have any interest for me.

"I went to the Ordination Day at the Cathedral; there were about twenty candidates—priests and deacons. Dr. King asked me to lunch with him to meet Bishop Mac-karness and his chaplains. The Bishop's wife was there! She is very pleasant. Altogether it was a very interesting lunch. Dr. Bright was very lively and amusing. *My* Doctor charming as usual; isn't he good to think of me when he believes it would be well for me to meet people? The Bishop ordained seated; it is much more dignified than doing it in a bunch. I do not regret at all my decision to stay here, for I am very happy. I have just finished Bos-suet and his contemporaries. I had the greatest admiration for him at the outset, but I must say I was exceedingly dis-appointed in him. It is sad to read of his end and his treatment of Fénelon. Have you read it? He had great longings for reunion and would have bitterly opposed in-fallibility, etc. . . . With best wishes for the New Year, the year of so much importance to us. . . ."

" Yours affectionately,

" HENRY."

" 31 IFFLEY ROAD, OXFORD,

" St. Stephen's Day, December 26, 1875.

" MY DEAR FRANCIS:

" . . . You ought to be here to look after me, for I am in a very dangerous state. The Cowley Fathers quite look upon me as one of themselves. What if I should be? I really think I have quite, if not altogether, a vocation for the religious life; whether as developed at Cowley or not, remains to be seen. I have been there a great deal lately, and enjoy keeping the canonical hours. I don't know if I had better keep on going or not, but I shall consult Dr. King as soon as he comes back. Perhaps it would be as well to try myself a little. There is no intention on my part of doing anything rash, so don't be alarmed. I shouldn't think of joining or doing anything definite before I am thirty years old. The Fathers I like very well. I took tea there and went to Vespers yesterday, but I declined dining, as I should have to write an account of my Christmas dinner to my mother; nor have I mentioned the dangerous proximity to the Mission House, it would worry or alarm her needlessly. I passed a very happy Christmas, though I missed the midnight mass.

" I went to High Celebration at St. Barnabas', and heard a very good sermon given by the curate, extempore, but very fluent and to the point. I much prefer him to the vicar. I had dinner solus; then, as I said before, had Vespers and tea at the Fathers, and went to Evensong at their church, where Father Benson preached an excellent sermon. I could scarcely realize it was Christmas Day, for it was like

Spring—a mild, pleasant day—and then so many services and so well attended. The evening service was crowded. Imagine it in our churches on Christmas! Why, everyone would be gorging himself at dinner!

" I went this afternoon to the Sisters with Father Prescott and read the lessons; it reminded me of last winter. The Father preached a little sermon. The chapel was very prettily decorated. It is so hard to believe that I am myself at all, everything is so strange. I am unnatural, I suppose, but quite happy here; of course I should like to be at home. And now if I thought you would answer any questions, I would ask you what you think of my case. Would you avoid the Fathers until the danger be passed, or not? Father Prescott seemed to insinuate to-night that it was a matter-of-course that I should join the Society. I need not say it is nothing of the kind; in fact, I have no desire to join an English Society. I think it would be much better to be trained in the United States if one is to be trained. My old tormentor, the Irish-American clergyman, has turned up again, but I have not had much to say to him; besides I am much more settled now than when he bothered me before. He is certainly most unfortunate—hasn't a cent of money and nothing to do. . . .

" Yours affectionately,

" HENRY."

"31 IFFLEY ROAD, OXFORD,

"January 12, 1876.

" MY DEAR FRANCIS:

"   .   .   .   It was delightful to hear that you had daily Celebration. How much you are gaining!   .   .   .   How primitive you are with your alb, but I did not know anybody but the celebrant wore the amice. I must tell you what I did on Epiphany—went with Father Maturin* to the nunnery and served him and acted as thurifer. I was dreadfully scared, as you know I have hardly ever served and did not know anything about the use of incense, at least very little. I have seen it used at St. Barnabas' twice, but not expecting to be thurifer myself, did not remark it especially. I got through very well, however. I swung the censer all through the Prayer of Consecration— I suppose you would call it the *Canon of the Mass*. I am exceedingly fond of incense and think it most beautiful and appropriate. I can scarcely write as I have chilblains, and my hands are much swollen, but I hope you can read this. I had to wear the most absurdly short cotta with deep lace. I am afraid I am decidedly elephantine in my movements, but console myself by thinking that even they have a certain amount of grace—I mean dignity.

" This week the *Mission* is in full force. And such a Mission! I would you were here with me. It began on Saturday by a service at the Cathedral which was crowded; the Bishop addressed the missioners in an episcopal style,

* Father Basil William Maturin, one time a Cowley Father, was received into the Church by Father Pope, S.J., at Beaumont, in 1897, and was ordained by Cardinal Vaughan in 1898.

70

with a little twaddle; still, as he had encouraged and invited them to come, knowing that the majority would assuredly do everything Catholicly, one easily overlooked any expression for the sake of the deed, and after all he really said nothing disagreeable.

"On Sunday I went, morning and evening, to St. Barnabas', where Mr. Randall of Clifton, a celebrity, and Mr. Coles, were the priests. Mr. Randall is quite an old man, over sixty I should say; he is the preacher. He gave a rousing sermon on the text, 'Friend, wherefore art thou come?' and it was very thrilling. In the evening he was still more impressive. He has a very grave, thin face, and looks as if he had fasted often; he has a good deal of gesture. He spoke most openly of confession, and gave an instance of a lady being saved from despair by a priest, which priest, at the end, he declared himself to be. No sooner is the sermon over than Mr. Coles mounts the pulpit to instruct. He is of an entirely different style, younger and stout; he is a great friend of Dr. King and has imitated him in his ways. I met him several months ago at the Doctor's house. Well, Mr. Randall has roused the people tremendously; then Mr. Coles proceeds to soothe them by his teaching; he is very calm and gentle and simple. He explained the first part of the Creed. At the door are stationed two other priests who hand everybody a tract and speak to those who they think require it.

"On Monday, Dr. King told me I ought to hear Walsham House, who was to preach, so I obediently went, but was not much edified, for it was at St. Mary the Virgin, which is high and dry exceedingly. It was not in the least like a mission, but only a Prot. parody. The sermon in itself was excellent, but there was nothing to follow it up; still it is a

71

good sign when such churches are willing to join in the movement instead of protesting.

Last night I went to St. Thomas the Martyr (Catholic), where a Mr. Ponsonby and the dear Dr. King are missioners. Oh, *such* a crowd of *such* people I never saw before. The church is in the worst part of Oxford, near the railroad and the canal. The men were there in smock frocks, with torn coats, and rags, and black hands and faces. The women with babies, and such poor, wretched people; it did one's heart good to see them in such a place. Mr. P. preached very well, really eloquent at times, and very lively, and the hymns, oh, the Methodistical tunes they sang! After the sermon Dr. King instructed about *Confession.* You should have heard him! It was the boldest, most courageous thing in him to do, for, just think of his position, and in Oxford, too! Confession is one of his hobbies. He was grand! He proved it most clearly out of the Bible and prayer-book—their prayer-book is much better than ours—and the people were most attentive. I talked with the Doctor after the service, and he said he enjoyed working among such people—think of it—he, the most *refined,* sensitive, gentle nature. It was delightful to hear him talk in such a way. You should have seen the assistant priests in their cassocks and birettas, talking to the people, going into the streets and bringing them in.

"The whole city is given up to the mission. All the shops are closed early every evening to give the people a chance to attend. We in the United States could never have such advantages, and then the clergy here can speak so much more authoritatively, particularly when the Bishop has sanctioned it. They are undoubtedly doing a grand work, but just think for a moment of such a thing at home!

Where would the priests come from? These missionaries are all secular, but they are very spiritual men as well as pretty thoroughly grounded in doctrine, though there is a good deal of machinery to work. But all in good time. First the seed—but how about the seed when such men as you say that we can't be ordained in the Church?

"Your idea of a Brotherhood of love at Hoboken is very engaging. I am very much interested in the Oratory and have been reading the life of Henri Perreyve, who revived the Oratory in France. He is a most lovely character. Couldn't we do something of the kind? The Bishop would never allow me to leave New York at present, I fear. I hope he won't be disagreeable to me. . . . I had a letter from —— to-day from Pisa; he is on his way home to rescue me from the Evangelist Fathers, as my letter to him alarmed him for my safety. He is very Protestant since being at Rome—alas, who isn't? It is a pity though for him, but he ought to have the sense to see beauty in the use of what is detestable when abused.

"As to vows, I have done nothing yet, for I had a correspondence with Mr. Carter of Clewer, but found it impossible to arrive at any conclusion by letters, so I expect to see him. They all say he is very, very cautious, and advises taking vows for a time as a probation. Be careful, then; do nothing rash, although it seems absurd for us who have thought of it so much and so long to talk about being rash and doing things in a hurry. Still, you are so young, but guard your name as much as possible from gossip. One can't be too careful; it is so horrid for those devoted to the Lord to be talked about. . . .

"Yours affectionately,

" HENRY."

" 31 IFFLEY ROAD, OXFORD,

" January 23, 1876.

" MY DEAR FRANCIS:

" . . . I don't remember exactly where I left off in my account of the mission. Did I speak of St. Frideswide? Well, it was too ultra to suit me. They were so very Catholic that they forgot their dignity and became mere Methodist ranters. The sermon was not so bad, but the instruction which took up the same subject was terrible to me. It was on the Crucifixion. The missioner imagined and invented all kinds of horrible jests and sarcasms said by the Roman soldiery, and drew the most revolting picture of Our Lord's appearance. It was sickening. I disliked the man's looks, too; he had *long* red hair and beard and wore a cassock with a short cape and silver cross in front. Now you know, I like a cassock and certainly a cross, but then there are different ways of wearing them. After the instruction the missioners went up and down the aisle making extempore prayers and ejaculations, in which Our Lord's name was, to my mind, most irreverently used, without any qualifying epithet. It struck me as being very forced. To cap the climax, the Irishman, my constant attendant, whose clerical clothes were concealed by his overcoat, was attacked by one of the priests, and inquiries made as to the state of his soul, and whether he received the message, but he didn't disclose his clerical character. I was utterly disgusted. It only shows that the step between the sublime and the ridiculous must be carefully attended to.

" It was very much the same thing at SS. Philip and

James', only everything was done in the most dignified way possible. The Canon, who is Principal of Cuddleston, was the missioner. He is an excellent preacher and drew well. The church is free, and the congregation would correspond to Trinity Chapel, with a sprinkling of poor people. He preached a fine sermon on religious presumption, which impressed me very strongly. He handled Confession most ably, introducing the subject in the most plausible way. Perhaps he left too much of a loop-hole for people to escape.

" Last Sunday afternoon there was an address for men, and the church, a large one, was well filled. The address was excellent, proving that religion was not in the least antagonistic to everyday life. He has a very manly and honest way of putting things that is very effective. In the evening, after the sermon, the assistant missioner made a few remarks and then read about self-examination on the Commandments, the idea being that a man's sins would be brought prominently forward, and he would be led to see the need of confession; the Canon meanwhile going about among the kneeling congregation and speaking as he saw fit. It was really the same thing as at St. Frideswide's, but the difference in the manner of doing things was very marked. I ought to say that I hear that the mission at St. Frideswide's has been successful, though it was a commoner congregation to be sure.

" There was a Mr. Boddington at St. Cross who was really splendid; he gave excellent addresses to men and had a wonderful flow of language. I heard him on non-communicating attendance. It was capital.

" At St. Barnabas' the mission has been so successful that they have kept it up all the week to follow up the impression they had made. Certainly Mr. Randall is the most striking speaker I ever listened to. Last Sunday the sermon on Hell was terrific, and yet not at all sensational, but only fearfully real and earnest. He has a great power in telling incidents, is very dramatic, without being stagey, is old and venerable looking, and his voice thrills you through and through. I would sit there trembling. It has made a wonderful impression on me. The very fact of seeing so many men at such a glorious work inspires me. What a wondrous power has been given to the priests here through retreats!

" I have been reading some of Newman's University sermons with great pleasure. What a splendid one that is on Responsibility. I have been very much interested in the life of Abbé Henri Perreyve, the favorite of Lacordaire, and a lovely character, a man of great ability, who came to an early grave through an utter disregard of his life. I am learning a lesson of the proper use of one's strength ' ad majorem Dei gloriam.' Père Gratry, who writes the book, speaks very plainly about the way Perreyve, who was the apple of his eye, overdid things, thus depriving the Church of a wondrous power. He was especially great with children. . . .

" Yours affectionately,

" HENRY."

" 31 IFFLEY ROAD, OXFORD,

" January 30, 1876.

" MY DEAR FRANCIS:

" . . . Speaking about Confession, I am convinced that multitudes of young men would be saved had they such a safeguard. . . . Last Sunday night the mission at St. Barnabas' ended. The church was thronged, the service grand, and they sang High Even-song. Do you know what that is? Perhaps not, so I will tell you. The priest wears a cope and biretta and says the service in the Sanctuary at one side of the altar, and incenses it. Mr. Randall preached a very fine sermon on St. Mary Magdalen. He is certainly a most striking preacher, and by no means minces matters. It was very good for the undergrads to hear. At the end of the service they sang Te Deum for the successful mission. It was grand. Mr. Noel was at the altar in his cope, a very handsome embroidered white one. The censer was kept swinging and the processional Cross was held facing the altar, with acolytes bearing candles on each side, and others carrying large handsome banners, with faces towards the altar. The Te Deum was plain-song, and all the large congregation joined in most heartily. The effect was splendid. At the conclusion the procession marched round the church, singing ' Crown Him with many Crowns.'

" On Monday I dined at Dr. King's to meet Mr. Randall and Mr. Coles, the two missioners. I had a charming time. They told many interesting anecdotes and reminiscences about Manning and Newman and Wilberforce. Mr. Randall is very entertaining indeed, and so is Mr. Coles. He very kindly asked me to come and stay with him and see a country parish. Very likely I shall go after Easter, D. V. . . .

" College men here do not mix even among themselves without a formal introduction. You see them sitting day by day in the lecture rooms and never speaking or making each other's acquaintance. You are on no account to imagine that I have not had a delightful and exceedingly profitable time at Oxford. I have kept pretty steadily at work, tried to cultivate the inner life, and have not cared much for external things at all. The friends I have made I have not followed up, simply because I did not care to waste time or distract myself. Undoubtedly I could have made many more had I cared to. I was very much pleased, on going to Canon Liddon's, to find that he remembered me perfectly and asked if I had gone to the East as I had planned. It was quite a thing to be remembered by one who sees so many. He made some very kind remarks about seeing me often. . . .

" Yours affectionately,

" HENRY."

" 31 IFFLEY ROAD, OXFORD,

" February 6, 1876.

" MY DEAR FRANCIS:

" . . . I have received a most charming letter from my Bishop in answer to mine. He wrote the day after receiving ' my welcome note,' expressing his pleasure at all the kindnesses I was being shown. He particularly commends me ' to his dear and honored friend, Dr. Pusey.' He encloses me his blessing and calls me ' his dear friend,' and concludes ' most affectionately.' He likewise sends me the most flattering commendatory letter, which could never possibly be shown to any one. He says, moreover, he had

intended to give it to me before I left, but had not the opportunity, and somehow his delicacy prevented his sending it
through my mother. Imagine my feelings on hearing of
such magnanimity. I was quite overcome, I assure you.
I have had many prickings of conscience on the subject of
my behavior to him. I really did not deserve much kindness
or politeness at his hands, for however he treated me, that
was no excuse for me. It has taken a great load off my
mind. All things work together for good; it must come
out right; I have great faith. Is it not wonderful how
everything seems to be coming about just as I have longed
for but scarcely dared to hope? . . .

" To go to Cowley would ruin my life, although I have,
I am sure, the most distinct call to the religious life, but
not exactly in that place. You are perfectly right about
doing what we are best fitted for—certainly mission preaching would not be my forte. What I long to do is some quiet,
unobtrusive work, much prayer, intercession, meditation,
with especial attention to be given to *men and the poor*.*
I am reading ' L'Oratoire '; if you read French well enough
to care for it, I will gladly send you a copy. I quote a
little paragraph: ' Tel est donc l'esprit de l'Oratoire: pour
but, la perfection du sacerdoce; pour *principe* et pour *moyen*
la *charite;* rien par vœu, tout par amour, rien de profane
et de seculier, tout par rapport à Jesus Christ, à l'église
et au sacerdoce.' I think that probably the ' Priestly Life '
is in great part taken from this book, which gives an
account of the Oratory of S. Philip Neri, de Bérulle and
the one of the present century in France, under Henri de

---

* A remarkable foreshadowing of his future work as a Jesuit priest.

Perreyve. How glorious is the idea! What if we could do some little work for Him in this way! His strength is made perfect in weakness; let us try and begin now by making it a perpetual subject of prayer, and that He will raise up some one who will be the Superior General. I dared not mention what was occupying so much of my thought to Dr. King, for fear I might seem presumptuous. To my great joy he told me a plan he had for something of the same kind. He had bought a house which will hold about twelve men to be a sort of training school for missionaries. Mr. Moberly, the Bishop's son, is to be the head; Dr. King, I suppose, the director. Well, the dear man asked me to stay another year. Now you will think me crazy, but I am going to decline; perhaps he would not really want me; at any rate, he suggested it, i. e., said he did want me, so then I told him about my aspirations, and he said he thought them not at all presumptuous and not by any means impracticable. I have not had a chance to say much more to him on the subject. Wouldn't it be a good plan, if you agree to it, to get him to help us to draw up a few simple rules to start with? He has a great deal of judgment and is good—so true and sympathetic. The reason why I cannot stay is that I cannot put off the priesthood for a moment. The sooner one of us can offer up the all-prevailing sacrifice the sooner must our plans begin to be realized. So don't, I beg you, write asking me to stay. I no longer think of Avenue C except, perhaps, as the beginning of my career; it is no longer the centre of my priestly life. How wonderful it all seems! too good almost to be possible. Let the Society of the Holy Cross (do you like the name?) be the subject of our intention especially once a week, Monday, when I go to the Sisters' chapel;

and when Dr. King celebrates, I will ask him to remember it. Have you still Daily Celebration? Have I led you to suppose that I have broken in any way with the Fathers? I have not, and hope to go to the house in Lent for Lauds. Father Benson gave us an excellent sermon this morning on the Gospel. He is decidedly above the congregation, though all his teaching seems to lead towards perfection. The lectures are all going on now. I enjoy Liddon's more this term than last. I am reading, with great pleasure, his Bamptons. Haven't I made an advance? I can hear him in fancy speaking each word, and I can bring before me every tone of his voice and look, and it adds wonderful interest to the reading.

" Dr. Bright is interesting in his treatment of the Ignatian Epistles. Dr. King is glorious on the Ordinal. This set of his lectures does not belong to the school, and is quite voluntary, yet not only his room is crowded, but the adjoining one likewise. He has been treating the separation of the Levite and Aaronic priesthood, the use of *media,* and that not any and everybody may be a priest, but that there is need of a distinct call. He is splendid. His meditations have begun, his little chapel filled to overflowing, and men standing all through. Last Friday his lecture was on self-examination, and very excellent it was. He discussed the different ways of meditating; the purgative, the illuminative, and the unitive, and then, after dilating to some extent upon each of them, said, ' No doubt some of you will think it is mere mediævalism,' and then he spoke about St. Clement of Alexandria's works, and especially the Paidagogos who is Christ, showing that St. Clement taught in that early age on exactly the same plan as the later saints. He then analyzed Wesley's rules of self-examination, thus combining to suit and not to offend any class of thinkers. He is wonderfully happy in his handling of such subjects.

" I have just come in from service at the Evangelist Fathers' Church. Father Benson preached on ' Oh, taste and see.' You can imagine it was a pretty high sermon, much too high for the understanding of the people, I fear. I enjoyed it very much, although it was rather long. You ask about the chanting; it is hard to say whether it is fast or slow; rather fast, I should say, pausing slightly at the commas, and not dwelling much on any one note. The accompaniment at St. Barnabas' is very brilliant; the organ is a fine one, the boys singing alternate verses. The congregation there is divided, men on the right side and women on the left. The women sing with the boys. In high services and on Sundays cadences are introduced in the intoning of the prayers. I don't think honestly that the English singing is any better or differs materially from ours; perhaps some of the boys' voices may be sweeter. . . .

" I agree with you entirely about the Mary banner; let the *first* banner, at least, be in honor of Our Lord, the Lamb, for instance, or the Good Shepherd, or Our Lord blessing little children, etc. . . .

> " Yours affectionately,
>
> " HENRY."

> " 31 IFFLEY ROAD, OXFORD,
>
> " February 13, 1876.

" MY DEAR FRANCIS:

" . . . Father Prescott has imbued me with the idea of extreme caution in regard to the enthusiasm which we young-blooded fellows feel. Without experience we are apt to sneer at his advice as conservatism. Surely, when we are playing for such high stakes we cannot be too careful. At least the great guns of Oxford impress me so.

"I hope to get back about the 21st of June, as I have engaged my passage on the Bothnia, which sails on the 10th. Secessions to Rome seem to be the order of the day. Mr. Hutton, a former curate of St. Barnabas', and a first class honor man, who composed a defence of Anglican Orders and was one of the Catholic party, has just been received by John Henry Newman at the Oratory. He went to see Dr. King, and the Doctor says he had absolutely no reason to give for his perversion except that there is no room 'for childlike faith in the English Church.' Certainly one would require a vast amount of that article unadulterated to turn Roman nowadays. Isn't it sickening to see the work of years and noble lives almost neutralized by such absurd monomania? But certainly everything preaches a lesson of caution to us to give people a thorough grounding in good, true, sound doctrine, before they are carried away by their feelings. But how can one account for first class men behaving in such a way?

"I went to a delightful dinner at Dr. King's on Thursday to meet Burgon, the new Dean of Chichester. It was quite a large affair,—fourteen of us. I was the only man under forty-five. I considered it quite a compliment. Half the party were ladies. The Dean was the most amusing company, full of anecdotes, some quite stale; a most lackadaisical looking person and with such a comical way of telling things that one laughed whenever one looked at him. Among the guests was Archdeacon Pott. He was very jolly and told very amusing things about Wilberforce; he looked so amusing in knee-breeches and apron; he reminded me strongly of Dr. Seymour. Imagine *him in that dress!* Another guest was a Rev. George Williams, very learned in Eastern Church concerns, who has travelled a great deal, and who gave us an interesting account of the steps the Orientals are making towards unity. There is also a Brotherhood at Athens, lay, I believe, for the improving of the education of the clergy. Professor Damalas, one of the Bonn men, is one of the leaders. We need something of the kind—our Oratory under another name. We heard of Dr. Eigenbrodt's dog-in-the-manger treatment of the St. Chrysostom Society. How contemptible it does seem!

"The weather is horrid; I never suffered so much from cold in my life; not that it is so cold, but such penetrating damp. My hands have been perfect sights from chilblains—all swollen and red mottled—and as for my feet, they are in a constant state of numbness. I shall certainly be glad when Spring comes.

"We went to a breakfast at Exeter College yesterday. Segur was our host; he is one of the best men I have ever met. We were a party of eight and had a very jolly time. We were told some very amusing college stories, and were greatly entertained. An Oxford breakfast is quite an imposing affair.

"Dr. King gave us a beautiful instruction on Pride. He is certainly a most charming man. He makes great use of Dante, rolling off the Italian very sweetly. I think he managed to convict us all of pride, in some of its shapes. He describes most graphically, and is particularly good about castle building, in which one is sure to be the lord of the castle oneself. 'Full,' gives you no idea what the little chapel is; men willing to stand, too, and such men, not the scrubs

84

one is apt to consider as the only Theologs, but fine-looking, manly, high-bred fellows. I find myself questioning whether it can be possible that they are really candidates, and yet the fact of their coming to extra lectures and meditations proves that they are not going into Holy Orders as a matter of business. What a contrast Dr. King is to our Professors! He gave us notice yesterday that to anyone who expected to be ordained at the Lent ordination, and had not heard his ' Parochialia,' he would be happy to give them privately. Wasn't that good in him? What a thing love is! How many people would take such extra trouble for any set of young men? I asked the dear soul to make a special memento of us and our plan on Monday mornings at Celebration; he seemed very pleased with the idea. A good talk with him on Monday sets me up for the rest of the week. I don't know what I should do without the daily Celebration. . . . Our friend B. has decided to pass the summer in Hanover or elsewhere in Germany. I wouldn't think of doing such a thing, for I consider it absolutely dangerous for one's spiritual life to live in a country where religion is a mere nonentity—no services but once a week, and those dreadful, and to live in an atmosphere of utter worldliness and pleasure-seeking. Decidedly Germany has no charm for me which could outweigh the evils. I am sorry to say that I have forgotten all the German I knew. Last summer seems like a blank. I might have learned so very much more than I did, but I suppose there is no use crying over spilt milk. . . .

" Yours affectionately,

" Henry."

CHAPTER VI.

Letters From Oxford (*Continued*)

" 31 Iffley Road, Oxford,

" February 20, 1876.

" My Dear Francis:

"   .   .   .   This morning Dr. Pusey preached before
the University. St. Mary's was crowded. The Undergrads' gallery was packed, and many were standing in the
aisles. I went early and got a good seat. Shall I tell you
how? I was very bold. I was modestly waiting near a
locked pew; a beauteous damsel was waiting likewise, amid
a throng of others. The pew-opener's heart warmed to so
much beauty, and the door was opened. I followed close to
the beauteous damsel and was locked in the pew with her—
was not that a successful dodge? The dear Doctor appeared in his *red* gown, which, although innocent of ritualistic tendencies, would have scared our respective mothers not
a little. The text was: ' As my Father has sent Me, even
so send I you.' The sermon opened with a description of
the ' Zeitgeist,' intellectual pride; unwillingness to accept
revealed truth which reason could not understand. He
then proceeded to consider several schemes of philosophy,
but was seized with a violent attack of coughing, which
threatened to put an end to the sermon. However, the brave

old soul is not one to give in; he struggled on and proved victorious. It was very painful, though, at times. Next he spoke of *media* in natural life, and then by analogy in our spiritual life, touching on the two great Sacraments and concluding with a splendid appeal to the Undergraduates on the Sacrament of Confession. He was wonderfully interesting. Just to look at him fascinated me. He filled me with a feeling of sadness—I know not why—there is something so pathetic about him. I must get Dr. King to introduce me to him as I am very anxious for his blessing.

"The precentor of Christ Church Cathedral, a fellow, offered to teach intoning to any of Dr. King's students, for love, of course. The Doctor very kindly asked him to take me. I supposed it would be a class, but to my surprise he gives us each a separate half-hour a week. He is a Catholic, a priest, and sings on great occasions at St. Barnabas'. I remembered hearing him there; he sings splendidly. He is very kind indeed and says, when I have practised a little, he will take me into the Cathedral to see how I can get on in a large church. Of course the Cathedral will be empty. He makes me take G. I think perhaps it is too high for me, but he says not. I have been practising breathing and since I have been in Oxford my chest has expanded an inch. I am very careful to articulate distinctly, and find that my practice stands me in good stead for my intoning.

"Dr. King's Friday evening conferences are literally thronged; the room is altogether too small, but the men don't seem to mind standing. He was on 'Envy' last time, and spoke about the great danger of it for fellow curates.

"I consulted Dr. King about the Canon. He quite consoled me and thought it would not be dishonest. I should have no scruple about telling the examiners if they see fit to ask me. I mean to have a walk and a talk with Dr. Liddon, and perhaps what he says may have more influence with you.

"I enjoy Dr. Liddon extremely this term. As for his Bampton lectures I am enraptured with them. I am getting quite a clear view of the Incarnation and the Trinity. I don't get on very quickly, though, with Bamptons, for there is so much matter in them for meditation that I read and re-read. What a beautiful style and what a devotional spirit pervades them!

"Dr. Bright is lecturing on the Gnostic heresies, which fit in very nicely; he makes them really very interesting. Do you remember all that bosh we learned the first year? Dr. Bright really brings the heretics and their views before you, and he is withal very fair to them, showing their points of contact with the Catholic faith, and how they arose. You can realize that the heresiarchs were men, and not fiends, as they are usually represented.

"I wish you were here that we might plan together, but one thing we can do, and that is, pray. It is a very serious thing—prayer—one must be very particular and regular; regularity and order are very excellent safeguards. Make a rule and stick to it as closely as possible. I find it the only way for me. You may think me a mere creature of habit! Amen, say I, provided the habit is good. Do you try to meditate, or have you given up in despair? Surely not. Don't trammel yourself with too many rules in meditation.

"How near Lent is; I rather dread it for some reasons. Do you ever speak about our plan or do you keep a religious secrecy? At all events we must have Associates. Do you make our Brotherhood a definite subject of prayer? I do

IFFLEY CHURCH, OXFORD.

every day, at Celebration, to say nothing of other times. I am still reading 'L'Oratoire' at odd times. In it is the life of the Père de Condren, one of the Superior Generals of the Order. It relates that Père de Bérulle had his eye upon him long before de Coudren thought of joining, and the Oratory offered up prayers that God would put it into his heart to join, which in due time came to pass. Now, why can't we do the same for those whom we think would be fit helpers in our work? . . .

"I have just come in from a sermon of Father Benson— very excellent—on the faults of omission, but he is certainly too long; three-quarters of an hour in the evening is too much, and then there is so much in his sermons; it would be better to divide them up into three, fifteen minutes each. I am positive they would have twice the effect. Let us make it a rule in the Brotherhood that no sermon shall exceed fifteen minutes. They sang one of my favorite hymns, 'Hark, Hark, My Soul.' What a power music is! Shall I bring out a selection of church music for 'our choir?' If so, what? How about 'our' Library? That is a very important thing; we can't get on without books.

"Yours affectionately,

"HENRY."

"31 IFFLEY ROAD, OXFORD,

QUINQUAGESIMA, February 27, 1876.

"MY DEAR FRANCIS:

" . . . Our lectures are very interesting now, and I enjoy Liddon very much more this term than I did the last.

89

The Oxford men all have a certain mannerism to which one must get accustomed. I can see you smile incredulously at the suggestion of any imperfection in Liddon, I do not think his mannerisms altogether objectionable, for it is a great comfort to feel that such men have their little failings. Liddon invariably says *jest* instead of *just,* and in lecturing he stutters and repeats the same thing over and over again, apparently waiting for a happy expression to follow out the thought. Of course, his sermons being written, there is no such defect. Dr. King, too, stutters in exactly the same way. It is very pleasing withal. Apparently all Englishmen have it more or less. But don't think that I am depreciating them, far from it, only it is ' jest ' as well for you not to idealize too tremendously.

"I haven't had my promised walk with Liddon yet; the weather has been disagreeable, the walking wretched. I know by experience he is far above caring about either, and so am waiting for a good day.

"Dr. King is giving us good lectures on the Apostolic Succession, Archbishop Parker's consecration, etc.; the Roman Catholics' objections and how to refute them, especially from their own writers. It is certainly most scholarly and impressive to quote by reading from the books quoted in the original language. Had Woodman* been thoroughly grounded, he couldn't have the impudence to say that he could not look upon us as anything but laymen. That Nag's Head story is the most palpably absurd thing ever invented. It is astonishing how Roman Catholic scholars, up to this day for the most part, implicitly accept it, and hand it

* Rev. Clarence Woodman, at that time a student of the General Theological Seminary, N. Y., afterwards joined the Church and became a Paulist.

down in their writings. The fact of Lingard rejecting it is almost authority enough, did not the various registers at Lambeth and different Cathedrals and State records prove the true consecration most convincingly. Considering that we all stand upon it, I think the clergy as a rule are culpably ignorant*.

" The Archbishop of Canterbury has been, as usual, talking in the most absurd and ignorant way about reunion with Dissenters. The other day at Convocation he talked a lot of bosh about Apostolic Succession of the Lutherans and the Swedish and Danish churches. It is a wonder he didn't mention our Methodist Episcopals; they have bishops, too, by name. In fact he did speak about the three bodies of the American Church, whatever that may mean—I don't know I am sure. He cannot mean high, low and broad, for he certainly has no desire for union with the high. It is sad such an old Erastian should be a Primate. He is doing his very best, although he cannot understand it, to undermine both Church and State, for they will certainly fall together. Mr. Boddington, one of the Missioners who was here, is to be tried in his, the Archbishop's court, for ritualism. I think he is able to defend himself pretty well. I do wish, though, they would try such a man as Liddon or Canon Gregory, but that, apparently, is not the Archbishop's line. They couldn't advertise Catholicism better, and you know Dr. Seymour's expression about the blood of the martyrs, etc.

" I am afraid this Lent will be too enjoyable for me,

---

*Whatever credence Catholic writers have given to the Nag's Head Story, the truth or falsity of the same in no way affects the incontrovertible arguments adduced against the validity of Anglican orders.

there are to be such good preachers. The Bampton lecturer is the Bishop of Derry, Dr. Alexander, the only Irish Bishop who voted for the Athanasian creed, I believe. They say he is exceedingly eloquent. The lectures take place every Sunday morning in Lent in the University Church.

"Dr. King preached this morning at the Cathedral on fasting. The opening part was admirable, but alas, he is far too charitable, for he qualifies so much that every man, woman and child could make a loop-hole through which to escape. I was disappointed, for I wanted someone who shall be nameless to have a good sermon on the subject. They sang a beautiful Te Deum by Mendelssohn.

"Did I tell you that I go every Thursday to have a lesson in intoning from the Rev. Mr. Hilton, a fellow of Christ Church? I get on pretty well. I have a tendency to slide up my first note at the beginning of a sentence, still I hope practice will cure the defect. . . .

"I have decided not to have anything to do with the work over on Avenue C, or the Sisters there. What a change of plans! All seems to be working for my end, however, for if I had gotten very much interested there, how could I ever leave it when our Society starts. But now, perhaps I shall have a little country parish, a few poor sheep to tend—how lovely that sounds—and there are sure to be a few wolves disguised among them. Well, I shall tend those few poor sheep and have time to devote to prayer, meditation and study. I suppose you are up in arms against me and are saying: 'Oh, he has gone back on himself and doesn't want to work; grown lazy and spoiled.' Quite wrong in each particular, I assure you—but all in good time. I am so afraid sometimes, that you are only jesting about our plans when I am dead in earnest. At all events, Dr. King says it is not ridiculous, and I can't tell you what comfort that is to me.

" Yours affectionately,

" HENRY."

" 31 IFFLEY ROAD, OXFORD,

March 16, 1876.

" MY DEAR FRANCIS:

"   .   .   .   I cannot believe it is so late in the year.   All the lectures are over for the Lent term, although Liddon is to give us two or three extra ones this week, as he wants to get through the Ephesians this year before the long vacation. Dr. King's upon the requirements for the priesthood have been very interesting this last week. He took St. Gregory on the Pastoral care, St. Ambrose on the priesthood, and St. Chrysostom on the same. He took them in turn, giving a day to each. They are, as you know, very tremendous on the subject, especially in the Eucharistic aspect. He concluded with an extract from St. Gregory Nazianzen. I am sorry to say the men pay very little attention, but read all the time—at least those in the room where we were. I am sure the majority are mere Erastians,* going in to please their families, etc. I was in hopes it had died out, but am

---

* " With Froude, Erastianism—that is, the union (so he viewed it) of Church and State—was the parent   .   .   .   of liberalism."—NEWMAN'S APOLOGIA, Part IV.

convinced of my mistake. One excuse is, I suppose, that coming to the lecture, as they do, in the midst of their ordinary University course, they know nothing at all about Ecclesiastical History or the Church itself, and so cannot be expected to care much about the opinion of writers of whom they are ignorant. Good seminarians are certainly desirable, if for nothing else, to make a break between the life of the University and that of priests or deacons; otherwise the transition is altogether too sudden.

" Dr. King's Friday Conferences came to a close last week. Literally the room was crowded, and men, as usual, standing. They seem to be a different set of men from those who attend the lectures. The Doctor was grand. We are going to hear him to-night at St. Barnabas'; I wish it were not so far away, as I enjoy the service there so much.

" We went this morning to hear the first Bampton lecture. The Bishop of Derry is a splendid man, and we were both delighted with him. The subject is the ' Messianic Psalms.' The lecture was on the 22nd. It was beautiful. He is quite old, but his voice clear and sympathetic. We were, as usual, fortunate in having such a lecturer for the year. Mr. Mylne, Bishop designated to Bombay, preached last Wednesday night upon ' Spiritual Progress.' He was quite good, but rather slow. He did not hesitate, yet seemed to weigh each word before uttering it, which rather spoiled the effect.

" I think I have heard Father Benson too often, for he palls upon one a little; he is too severe and hard, and takes too gloomy a view of the state of mankind in general. It is the way with monks. They wind themselves up beyond the level of ordinary mortals, and then look down with scorn upon the efforts of the poor ones who must live in the world, however much they may be trying not to be of it. If we want to reach the hearts of the multitude, we must be gentle and loving and sympathetic, and that monks cannot be as a general rule, for their vocation is to live apart from their fellows and even themselves.

" It is a relief to turn to the gentle Dr. King, whose influence is wonderful. I couldn't possibly be striving for a more difficult thing than to be gentle, forbearing and sympathetic; for you know that, in general, I have a certain amount of reserve and an immense amount of pride and disagreeableness. Still I am convinced it is *the* way.

" You speak about my coming to Hoboken. What does Mr. P. say? Or is he willing to take curates ad lib.? It would be a good beginning for the Society of the Holy Cross.

" I went on Friday to take my intoning lesson in the Cathedral. It is rather trying to one's voice, as Hilton puts me under the lantern tower and himself at the worst point for hearing. By way of variety, I sharped a little instead of flatting. I have bought a pitch pipe. You would be quite horrified at the number of my books. Tell me of any in particular you think would be useful; and do tell me about the Fathers we certainly must have.

" My sister tells me of my mother's reason for advising me to stay abroad—to keep me from the Sisters. She does not dream of the Society of the Holy Cross. .   .   .

" Yours affectionately,

" HENRY "

" 31 IFFLEY ROAD, OXFORD,

" MID-LENT SUNDAY, March 26, 1876.

" MY DEAR FRANCIS:

" .   .   . Nothing very interesting is going on here; time, as usual, is passing very quickly. The term is over, and the city is very quiet. We have had two of the eight Bampton lectures, which were very fine. Perhaps you may hear some of them, as they will be resumed after Easter.

" I go, as usual, to the Mission House every morning at six, but am getting bravely over my fancy for their phase of the religious life. I want something a little *broader*. I should hate to be a mere machine. . .

" In the afternoon I had a treat—Liddon at St. Paul's, on the Personality of Satan. I had a splendid seat and enjoyed myself immensely. Of course he was grand; calls the evil one *Sattan,* and so do most people here. He was very eloquent, and drew an immense crowd. The next day I went to St. Alban's, as I had a letter of introduction to Mr. Maconochie from Father Benson, but after I got nearly there, I thought how wrong it was to take a priest's time in Passiontide, and I said so to Mr. M. He was very polite and asked me to go there any time at one, and lunch, as I should be sure to find him at home. Of course he was very busy, and so I took my leave.

" I went to Even-song at St. Andrew's, Well street, where Barnby is organist, and where they are supposed to have the best singing in Europe. The chanting was splendid; so precise and steady, but the anthem, a beautiful one—' O

96

daughters of Jerusalem '—was marred by the solo treble boy having a horrible cold. . . .

" You don't know how you have misjudged me if you fancy that I am aristocratic with poor people. Burgess is constantly telling me that I err on the opposite side, and am too easy and familiar with them. And as to children, I have grown to love them. My nature, perhaps, has changed under Dr. King's influence. My only wish is to work among the poor. Burgess says that I carry it to such an extreme that one would think that the rich ought not to be preached to at all. Do you imagine that I have become puffed up since I have been here? Oh, no! Or did you fancy because I spoke of not going to Avenue C that I was beginning to repent of my determination to go among the poor and the uncared for? . . .

" I have not been at all satisfied with this Lent. I have not made progress, I grieve to say, but have had a long spell of dryness. It was good for me, no doubt, as it helped to save me from pride and presumption, which, alas, I had fallen into, I fear. It is a temptation, but it is hard to be spiritually dry. I hope now that the worst is over, and that Easter will bring me peace. I feel utterly fagged out and good for nothing. I went up to London, hoping the change would set me up, but it has only made me more tired.

" Mr. Lang came for us to go rowing yesterday as it is much nicer for them to have me to steer them. I went, although really I have not strength enough, and they always expect me to do some rowing. In Lent one has not much extra strength. Fasting doesn't make me cross, and I find that I shall be able to manage High Celebrations very well; still one doesn't have much energy. The air here is not bracing as at home. Spring is now here, and the birds sing most delightfully. There are quantities of larks. Today has been very warm; the hedges will soon be in bloom, and the country will be lovely. I do enjoy the country so much.

" I should like to have some work to relieve the monotony of study. Dr. King preached to-night, Wednesday, an excellent sermon: ' Rest after labor, and sympathy for others.' I long for you to hear him.

" I looked at some of the Arundel Society pictures in London. I liked one of Perugino's, Raphael's master, you know; it is in three compartments: central one, Our Lord on the Cross, with one figure at the foot; the side ones, each, two figures gazing at Him. I have often admired it at Dr. King's. There is another by Fra Angelico, but it has too many Popey people in it. Would you buy the first, and brass cross and candle-sticks for our private monastery chapel? . . .

" Yours affectionately,

" HENRY."

" 31 IFFLEY ROAD, OXFORD,

" EASTER DAY, 1876.

" MY DEAR FRANCIS:

" . . . An Easter greeting to you. What a comfort it is to reach Easter after the long, long fast. Well, upon the whole, I think Holy Week was a very profitable one for me. We revelled in having a great deal of Dr. King. He gave beautiful Meditations on the Mondays, Tuesdays and Wednesdays, upon the types of the Old Testament, selecting the Tree of Life, the Sacrifice of Abraham and the Brazen Serpent, subjects that actually suit his devotional mind. On Monday, Wednesday and Friday he preached in the evening at the Cathedral—of course, equally well. I was to have gone with him on Friday to Abingdon, but there was a misunderstanding about the hour, and I missed him. However, I was quite reconciled to the disappointment by the thought that there would have been too much pleasure in being with and hearing Dr. King on Good Friday. I went instead to the Cowley Fathers' Church. Father Benson made the address on the Seven Last Words, and was particularly good. There was a large congregation. The service was wonderfully melancholic. The whole choir was hung in black, the altar perfectly black, not even relieved by any white. The exercises began in the morning with a meditation at 7.30; then there was a children's service, followed by Matins and the Seven Words.

"For three hours the bell at the Mission House tolled every minute, and from two to three the church bell also. The day itself was gloomy. I never heard anything like the whistling of the wind the night before; there was a heavy fall of snow, and it was bitterly cold, altogether calculated to make one exceedingly mournful. By the evening the snow had completely vanished, and it had become mild and pleasant.

"We had also an appropriate service on Easter Eve. The church was prettily decorated, and the music joyful and inspiriting. Father Benson, however, gave us a very *woful* sermon, in which he told us we must go through the world like the corpses that we are. I could not agree with his gloomy views of the Christian life. It is one thing to be dead unto sin, and quite another to be forever storming

99

and raging against the world, which we must abandon, alas, to the unconverted sinners, if all the true followers of Our Lord leave them to themselves. Dr. King preached a splendid sermon at the Cathedral, but the service was miserably cold and un-Easterlike. I got to the Cowley Fathers' in time for the Celebration, and afterwards went to the Mission House to dinner, at Father Benson's invitation.

" In the evening I went to St. Barnabas' where they had a grand Te Deum, such as I described to you at the end of the Mission. There was an immense procession, in which all the Sunday-school children took part and, although it extended all around the church, there was not the slightest confusion. But I am writing all this one week after the date, to-day being Low Sunday. I can scarcely realize that it is only a week since then, but I really despair of ever finishing this letter, as this is my third attempt. I must tell you one very good reason why I was interrupted. I have taken a little jaunt this week, and where do you suppose I went to? Stoke-on-Tern, where the Society of the Holy Ghost abides. I went very boldly, unannounced, as I thought it better, and had no time to wait for a letter to be answered; moreover, if they would not show hospitality, I should know what to think of them; but I have no charge of that kind to make against them. It was a four hours' journey by rail. Just as I reached the last junction I spied a little crowd of cassocked and cloaked creatures, and I guessed correctly that they belonged to Stoke. When we got to the station I marched boldly to the crowd and asked if Father Bicknall were there. Luckily he was. I said that Canon King had commended me to him, etc., and was very warmly received by him. They had all been off on an excursion to celebrate the Easter festival. Stoke

100

can scarcely be defined by the name of a village, for it is hardly a hamlet, yet there is a handsome stone church, large and lately restored. The rectory is a huge house for such a tiny parish, with beautiful grounds, a succession of terraced lawns sloping down to a little stream, and the churchyard adjoining. The house seemed just fitted for what it is now used. There are six Fathers, two were away, one being the Superior, Father Corbet, a fine man, they say. I was charmed with Father Bicknall; he is so unaffected and pleasant, and seems to be really fatherly. I liked another one very much, Father Douglas, a genuine, whole-souled creature. There are besides five or six lay brothers. They are pretty advanced in ritual and have holy water for crossing etc. The great objection I find is that they have no definite aim at present, except community life and individual perfection. To be sure they do give occasional retreats, still home life seems to be their aim. Now, of course, one must, and one ought to, aim at one's own perfection, still I cannot help feeling and saying that it seems to me somewhat too narrow and selfish an aim. At least, I could not be happy there. I was really oppressed, or rather depressed, during my visit of two and a half days, although the services were bright Easter ones. I don't mean to be condemning them if they are called to such a life, but only that it is not my ideal.

" The Church is wide enough for all kinds. I was most kindly treated and liked them personally, still——. In the evening from nine to half-past, all the Fathers and lay brethren met in the community room for a chat. There was one fine-looking lay brother to whom my heart went out. Father told me to stay as long as I wanted, but I thought it better not to trespass too long upon their hospitality. He gave me a letter to their curate, who was staying in Lichfield, where I was going to see the Cathedral. Really I cannot say too much of the kindness with which I was treated everywhere.

"The curate is a very agreeable little man. The Fathers do not care to do parish work and so engage him for the purpose. He has a wife, who is also very pleasant. I dined at his mother's afterwards, and we went over the Cathedral and library together. It is a very interesting place, built partly in 715, and dedicated to St. Chad. We saw that old gentleman's gospels in Latin with Anglo-Saxon notes, much coveted by the British Museum. It is so encouraging to meet Catholics scattered broadcast over the country. It is good for them, too, to hear about the United States.

"I was very glad to get back to Oxford to-day. We had a Bampton lecture and a sermon by Canon Lightfoot. Another to-night by Mr. Mylne, Bishop-elect of Bombay; very excellent. It is splendid to have good churchmen at last, for Bishops, and such young men, too. Not a bit Erastian or cowards. I had a most unsettling letter from my mother, saying she had bearded the lion, Bishop Potter, in his den, and that he had heartily agreed to my staying over here until the Autumn to travel with my sister. . . . Liddon will be in residence in August. . . . My mother hopes that I have become moderate. What think you? Dr. King conveys a feeling of safety, in name at least, to her mind, but the reality—— . . .

"Yours affectionately,

"HENRY."

"31 IFFLEY ROAD, OXFORD,

"May 19, 1876.

"MY DEAR FRANCIS:

" .   .   .   I ought to be willing to make a little sacrifice, to prepare myself for the awful responsibility of taking charge of many souls. I should not mind being in the country, the people are so much simpler than city people. We walked out on Sunday afternoon to Littlemore for Even-song. It was a most lovely afternoon, the sky cloudless, and the church was much brighter than when I last saw it. There was a good congregation, the service choral and well sung. The Vicar was rather a depressing little man, and to our regret he preached; he had not much to say nor did he say it well. Still one must be charitable, for Dr. King told that once when Keble preached for him, an old farmer remarked to him afterwards, that 'it was a pity that the old gentleman should be allowed to preach.' Think of Keble being thus criticised.

"The Doctor is giving us a very good course of lectures on Preaching; of course, coming from such a good preacher, they fall with double effect. On Friday evenings he is treating the Lord's Prayer to a crowded oratory, although it is a gay term, given up in great measure to boating. The men requested him to make the hour nine instead of eight, to give them a chance to get there. So you see that they really enjoy the 'talks.' The Doctor thought seriously of not having them on account of the term, but was delighted to continue them when they were wanted.   .   .   .   I mean to try and study very hard though it is discouraging—I have such a poor memory. I will make a good house Father or parish visitor perhaps, which may not require very great learning.   .   .   .

"Yours affectionately,

"Henry."

"31 Iffley Road, Oxford,

"May 26, 1876.

"My Dear Francis:

".   .   .   Just think what a state I should be in if I were going to sail to-morrow, and on some accounts I do wish that I were.   One reason being that I should see you.   .   .   .

"How much Keble's life is abused.   He seems to be used by people as an example of combining the worldly and the heavenly.   Of course it isn't a bit true.   Burgess is very much afraid of leaving me here on account of the Fathers. He seems to imagine that I shall fall an easy victim after the fright I gave him last winter when he was away, but I don't believe there is any danger; at any rate my sister will soon be over to preserve me from the allurements.   Frankly, though, there is no reason for his fears.   I like them very well as individuals, and I like the religious life, but never would join an English Order or care to be under Father Benson.   I must say I prefer a limited monarchy to an autocracy such as his.   .   .   .

"We went on Sunday evening to St. Barnabas'.   Mr. Holland preached.   He is a senior student (fellow) of Christ Church, and tutor, and is considered, perhaps, the rising man; I believe Dr. Liddon thinks so.   I liked him very well, though it was not a remarkable sermon in any way, but he may have suited himself to the St. Barnabas' people and aimed particularly at simplicity. He is to preach at the Cathedral on Sunday.

"This week there have been quite exciting boat races every day. We went three times. The unattached, in whom we took special interest on account of our friend Lang being one of the eight, did most wretchedly. Did I tell you how they race here? I will repeat anyhow. The river is so narrow that ten boats could not possibly go abreast, so they row in a string, and the thing to do is to 'bump' the one just in front and so work one's way up. They row in two divisions, the best ten at 7 P. M., the second best at 5.30; the head of the second best ten rowing twice, in the race at 5.30, and last in the race at 7 P. M. Brasenose came off victorious. There is a narrow bank path along which the college men run, keeping up with their boats and yelling encouragement at the top of their lungs. It is very amusing indeed to see them. There are a great many people 'up,' as they are wont to come for Commemoration. Now that is closed to the public, they come for the races instead. The week unfortunately has been cloudy and showery. They have been playing cricket matches in Christ Church meadow in front of our house every day this week. It seems to me very stupid. The men are very swell and come out in a four-horse wagon. The Oxford and London coach makes quite an excitement when it passes. You know it is driven by gentlemen. They always sound their horn when they pass, and Burgess laughs because I rush to the window to see it.

"We are going on a rowing expedition to-morrow to commemorate Burgess's last week-day in Oxford. The party is to be the two Langs and ourselves. We start at

105

noon and expect to be gone the whole afternoon. We are
going to surprise them with a very recherché hamper to
sustain us by the way. Would that you were here to help
us discuss and enjoy it. We like the Langs very much.
. . .

" May 29, 1876.

" I had to break off and go to a Missionary meeting at
Corpus Christi College. Bishop Mylne, of Bombay, was to
address the people. It was quite interesting. You remember, he is from Keble College, where I dined with him. He
is very popular and has had fifteen men promise to go out to
India to work under him. None of them are yet in orders.
The Bishop's idea is to have a sort of Brotherhood system;
at least associated work, under his direction, and it is owing
to that he has got so many men. One does dread the idea
of working all alone so far away. They are to agree not to
marry for a term of years. . . .

" On Saturday we had a very jolly time indeed. The
day passed charmingly without a mishap of any kind. We
started at 12 and got back at 8 P. M. We took turns in
rowing and towing the nine miles to Abingdon, where
there is a singular old church with five aisles. It is
in good Catholic hands. There is also a ruined Abbey
there. We picnicked on a very pretty spot by the river side,
and enjoyed the good things that Mrs. Aldridge had provided for us. We all had a very pleasant time. It was
certainly very unlike the common run of days with me.

" Yesterday Mr. Holland preached at the Cathedral a
very excellent sermon. Dr. King very kindly asked us to
take a farewell lunch with them. Then we heard the Dean

of Rochester, Scott (Liddell and Scott, you know). I forgot to say Canon Liddon was to have lunched at Dr. King's, but was not well. I have been going a good deal to the Cathedral lately. . . . I have been reading Keble's memoirs and have been enjoying the Lyra Innocentium. How exquisite those lines upon the death of the New Baptized and Disuse of Infant Communion. The last is enough to convince anyone but an *intelligent layman* of the beauty and need of it. And now there is to be a month of quiet all to myself, then wandering for two months, and after that home. I am sure that I have done right in staying; my sister was so disappointed when she thought I would not travel with her.

" The weather is very pleasant now, the country lovely, the birds sing more delightfully, and the hawthorn hedges and the wild flowers are charming. We heard some cuckoos on Saturday and are hoping for the nightingales.

" Dr. King's lectures on Parochialia are really a help.

. . .

" Yours affectionately,

" HENRY."

" 31 IFFLEY ROAD, OXFORD,

" Whitsun Eve, June 3, 1876.

" MY DEAR FRANCIS:

" . . . You can never make your letters more interesting than by telling me about your boys and what you are doing with and for them. That is the real way to get at the older people—through the younger; one can see how natural it is too. . . . As to the idea of dying young, one ought not to indulge fancies. For your own dear self, to depart and be with Christ, must be better, but for those who are left, or would have to be left, it may be more expedient for you to tarry. About one thing there can be no doubt; that until He calls we are not to go. We must do all in our power to preserve our lives. You, of course, understand that I do not mean one is to neglect any plain duty, or coddle himself, but use ordinary and necessary precautions. For myself, I do not feel any terror now at the possibility of dying, only that I have done and am doing so very, very little, and that little so feebly and imperfectly for Him. One would like to feel that one has fought the battle before reaching the resting place. . . .

" I am very much interested in Keble's Memoirs, although I do think that Coleridge makes himself too prominent by far. Keble used to take a good many trips for his wife's health, didn't he? Or perhaps they seem more frequent by reading about them in such close connection in a book. Dr. King has been upon Confession in his last two lectures, introduced by the reading of the Visitation Office. Last night we had a choice little conference on ' Thy will be done.' We are to have a treat to-morrow; Dr. Liddon is to preach before the University. Was I harsh in telling you what he said about the League of Saint Cross? or did I have the tone of, ' I told you so '? If so, forget and forgive.

" If you come to Keble you will have great temptation to go into the delights of college life. I feel that even I, staid and old as I am, could very easily be led away by them; not that they are in any way sinful, but only not exactly a help to spirituality. I do not mean to speak of Keble especially, but college life in general—unattached. I don't like it at all—lectures and no congenial society—nor do I think Cowley and college at the same time a desirable mixture, but more of that hereafter. As to being allowed to work in a London parish, I am sure there would be no difficulty, for they are always glad of helpers, especially if you didn't need a stipend. I am rather lonely, but am sure it is good training for me. Let me hear from you as often as you can; write scraps in pencil in any kind of way, they will always be most acceptable. . . .

" You know well that I should love to be with you at the Monastery next winter—if you are there. Do pray for me that I may not waste this summer; not that travelling is a waste of time, but there are so many and great temptations in travelling that one finds many excuses for neglecting ' exercises ' and church duties. And now for the present farewell. Let us continue and increase our prayers for the L. S. C. . . .

" Yours affectionately,

" HENRY."

" 31 IFFLEY ROAD, OXFORD,

" EVE OF TRINITY SUNDAY, June 10, 1876.

" MY DEAR FRANCIS:

" . . . Dr. Liddon preached a beautiful sermon last Sunday before the University. I am going to send you the paper which has it, though very much of the charm is in the man himself. His red Doctor's gown was very becoming. I had a delightful walk with him on Friday; he was very agreeable. I asked him a good deal about the Roman question, as it has been brought before me lately by the perversion of a friend of Lang's. The Doctor, of course, was very satisfactory. ' Did you ever read " Loss and Gain," by John Henry Newman? If not I shouldn't advise you to do so,' said the Doctor. But the way it came up was, he took me to see St. Bartholomew's Chapel, which is mentioned in that work. It is such a disgrace to Oriel. The religious house, of which this was the chapel, was suppressed and given to Oriel. The chapel, a pretty stone one, of very good style, is used by the tenant, a farmer, for rubbish. Think of the desecration! The elevation for the altar is still there; the chancel steps, the gravestones, the rood-screen still stands, but the whole of the sacred place is filled with old wagon wheels, doors, barrels, etc. Isn't it shocking? The Doctor said it is the kind of place that would suit our purpose, referring to the League of Saint Cross, which he had not forgotten, although I had not mentioned it again. He is so kind and considerate. He asked me if I would not ever come to England again, and when I said I thought not, he said he was sorry, and asked me particularly to let him know about my ordination— all this spontaneously. I had not been speaking of it at all, and he did it in the midst of our walk, and not merely when he was saying good-bye. He said he would be in Oxford ten days longer, and if I would look him up he would be happy to take another walk. Now I tell you all this not from any feeling of conceit, but just to show you how kind he is. He seems to be rather provoked at Dr.

Nevins' Preface to the Bonn Conference, as he alludes in it very disparagingly to Dr. Pusey. I hope that Dr. Nevins will not be at Bonn this year, but someone who really understands the importance of the subject.

" Dr. King criticised one of my sermons most carefully. He does take so much trouble; he analyzed it and paged it and read it three times; marked the good points and the weak ones. He thinks that Dr. Pusey is the best example of style for me to study. I am quite pleased. What I most lack is analysis and due proportion.

" On Tuesday is the Cuddesdon Festival, and Dr. King has got me an invitation. I went to his last lecture on Saturday; he has been dwelling upon the good points of the sectarian bodies and urging us to develop those same points in the Church—the personal holiness they so desire, the closer feeling of brotherhood of the Congregationalists, and their longing for an immediate union with Our Lord— all of which the Church, of course, ought to and does supply. No wonder right-minded and earnest people detested the cold Erastianism of the last century; but surely the time has come for the Church to try and bring back her wandering children. If only the Roman Catholics in power were like the men we read about with such intense interest, how might we hope for unity; but alas, the Vaticanists are too hideous in some of their teaching. The notices or books of devotion for the month of May lead one almost to despair of their ever being brought back from their Saint-worship to the worship of Him who is Himself the Brother, the Friend of sinners, and not the angry Son of a merciful, forgiving Mother. I read with great interest Mr. Oxenham's Preface to Dr. Döllinger's lectures on the reunion of the Churches. By the way, it was dedicated by Mr. Oxenham to

Liddon. I asked the Doctor about it, and he said that the Roman Catholics were very angry and had sat upon Mr. Oxenham in consequence. The Doctor said he was afraid that Mr. Oxenham had gone back a little in the last year—certainly the preface was wonderfully liberal. Let us pray that there may be thousands of others like him, longing for unity. Do you pray for it? I think that we ought to teach people the necessity for intercessory prayer more than we do. It is a thing about which there is most woful ignorance, even with myself, until very lately, not wilfully but because I knew no better.

"There have been two interesting lectures on India by the Professor of Sanskrit. Really the way that an educated Brahman explains their idolatry is identically the same as the Roman Catholics'. Apparently they, too, have vague ideas about the Trinity, and the need of an incarnation of God. It is most interesting. . . .

"Yours affectionately,

"HENRY."

"31 IFFLEY ROAD, OXFORD,

"June 17, 1876.

"MY DEAR FRANCIS:

"For the last time do I write you from Oxford. By Saturday next, I hope my sister will be safely here. I sup-

CHRIST CHURCH CATHEDRAL, OXFORD.

pose I am the most absurd person, but really I have not the least desire to go travelling this summer, not the least. Oughtn't I to be ashamed of myself not to appreciate the opportunities that are given me? Well, I am ashamed, but I cannot excite the smallest enthusiasm. Perhaps, though, when my sister is with me, it will be different. At any rate I have no intention of putting any damper upon her enjoyment by seeming uninterested or bored. It is not that I am lazy and don't want to move, for I should like to have some active work. The dangers of travelling are fearful. I don't mean the risk of one's life, physical life, but the spiritual. It is so extremely easy to omit one's duties. I suppose a good way to keep them is not to have too many, but to be very particular about those rules you do make. Dr. King made some very sensible remarks apropos of this last night—that it is much better to propose to read one book, and do it, than to lug about in one's bag a small library.

" I dined at Exeter College on Sunday, and went to Compline in the rooms of my host. It is very helpful to see a lot of University men not ashamed but glad to meet for extra prayers.

" I went over to Cuddesdon on Tuesday for the festival. It was silly for me to go on an anniversary day, for naturally everyone had his friends to look after, and so I felt rather in the way; not that anything was done to make me feel so. There was a surpliced procession of about one hundred and fifty men, headed by a cross bearer and followed by a chaplain with the pastoral staff and the Lord Bishops of Oxford and Maritzburg. They sang as they walked from the college to the parish church. After the service of Matins there was a luncheon in a tent on the lawn. . . . They certainly have wonderfully good officers at Cuddesdon; Dr. King, Dr. Liddon, who was vice-president for five years, and now Canon Furse, who is a splendid man. They only have three officers, president, vice-president and chaplain. They generally have about twenty men, and the term is only one year. Certainly the men they turn out are excellent specimens. I have met a good many at Dr. King's, who all say it was the happiest year of their lives. They have good buildings and chapel and library. It is in a very quiet little village, seven and a half miles from Oxford. The atmosphere is thoroughly Catholic, and the president, vice-president and chaplain are all of one mind; so naturally the influence is both strong and good. After the festival they have a retreat for old students, of whom there were a great many present. It really made me envious. Would that the G. T. S. could become more like it! How wonderful it would be! Perhaps the little League of Saint Cross may be able to help a few along. Let us hope at any rate and pray.

"I should like to know what is to become of yourself and myself. One cannot forecast at all. If it so happens that for a time we may not be able to live together, I see no reason why a solemn league and covenant might not be made by which we could agree to meet if possible at one of our rectories for mutual counsel and encouragement, and perhaps for a retreat. Why, at least, shouldn't we have an association of prayer called the League of St. Cross, and about which there need be no secret? It is a great thing to get people to help us with their prayers. I am the precipitate one, am I not?

"Which would be a good motto? Galatians, VI, 14. either whole, or first or latter half; or Galatians, II, 20; or Philippians, IV, 13; or the old Oratorian one, 'Omnia vestra

114

in caritate fiant ' ?* What do you say to a cross with a motto for associates? Tell me which motto you prefer, or suggest others.

> " Yours affectionately,

> > " HENRY."

In June Van Rensselaer's only unmarried sister came over to England, and they travelled together all that summer. Fortunately we have three letters, which we subjoin, giving an account of his last student days at Oxford, and of the trip through England and Scotland.

> WINDERMERE,

> > " June 25, 1876.

" MY DEAR FRANCIS:

" . . . I am really off on my summer tour, you see, and so far, so well. I left Oxford on Friday for Liverpool, and on Saturday, at noon, the Scythia arrived. It was

---

* The passages taken from the Protestant version and referred to as suitable for a motto for the projected League of Saint Cross, or Society of the Holy Cross, are:

"But God forbid that I should glory save in the cross of our Lord Jesus Christ by whom the world is crucified unto me, and I unto the world."

"I am crucified with Christ: nevertheless I live; yet not I, but Christ liveth in me: and the life which I now live in the flesh I live by the faith of the Son of God, who loved me and gave Himself for me."

"I can do all things through Christ which strengtheneth me."

very pleasant to see so many home faces again—one new one, too, in my smallest niece, a very beautiful child. Our family party broke up, part going to London and the rest to the Lake districts. You will be amused to hear that my sister and I have, as our travelling companion, Dr. Tyng's new associate rector, Dr. Williams. They all liked him very much on the steamer, and he was proposing to himself the same tour as my sister and I, so we thought it would be pleasant to join company, as he is alone. He is about forty-five, and is very companionable, an excellent churchman in many respects, and very liberal. He is by birth a Virginian, has had a parish at Georgetown, D. C., for ten years, and regrets the lack of church discipline in the diocese. He has really some excellent ideas upon the subjects which we have discussed; that is, he has always made a rule never to allow any persons to be sponsors unless they were communicants. Good and brave, isn't it?

" We are spending Sunday in just the very loveliest place imaginable, a pretty little village on Lake Windermere; the hotel on a hill overlooking the lake, beautiful trees, flowering shrubs on all sides, the water blue. There is a quaint old church here, prettily decorated, surpliced choir, etc. We were so disappointed to find that there had been a Celebration at 9. We asked at the hotel, and they said there was no service until 10:45.

" I went yesterday to an early Celebration at St. Margaret's, Liverpool—a beautiful church. I never saw one I liked better. I must go backward a little and tell you about leaving Oxford. I went to the Commemoration on Wednesday, and it is a stupid enough affair, I assure you. There was some fun, though, before it began. The undergrads made funny remarks, and gave cheers for people, etc., Girton

116

College (women, you know) among them. The Vice-Chancellor made a Latin speech, encouraged by such remarks as ' Cut it short,' ' Wind her up,' etc. When he conferred D. C. L.'s, he had to repeat the same form of words about ten times, and after doing it once or twice he was told not to do it again. The poor old gentleman didn't exactly enjoy it, and whenever a popular man got the D. C. L. the wretched undergraduates would cap the Vice-Chancellor's speech with a chorus of ' For he's a jolly good fellow,' etc., and it was very funny. By far the best looking man who received the degree was Lieutenant Cameron, of African fame. He really was intelligent looking. Some of the others looked as though they had been brought up on Latin and Greek roots, and the diet had not agreed with them. The Bishop of Derry was an exception.

" I must tell you about Liddon. He told his class if they wanted the conclusion of his analysis to go to his rooms on Tuesday. So I went. I was going to say good-bye, but he asked me if I wouldn't like to walk. Of course I did, so we went out walking. He again alluded to the League of Saint Cross of his own accord, and wanted to know if we couldn't start by having a clergy house; so you see he would seem to approve of our beginning at once. I suggested an association of prayer, which he thought would be excellent. He promised to compose a prayer for us to use, if I should write and tell him what we wanted. He takes great interest in our spiritual welfare. Why shouldn't we have an association? Did I speak of it in my last letter? One of our friends wrote that he had a strong longing for the Religious life, but would not allow himself to think about it for several years, which would amount to his being engaged in the meanwhile, if not married. Now, we ought to see what we can do to help each other along; he might be very useful in the L. S. C. Why shouldn't we have a form of prayer and intercession and a few rules like those of the Brotherhood of the Holy Trinity at Oxford and Cambridge. They are not severe and are good for a beginning. Then, if we could meet each other occasionally, at least once a year, for a retreat and a conference, in a little while we might try in good earnest. I feel sure that there must be many other men like ourselves, only waiting for something to turn up and help them.

" Yours affectionately,

" HENRY."

MELROSE,

" St. Peter's Day, June 29, 1876.

" MY DEAR FRANCIS:

" I did hope to have sent this off before now, but one has so very little time in travelling, and we are travelling with a vengeance. To-morrow night we hope to be in England again. I am sorry to say that the saying—*l'appetit vient en mangeant*—in my case, is untrue of travelling; for the more I travel the less I care for it. I cannot get up any excitement at all, and it is really most tiresome to me. My sister and Dr. Williams enjoy it all immensely. On some accounts I would just as lief not have him. My sister says it is fortunate that he is with us, as I should be tempted to hurry her past a great many interesting places, which is rather mean, considering that I am here entirely on her account.

" We saw the English lakes under the most favorable conditions; shed some tears over Wordsworth, Southey, etc., and came to Edinburgh. Holyrood, of course, is very interesting, but I hate to be in Scotland on account of the prevailing religion. Everything speaks to me of desecration, ruined abbeys, or, sadder yet, cathedrals and churches transformed into kirks and meeting-houses. No doubt the monks were bad, but——and to think of people daring to destroy the houses of God, and to use the materials to build themselves houses—how dare they do it? No, I may be narrowminded, but it is a fact all the same, that I cannot see anything nowadays except in connection with the Church and the Church's Head.

" On Tuesday we went to Roslyn Chapel, a most exquisite thing, built in the fifteenth century, apparently regardless of expense, entirely of stone; every stone, almost, beautifully carved. It is really a wonderful piece of work. In those days nothing was too rich or too expensive for the glory of God. The present Earl of Roslyn, a Catholic (not Roman Catholic) has restored it to the service and ' ad majorem Dei gloriam,' as he calls it—keeps a chaplain and has the chapel properly equipped, cross, candles, etc., and services, although he does not himself live near. It is encouraging in such a dead level of Presbyterianism.

" This morning we went to an early Celebration of All Saints' Cathedral, Edinburgh. It is Catholic, too. They used the Scotch Liturgy, which is more like the Roman than ours. The Consecration and oblation come first, then the prayer for the Church and the Lord's Prayer before Communion. I rather like it. Yesterday we made a tour of the

119

Scotch lakes, Lomond and Katrine, and Stirling Castle, and to-day we have been to the Abbey here and to Dryburgh. The latter is most beautiful, although very ruinous, and is situated in the midst of exclusive grounds. Sir Walter Scott is buried in one of the ruined chapels; but it is altogether sad to my mind to see such ruins. To-morrow morning we go to Abbotsford, and then on to Durham and York, etc.

" Perhaps you will be glad to hear that I have taken our passage for September 9th, in the Scythia, and I hope that we shall get off then, though our departure may be postponed until a little later if necessary. I shall be so glad to get back. Can't you wait for my return for your retreat at Boston, and we shall go together?

" I did not tell you about Liddon's farewell. I asked him for his blessing, and he not only gave me that, but went up-stairs and tried to find a little book of Bishop Andrews on Devotion for the Sick, for which he had written a preface. He did not find it, and he brought me ' Some Elements ' instead. He asked me if I had it; I said that I had. I didn't know what the other book was and rather wanted it. So he rummaged round and found a copy, in which he wrote: ' From his affectionate friend, H. P. Liddon,' and in Greek, ' Contend for the faith once delivered to the Saints.' He asked me to write to him, as if he really cared to hear, and said that I mustn't mind sometimes if he could not always answer on account of business. Wasn't it good of him? Well, you know, I did hanker for the ' Some Elements ' dreadfully, but didn't like to tell him so. The other little book is nice, but mostly Bishop Andrews', which was proba-bly the reason why he selected it, being like most truly great men—modest. I could not resist writing him a little note the next day, asking him if I could not have ' Some Elements,' he had meant to give me. The book came in reply with the motto from St. Augustine—'*Ama et fac quod vis*'—and of course my name, and from him. The angelic Dr. King gave me a copy of St. Anselm's Meditations, with a very touching inscription. My friend Lang gave me ' Prometheus Vinctus,' done into English verse by himself at the age of 17. It was quite a wrench for me to leave Oxford. I have forgotten a most unlooked-for token from my fellow boarder, Miss Seal, a beautifully worked chalice veil, corporal, etc., done by herself, lace and all. I had my photograph taken for my Oxford friends in ordinary dress; I will send you one. Don't think about St. Clement's, I beg you. If you take a holiday do write: have heard nothing more about Keble College.

" Yours affectionately,

" HENRY."

After the visit to Scotland, the little party then crossed over to Holland and Belgium. The Low Countries infected Van Rensselaer with malaria, so that, when they got into Switzerland via the Rhine, he was taken down with a fever. This interrupted his plans somewhat, for towards the close of August he was again at Oxford, where he remained until his departure for America a fortnight later. By this time he had definitely abandoned his purpose of working among the poor on the East Side, but he still clung to the dream of founding a religious community that would fill a very noticeable gap in the American branch of the Anglican Church. He again refers to the subject in these two letters, which were the last he wrote from England.

" 31 Iffley Road, Oxford,

" St. Bartholomew's Day, August 24, 1876.

" My Dear Francis:

" I am once more comfortably installed in my old quarters here, and it seems natural and pleasant. . . . I don't see the advantage for you of a year spent working in London as a member of the League of Saint Cross. Of course I understand your idea of learning to work among the poor, but after all the Oratorian work and life is not one devoted to parish work, but more one to be spent in trying to promote spirituality among the seminarians and clergy, one to try and raise the tone of the clergy both intellectually and spiritually. But how will a year of hard work among the poor conduce to fitting you for it? It strikes me that what we need is enough, not overmuch, work, time for meditation and prayer, and as much retirement as possible. As you say, we should not get too much interested in individuals and places. That was one of my chief reasons for giving up Avenue C. I knew I should be much interested, and that it would be almost impossible to tear myself away from it after having once taken it up. We really ought to exert ourselves to the utmost to be together, and near enough New York to have an influence at the General Theological Seminary. . . .

" I am sure it will all come out right, and I have the liveliest hopes for the League of Saint Cross. Don't you think you have overlooked the main object of ' L'Oratoire ' in your desire to be an efficient parish priest? . . .

" It is very pleasant to be settled again within sound of the church bells. I go to a retreat at the Fathers' on Monday to last until Friday evening. I hope I shall get back some spirituality, for I feel so hard and dry now.   How true it is that if one does not go forward in the spiritual life one does not stand still but goes backward.   The retreat is to be for priests, so I suppose I shall have to don my clericals, cassock at least, so as not to be conspicuous.   I received a warm welcome from the Fathers and dined there yesterday.   They never try to convert me: only Father Prescott does that.

"What a work there is to be done, and doesn't it seem well nigh presumptuous for us young men to try to do the little we can.   It would be so indeed if we did not firmly believe the truth: 'Ye have not chosen me, but I have chosen you.' How that alters everything.   No longer presumptuous, no longer hopeless, but in quiet confidence and with an holy boldness, being called, we obey the Master's voice.   People are sure to say: 'You ought to wait for some older and more experienced person to lead the way'; but look at the founders of the Religious Orders; none of them were old men when they started them.   All began their work young, even if the completion was long deferred.   .   .   .

" Yours affectionately,

" HENRY."

" 31 IFFLEY ROAD, OXFORD,

" September 1, 1876.

" MY DEAR FRANCIS:

" .   .   .   I am now writing to you for the very last time from Oxford, at least so far as I can tell.   This night

123

week we shall be in Liverpool ready to sail on Saturday. I am sure you are pining to go to New York. Do come on to meet me, or if not that, as soon as possible. You may have been expecting to hear of Mr. Lowder's decision, but you know one can read no letters during retreat, and so I did not get his answer until to-day. He says that he is sorry that he has no room for you, but advises me to apply to Father Benson, who can doubtless assist me to find a place. I still cling to the idea of Hoboken. Do have a letter waiting for me at home telling me whether Mr. Wetherill is at the Holy Innocents' or not. If he is I shall go over and see him before calling on the Bishop, as it would be well to have my plans laid before seeing him. I don't think there is a chance of my going back to England, certainly not at once; not for any lukewarmness for the interest of the L. S. C., I assure you.

" I don't see how its interests will be advanced by such a step. I am reading Mrs. Oliphant's Life of St. Francis of Assisi, and am almost convinced that his example might be followed with advantage in this century. What think you of turning Franciscan? I am not jesting, I have really been thinking of it; not the Roman Catholic Order, but one like it; yet I fear you will laugh at me and say it does not look much like it to be buying lots of clothes and books, etc. It is a little contradictory, to be sure.

" The retreat ended this morning; there were eighteen priests and your brother Henry, disguised as a priest in cassock and clerical colar. It seemed quite natural for me. Father Benson was the conductor and gave very good addresses, although a trifle transcendental. He has a deep insight into spiritual things. I think, though, that in all my life I never passed three longer days. It seemed as if the day would never come to an end. There were four addresses a day—think of it! On Wednesday they had special services for missions and a litany which seemed perfectly endless. You think me very bad, but I can't help it. I am afraid I have no vocation for the Evangelist Fathers' life. God grant I may have for another phase of the Religious life. After being silent all the week, it seemed as if I could not sing enough when I got back here. My landlady says she likes me to do it.

" . . . I gave a hint of our plan to Tompkins, who takes the greatest possible interest in the League of Saint Cross and longs to help us. He already does so with his prayers. A lady member of the Confraternity of the Blessed Sacrament is his right-hand helper. Poor fellow, he has a hard struggle out there in the West. You should hear him speak about Sectarianism. It would do your heart good. I cannot but feel that, under God, I have had influence on him, which only shows how much a little sympathy and kindness can effect. Let us be encouraged, dear friend, to try what we can do for others.

" What a delight it will be to see you again, but I also dread it, too. You may have imagined or hoped that you would see a great change for the better in me. Alas! I fear that the improvement is but small, but I do not despair.

" Yours affectionately,

" Henry, L. S. C.

CHAPTER VII.

Anglican Deacon.

IN mid-September Van Rensselaer arrived in America, and about a month later, on St. Luke's Day, October 18, 1876, Bishop Horatio Potter ordained him deacon. He had made up his mind that he would always teach exactly what he believed, and he had quite definite ideas on religious matters. Being independent of salary, he determined to cast his lot with his friend at the seminary, Francis P. Mackall, also a deacon, who had decided to work in the new parish of the Holy Innocents, Hoboken. The rector was pleased to have their services for nothing, and gave them free fling. Opposite the church they took an apartment, which they fitted up in monastic style, with a chapel and altar. Indoors they always wore cassock and biretta.

Thus was Van Rensselaer installed in his new field of work as an ordained deacon of the Anglican Church in America. New experiences crowded in upon him, and all the while he was drawing nearer, albeit unconsciously, to the truth, the evidences of which could not be long delayed. The rector was supposed to be a very high churchman. At all events he liked ritualism. To check his exalted views, the trustees of the church had named an assistant of the lowest type of churchmen. The other assistants deemed him unorthodox, and with the rector's connivance and cooperation, they denounced him to the Bishop of New Jersey, Dr. Odenheimer, on the charge of Nestorianism. The Bishop suspended him. This, however, the good assistant declared he did not mind, as he was simply relieved of his duties. He continued to draw his salary.

At times there were extravagant exhibitions of ritualism. "I shall never forget the midnight Mass that Christmas in the Holy Innocents," he says. "We were to appear for the first time in vestments. As these were tentative, they were made of linen. The effect, especially of the dalmatics, was startling, and when the choristers beheld us they burst out laughing and whispered audibly, ' night shirts.' But we went out all the same in solemn procession through the church, to the great admiration of the people.

"Those were wonderful functions of the go-as-you-please style, and necessarily so, for the Book of Common Prayer makes no provision for such Popish ceremonies.

"Another sample of the absurdity of ritualism was given at a funeral of one of our choristers. We decided to have a Requiem Mass. Of course, there is no provision made in the Book of Common Prayer for a Mass of any kind, as the Articles of Religion in that book denounce Masses as an abomination and a Popish invention. But such a denunciation only whets the desire of a ritualist. So a Mass of Requiem was to be sung. But how about vestments? Our church had not risen to the height of colored vestments, except stoles. They had to be borrowed. We selected violet ones as being less lugubrious. Violet ones were, therefore, procured for the occasion from a very high church in New York. But our troubles did not end with getting vestments. How were we to transform the Communion service in the Prayer Book into a Requiem Mass? Some parts would do, but others were very inappropriate. What connection could there be between the dead and the recital of the ten commandments with the response: ' Lord, have mercy upon us and incline our hearts to keep this law '? So we eliminated the ten commandments. But how about the

' Gloria in Excelsis ' ? This seemed too joyous, so out it went from our constructed Mass. The ceremony, in fact, was a very remarkable one and evoked much comment, as well it might, for neither celebrant nor assistants knew what was to be done, as there were no rubrics in our Prayer Book to direct us."

Life in church matters became rather discouraging for Van Renssalaer and Mackall. The assistant minister had been evicted, it is true, but there was no responsive chord in the congregation. It was dreary, indeed, to say morning and evening prayer for one person, and to address this one person, a woman, as " dearly beloved brethren." To make matters worse they were only a couple of blocks away from a Catholic Church. It made them green with envy when they saw the crowds that poured into it on Sunday, and even on week-days. What a contrast was St. Mary's Catholic Church to their poor Holy Innocents' !

The rector was hardly the man to help them in their difficulties, as may be judged from the following incident :—

" We had a trial in Lent, when the rector slated himself for a course of sermons. Perhaps the most read book in those days in religious circles was Farrar's ' Life of Christ.' There were many cheap editions, and every Protestant household was likely to possess a copy. What was our dismay when the opening sermon of the course was a chapter, word for word, from this book, carefully copied and read. Now Farrar is absolutely heretical in his teaching about the temptations of Christ, stating, as he does, that Christ could have sinned. What was to be done to ward off the reading of such a doctrine ? It was bad enough to have any of the book read, for we knew that members of the congregation had it at home, and would probably recognize the steal. So, as that Sunday he was to dine with us, we put our copy of the book, opened at the chapter, in a most prominent place. But as it did not seem to attract his attention, we deliberately brought up the subject of Farrar's heretical teaching on that point. The shaft went home. The rector became excited and, saying that he had a few finishing touches to put to that night's sermon, excused himself and went home. So that night we had Farrar amended."

After a couple of months Van Rensselaer became convinced that the Protestant Episcopal Church had no authoritative teaching, nor the authority to teach. People believed as much or as little as they liked. The reading of Allies' " See of Peter," which deals with authority and jurisdiction, made a serious impression upon him. Newman's " Anglican Difficulties " did not improve the Anglican position in his eyes. But he was fair and read the other side as well. Hessey's " Rise of the Papal Power " and Pusey's " Eirenicon " were supposed to be antidotes to Allies' " See of Peter " and Newman's " Apologia." The more he read the Anglican side the more disposed was he to the Roman.

These views were all shared by his clerical friend, to whom he had written frequently from Oxford, and who was now associated with him, as fellow assistant, at the Holy Innocents, Hoboken. Yet they would not make their submission to Rome while they had any misgivings as to the step, or while there was a single loop-hole of escape. He writes:

" When our position became unbearable, we turned to our erstwhile confessor of seminary days, and wrote to him of our troubles. The answer was: ' Come on to the Church of the Advent in Boston '—where he was the Superior and Rector. This was the old ' Advent ' in Bowdoin Street, not the new one of the name in Mt. Vernon Street. So to Boston we betook ourselves, my friend and I. We met with a warm welcome and the assurance that we had no real difficulties, but that our dissatisfaction was the natural result of our being unsuccessful in Catholicizing our congregation. This did not satisfy our doubts; so we began to question some of the other 'Fathers,' to the chagrin of the Superior, who made the proud claim that he was the first monk ordained in England since the Reformation. Had he qualified the assertion by prefixing Protestant to the monk, it might have been true. Among the daily prayers recited in community was one that struck us as being peculiar. It was for the restoration of the abbey lands in England. I asked the Superior the meaning of the prayer, and to whom should the lands, in his estimation, be returned. This was an unexpected question, and he was nonplussed for a while; then he said: 'Why, to us, of course; the rightful successors.' This was a little too much; so I asked in what conceivable way the Cowley Fathers could be the rightful successors of Carthusians, Cistercians, Augustinians, Franciscans and Dominicans? The only reply was a contemptuous 'Bosh!' But he saw clearly that we had difficulties beyond his reach; so he said we had too strong an attack of the Roman fever to be cured by him, and that we had better go where we belonged. Yet, his advice would be for us to go to some congenial parish, where we might meet with the success we yearned for. We were really docile. My friend was shipped to St. Clement's, Philadelphia, and I to the House of Prayer, Newark. The game was to separate us. We made no opposition.

"I was perfectly frank with the rector in Newark and told him exactly the state of my mind, adding that, under the circumstances, I did not think I could take any active part in the church work. He said that he under-

130

stood the case perfectly, as he had himself passed through the same ordeal, and that he would leave me perfectly free; that he had a large controversial library which was at my disposal. So I settled down supposedly to study. In reality his intention was to keep me so busy that I should not have time to think. Among other things, I was to have charge of the men's Bible class. I had not been long in Newark when my friend wrote me that his position in Philadelphia was unbearable and suggested that he join me. I proposed the matter to the rector, and he approved the plan, with a full understanding of the state of our minds. So my friend came on to Newark, and we again set up a monastery on a small scale. The charge of the Sunday-school was given to my friend, and he was kept busy preparing children for Communion and Confirmation.

"There was a 'mission' given in our church by the Cowley Fathers, and the well-known Father Maturin was the chief preacher. He labored manfully to prove the catholicity of the Protestant Episcopal Church, but the cause was a hopeless one, and his failure to prove his point a help to us. He was unsuccessful in his efforts to bring people to confession. A handful of women were the only penitents. I remember well, on the Sunday afternoon of the mission, the members of one of the regiments of Newark, of which the rector was chaplain, were invited to attend. I happened to be standing just outside the church door in cassock and biretta. An unmistakable son of Erin sauntered up and took off his hat to me. I at once asked him what church he attended. He answered that he went to St. James'. I asked him what he was doing at the House of Prayer. He said that he thought it no harm. I bade him go home. He went. My action in this matter shows how the wind was blowing Romeward. The breeze was stiffening."

CHAPTER VIII.

His Conversion.

THE weeks wore on, but no peace came to Henry's mind. Catholicism did not seem any more attractive, but Protestant Episcopalianism had no more staying power for him. It was impossible to continue in such a frame of mind. What was to improve it? Of Rome, personally he knew nothing. He had never spoken to a priest on the subject, had attended very few Catholic services, and had a mass of prejudices against Rome.

In the story of his conversion Van Rensselaer gives a vivid picture of the doubt and torture of a mind on the threshold of the Catholic Church.

"No one," he says, "who has not passed through the experience can realize the agony of mind of one in the process of conversion. The ground seems slipping from his feet, and there is no coign of vantage for him. He knows his own church, but he is ignorant of the one he may enter. Perhaps he may not be any better satisfied in the new than in the old. Why venture in the uncertainty? Besides, by leaving his own church a person cuts loose from all the ties that have bound him to relatives and friends, and is thrown upon the possible friendship of strangers. Then what a deep gulf of prejudices is opened up, and one that may be unbridgable! How much to hold a doubter back, and what to draw him on to take the crucial step! If, after the step is taken, he finds out his mistake, how will he ever have the courage to acknowledge it and retrace his steps? Then, too, what an audacious thing it is for him to sit in judgment on what, until then, he has held to be the church of his fathers. Is he wiser than they? What a reflection upon their judgment! What was good enough for them should be good enough for him. Then every scandal that can be raked up is brought forward as damning proof against the Catholic Church. As if, forsooth, the violators of the Church's laws could be adduced as witnesses against the laws. Just as if the black sheep of the flock was the one by which the whole flock should be judged."

One thing was certain; it was impossible for Van Rensselaer to continue to act as minister of a church whose claims to be the Church of Christ were more than doubtful. He therefore resolved to lay aside his charge. His rector, unable to convince him, begged him not to go to Rome from his church. As he had not been with the rector long enough to make any impression upon the congregation, Van Rensselaer agreed to the request.

He next informed his mother of the probable necessity of his becoming a Catholic. She had long been in the habit of saying: " You had better go where you belong "; but of course when the time came to follow her advice, she felt it keenly. She suggested his going back to Oxford to see his former friends, the canons and professors. He was nothing loath, especially if it would give her satisfaction, and he explained to her he had no desire at all to go over to Rome; quite the contrary, he had no friends in that Church, and nothing in it appealed to him except the truth which it seemed to possess in its entirety. So to Oxford he went. He always regretted that he did not visit Birmingham to make a pilgrimage to the Oratory at Edgbaston, where Newman was living; undoubtedly the life and writings of the Cardinal had much effect in leading him to the light. The " Apologia " and " Anglican Difficulties " cleared the way, which Pusey's " Eirenicon " failed to obstruct again.

Henry's first visit in Oxford was to Canon King. The Canon received him as of yore, most cordially, until he learned his errand, then he grew sad. Arguments he had none, except the special pleading: " Be loyal to your Mother." " That," writes Van Rensselaer, " I always was; but that was begging the question. My inquiry was about the identity of my Mother, the Church. I have grave doubts about the maternal claims of the Church of England and her offspring, the Protestant Episcopal Church in the United States. As the good Canon said, my difficulties were historical, and he did not attempt to answer them, but referred me to Canon Bright, my former professor of ecclesiastical history. I never called again on my dear old friend, Canon King, as I saw that my defection grieved him. Since then he has become Anglican Bishop of Lincoln, and has had his own troubles with the Court of Arches for ritualistic practices. Would that the great St. Hugh of Lincoln might obtain for the nineteenth-century Protestant intruder into his ancient see the gift of faith! Imagine St. Hugh being tried by a secular court for wearing a cope and mitre! "

He next turned his steps to Canon Bright. The Canon was one of the lecturers whose courses he attended during his earlier stay at the great English university. Van Rensselaer describes him as a very nervous and eccentric man, learned but not entertaining. " I never fancied him and never counted him among my friends "; but in the search for truth, personal dislikes were repressed. And here follows an account of the visit to Canon Bright :—

" Now it happened that just at that time a controversy

was being waged over a book called 'The Priest and Absolution.' It was in reality an English translation of a Latin manual of moral theology, and intended by the translators for the use of 'Anglo-Catholic' priests (?). A low-church peer, Earl Redesdale, had produced this book in the House of Lords and treated his confrères to choice selections from the chapters concerning the commandment which is the Catholic sixth, but the Protestant seventh. 'Such are the matters,' quoth the Earl, 'which the parsons, now dubbed priests, discuss with your wives and daughters.' Of course the insinuation was manifestly unfair. He might as well have brought in a medical book and have read passages, with the comment that such were the matters that doctors discuss with their patients. Nevertheless the shot hit the mark, and when the question of confession and absolution was put to the vote of the bishops in England, they promptly disclaimed the doctrine and the practice. At this juncture I called on Canon Bright and asked how he accounted for the action of the bishops. He answered that if he wanted to know anything about the sea, he would not apply for information to a landsman. I admitted his wisdom in this, but failed to see the application. He then explained that the bishops knew nothing about confession. 'That's strange,' I said. 'If the so-called priests of the Church of England have any power to forgive sins, it must come from the bishops. How, then, can it be that the bishops do not recognize any such power resident in them?' 'Oh,' said the Canon, 'the Church of England is in a topsy-turvy condition.' 'Do you admit that?' I asked. 'Of course I do,' he replied. 'Then she cannot be the Church of God,' I answered. 'For though the Church may contain disorderly persons in her borders, she cannot herself be in a state of

disorder, especially in essential teachings, such as the forgiveness of sins.' So, far from holding me back, the Canon
only helped to drive me out of the fold, which was becoming
more and more evidently that of the hireling and not of
the Good Shepherd."

The visit to Oxford, then, had not strengthened the Anglican position. Still Van Rensselaer was loath to leave the
Anglican Church without making one more effort to clear
up his difficulties, so he next turned to his old friend, Canon
Liddon, then in residence in Amen Corner, London, where
the Canons of St. Paul's Cathedral lived.

"The Canon," he tells us, "was very friendly and listened patiently. It was not a new story for him. As he
admitted, he had often travelled the same road himself.
But, as he asserted, he always managed to steady his waver-
ing steps by reading the works of the Fathers of the Church.
What would he advise me to do? Read two books, one on
either side, treating the same texts of Scripture and quotations from the Fathers, and then decide for myself which
was the correct interpreter. Was not this true Protestant
theory and practice of the right of private judgment? If
he were a Catholic priest, would he give such advice?
Fancy a young man going to a priest and telling him that
he was in doubt about his faith. Would the priest tell him
to read Ingersoll and Lambert and then decide for himself? Would he not be bound to give reasons for his faith,
refute the sophisms and bid the young man avoid reading
poisonous literature, and strengthen his faith by sound
books, prayer and reception of the Sacraments of Penance
and Holy Eucharist? Such was not the method of Canon
Liddon, but he threw me back on my own private judgment.
What two books would he advise me to read? Hessey's

' Rise of the Papal Power,' on the Protestant, and Allies'
' See of Peter,' on the Catholic side. I had already read
them both. However, perhaps I had not pondered them
sufficiently, for I had to admit that Allies seemed to be the
genuine expounder of the texts of Scripture and the Fathers.
Canon Liddon had, I afterward learned, and as he himself
had hinted, often been on the verge of submitting to the
authority of Rome, and had even consulted Catholic priests
about it. Did the possession of a Canonry of St. Paul's
and a professor's chair in Oxford weigh down the scale on
the Anglican side? I did not call again; what was the use?
It would be a case of the blind leading the blind."

It should be stated here that Henry had already looked up
and settled to his satisfaction certain matters of prime importance. On a visit to the Bodleian Library, before meeting Dr. King, he recalled the difficulty of papal infallibility
which Dr. Döllinger adduced as a reason for rejecting the
authority of the Vatican Council. He says: " I turned to the
chapter on ' Papal Supremacy ' in the ' Church History,'
published by the said Dr. Döllinger in 1845, that is, twenty-
five years before the definition of Papal Infallibility in the
Council of the Vatican, in 1870. My reading of this chapter convinced me of true Papal supremacy, which would, of
course, include infallibility. Another point was cleared up
regarding the early Church, by reading Hefele's ' History of
the Councils,' which, to be sure, contained the ecumenical
letters. I was startled to find that these councils of the
much-referred-to undivided Church of the first four centuries, in their synodal letters, spoke of the occupant of the
See of Rome, precisely as the Church of after-centuries, up to
the present day addresses the Pope, successor of St. Peter,
Prince of the Apostles, Vicar of Christ on Earth. At the

Protestant seminary in New York, we had used as a textbook an *Index Canonum* of these very councils, but the compiler had very wisely, from his point of view, omitted the ecumenical letters. The discovery of their existence was a revelation and a shock. The stronghold of Protestantism had crumbled at its foundation."

Van Rensselaer still had many difficulties in regard to the Catholic Church. Many of her doctrines were not clear to his mind, and many of her devotions did not appeal to his taste. But, if Christ had built his Church on Peter, the rock against which the gates of hell should not prevail, had given him the keys of the Kingdom of Heaven, had promised to be with him always to the end of the world, and had bestowed the Holy Ghost, the Spirit of Truth, to guide His Church into all truth, then he felt convinced that whatever this Church taught must be true and should be accepted by all. The identity of the true Church was no longer doubtful. Submission to authority was the only course open to him. It was an intellectual conviction, without any sensible attraction.

The following letter to one of the family, written two weeks before his formal reception into the Church, sums up tersely the visit to Oxford and its result:

" PARIS,

" September 4, 1877.

" I have not written for some time because I have been, and am, too unhappy to want to put my feelings on paper. Dr. King was entirely unable to help me, and not being well up on the Roman side, he could not command that respect for his opinion which he otherwise would have. His argument is exactly Keble's: Born in the Anglican Communion, stay there. Why not equally well say: Born in the Church of Scotland, stay there?

"While I was in Oxford before Dr. King came, I obtained access to a library there, and read Döllinger's History, which convinced me that his present position as a schismatic is untenable from his own book, which, unlike those written by Anglicans who 'verted, has never been retracted, but still holds its position as true history. I also read Cardinal Manning's 'True History of the Vatican Council,' which gives one a very different idea from the one usually entertained in regard to Infallibility. It was quite strange that the day I went by appointment to see Dr. King I was kept waiting in the dining-room and picked up Macaulay's History and read the preface. His account of the formation of the Church of England by Elizabeth was startling and an ill preparation for my first talk with the Doctor upon the position and claim of the Church of England.

"Dr. Bright, to whom I spoke for only a moment, said he thought the present state of the Church to be anomalous. Is it possible that Almighty God has revealed doctrines such as the Real Presence and Confession, and yet it can be a matter of no importance whether a professing churchman believe them or not? St. Paul speaks very plainly of the necessity of the trumpet giving a distinct sound.

"But you must read and decide for yourself, which is exactly the advice given me by Dr. Liddon. I had several interviews with him, and he was very good and kind and, of course, what such a man says cannot but command respect. I had already read the books he recommended, but began to study Hefele's 'History of the Councils,' finding him very strong *on the Roman side.* Both Dr. Liddon and Dr. Bright say that he is very reliable. The attitude of the Council of Chalcedon towards the Pope, Leo, is exactly what one would expect from the standpoint of Rome, and entirely goes against the Anglican position.

" Well, Dr. Liddon could not satisfy me at all, and, as you already know by my letter to mother, I have decided to become a Catholic in deed and not only in intention, and so has Mackall, and so has E. It is useless to wait unless I am to become cold and indifferent, for my mind is thoroughly made up on good, strong, sensible, intellectual grounds.

" Your devoted brother,

" HENRY."

The collapse of the appeal to Canon Liddon, and subsequent readings on the subject, seem to have definitely settled for Van Rensselaer the question he had so long and so perseveringly sought to solve. There could no longer be any doubt as to which was the true Church of Christ. It was now high time to turn to the Church of Rome. Up to this point his progress had been slow enough, nor had he tried to free himself from Anglican influences. While he was studying the question, he had conscientiously abstained from going inside a Catholic Church or speaking to a Catholic priest. He had frequented the ultra-ritualistic churches, and in them he had seen the ceremonies of the Catholic Church carried out exactly. Externally the imitation was perfect.

140

The altar with its appointments, the ministers in colored silken vestments, the music and incense, all was there as in the true Church, but it was " Hamlet " with the Prince left out. The Real Presence of Christ was not there. The essential lack became so oppressive to him that he resolved never again to be present at such hollow mockeries, as they now seemed to be. He declares:—

" Protestant England had become so distasteful to me that I longed to be in a Catholic country. Before leaving London, we called, my friend and I, at the Brompton Oratory and were warmly received. The priest whom we saw was anxious to have us make our abjuration of errors and profession of faith then and there. He said that he would not dare to cross the channel in our frame of mind. We answered that having dared the dangers of the Atlantic we thought we could risk the English Channel, as our intention then was to make our submission in Rome itself."

In the meantime, his sister, who had preceded him in England, was also fully convinced of the untenableness of the Anglican position. She had come by strict orders of her director, who had also been his, to join the All Saints' Sisterhood in Margaret street, London. There she was nurtured on purely Catholic literature—lives of the saints and spiritual books of Roman, not Anglican, authors. They kept the feast of St. Francis Xavier, among others purely Roman. The Reverend Mother was in the habit of going to Paris to keep the feasts of the Immaculate Conception and the Assumption of the Blessed Virgin. When his sister stated her difficulties to her London confessor, he parried them by saying that it was well to have two strings to one's bow, and that if the Anglican were wrong the Greek might be right. When she remarked that her brother, who was a

141

minister, and his friend, also a minister, were troubled in the same way as herself, he only sneered at their youth. She soon decided that she could not persevere in Anglicanism, though she was unable to leave the Sisters just then, as there was no one to fill her position. So she remained a couple of weeks after her brother had left for Paris, and at the expiration of her time of warning to the Sisters, joined him and his friend there.

In view of his subsequent career it is strange that his first meeting with a member of the Society of Jesus was not auspicious. The circumstances were as follows:—

"We had determined to be received into the Church in Rome itself. Thinking that we should enjoy our stay in Paris and our journey through France and Italy more as Catholics, we resolved to take the important step in Paris. My sister and my friend were admirers of the Jesuits, which admiration I did not share. They accordingly paid a visit to the Jesuit house in the Rue de Sèvres and made arrangements for our reception. I noticed that they were not nearly so enthusiastic after their visit, and they discreetly said little about it. My friend had arranged that he and I should make a preparatory retreat of three days under a Jesuit Father's direction. The first day came for our instruction. I had forebodings. Our instructor had neuralgia and a much swollen face. He was not a representative of the wily Jesuit at all. He began by informing us we knew nothing. As he had not examined us, I felt he was not qualified to give the verdict. He insisted on instructing us. According to him we did not understand Infallibility. I insisted that we did. We had studied the authorized exponent's book, and Dr. Fessler was the best authority on the matter. The Rev. Jesuit pooh-poohed him and said he would enlighten us. I replied that he was losing time. He was sure we had difficulties. We were sure we had none. The visit was unsatisfactory, and when we got out of the house I declared that the others might do as they pleased, but that I would not repeat the visit, and the retreat could be called off. I wished to have my coming into the Church a pleasant memory, which under such auspices was impossible. My companions seemed nothing loath to follow my example, although we had committed ourselves with the Jesuit. I said it was a simple thing to write to him that we had changed our plan; foolishly, perhaps, I added that we preferred to go to one who was accustomed to deal with Anglican converts and could understand them. That same day his answer came in shape of a pamphlet written by him on Anglicanism."

The retreat was thus abruptly brought to an end. It was an awkward way out of an awkward situation, which might have been easily relieved by some display of tact on either side. The next step was to find some one to take the would-be converts in hand. They had brought letters to a dear old English priest, Mgr. Rogerson, who had a confessional for English-speaking people in the Church of St. Roch, so they presented their letters to him and were welcomed in a truly fatherly way. They felt at home with him at once. He told them that their experience had been that of many others, who, like themselves, had ended by coming to him. He examined them a little, saw that they knew what they were doing, and then, on the 17th of September, 1877, received their abjuration and profession of faith, and baptized them conditionally in the Church of St. Roch.

The narrative of those early days spent as a Catholic becomes of increasing interest as it tells of the efforts made to overcome life-long prejudices in accepting without questioning the devout practices so common in Catholic countries, but which usually repel the new convert. With his usual candor he informs us:—

"As Protestants we had many prejudices against certain practices in the Catholic Church. Among other things, we disliked very much to see old women selling candles in the churches to be burned before the statues. Having become Catholics, we determined not to do things by halves. If the Church approves of these practices, they must be right, whether they appealed to us or not. So, when we were passing out of the Chapel of the Calvary, where we had been received, we stopped at the grotto representing the Holy Sepulchre with the dead Christ and lighted candles, which we purchased from our quondam aversion—the old dame who sold candles."

On the feast of St. Matthew they made their First Communion in the Chapel of the Convent of the Sacred Heart in the Rue de Varennes. The Mass was said by their good old friend in need, Mgr. Rogerson, who did much during their stay in Paris to make them feel at home in their new religious surroundings.

CHAPTER IX.

A Catholic.

" 'BY the help of my God have I leaped over the wall.'
And what a wall it was! A wall that has proved
an impassable barrier to millions! This was the wall laid
by the leaders of the great revolt against the Church in the
sixteenth century, and raised higher and higher in succeeding
centuries by the accumulation of false accusations and
prejudices. By the powerful help of God alone can one have
strength to leap over this wall. And the leap supposes a
combined action of man's mind and will with the grace of
God. A leap it is, and, owing to the nature of faith, it seems
to be a leap in the dark. For there is always a latent appre-
hension that perhaps the action may be a mistake."

Such are the words with which Van Rensselaer gratefully
acknowledges that only through God's grace could he have
threaded the labyrinth of error and have found his way to
the Church, the pillar and ground of truth.

Naturally enough, he thought he would visit Rome and
tender his submission to the Vicar of Christ. How different
his sentiments now from those which animated him on a
previous visit! Still it was with no little difficulty he ad-
justed himself to some of the popular observances of his
new faith. His narrative continues: " Being now quite
Catholicized, we set our faces Romeward to visit the centre
of unity and the Vicar of Christ on earth. The saintly

145

Pius IX sat in the chair of Peter. His long reign was nearing its close, and he was then rather feeble. At our audience he had to be borne into the hall on a portable chair. He was surrounded by a brilliant retinue of cardinals, monsignori, and other attendants in bright uniforms. He was very benevolent and gracious. He gave us a special blessing on hearing that we were converts and bade us to go back to America to spread the faith. We have tried to carry out his injunction.

" I recall an incident in the Vatican. The first time we visited the great basilica we knew the correct thing to do was to kiss the foot of the bronze statue of St. Peter, which unbelieving Protestants claim to be a converted image of Jupiter Tonans. Our Protestant prejudices revived for a moment, and we passed it by unkissed. After going around for some time, I made a dart at the statue, conquered my antipathy, and kissed the foot. Thenceforth we had no difficulty in kissing, after the manner of the Italians, pictures, statues, and all other objects of devotion.

" My friend and I thought of remaining in Rome to make our studies for the priesthood, as we had no doubt of our vocation to the altar. But we could not well leave my sister alone so far from home, so we decided to return to Paris after we had seen the sights of Rome. We journeyed thither by easy stages. My sister went *en pension* to the Convent of the Sacred Heart, while we took up our residence at the French Oratory in the Rue de Regard."

Hearing that Cardinal Manning was passing through Paris, the traveller called on him, in hopes that he would administer to them the Sacrament of Confirmation. But this necessitated permission from Cardinal Guibert, then

146

Archbishop of Paris, and other formalities, so they had to forego the privilege. Shortly after, they were confirmed by the Coadjutor Archbishop, Mgr. Richard.

"Cardinal Manning," he writes, " was very cordial and gave us each a copy of one of his celebrated books on the Mission of the Holy Ghost. He made a deep impression on us by his austere appearance. The newspapers were then making much of his championing the total abstinence movement in England, not only by word but by example. This latter meant much, for the aged Cardinal had, like most Englishmen, been accustomed all his life to take his wine. His doctor forbade him to abstain, and told him it would shorten his life, but his indomitable will triumphed."

Van Rensselaer was not satisfied with the reception of the Sacraments of Baptism and Confirmation. He had already cast his lot in the service of the Church, and he was anxious to take the first steps towards entering the clerical life. Another Cardinal came to Paris on his way to Rome. It was our own first American Cardinal, the venerable Archbishop McCloskey. Van Rensselaer took advantage of his presence there to receive the tonsure and then, with a view to preparing for the priesthood, took up his theological studies in Paris, with the Fathers of Oratory. Of this period of his life he tells us :—

" My friend and I undertook to study theology under one of the Oratorian Fathers, but our work was, to say the least, desultory. We were determined to acquire the Catholic spirit, and to this end we attended all the religious functions we could, and they were many. The services at Notre Dame had especial attractions for us, and there we saw for the first time the impressive ceremonies of Holy Week. What struck us as strange was the easy-going behavior of the people in the churches. They seemed perfectly at home in what they rightly considered their Father's house. This was quite noticeable at Vespers in Notre Dame. While the Canons and choristers chanted the Psalms in the choir, the faithful of both sexes would saunter leisurely in the aisles outside the choir, joining in the Psalms, which they knew by heart. French boys have singularly beautiful voices, and, as at Notre Dame they have a 'maitrise,' or choir school, in which the boys live and receive their education, intellectual and musical, they are properly nurtured and guarded from injuring their voices by shouting in the streets. One of the great privileges of the year was our attendance at the Lenten Conferences of the Dominican, Monsabré. It was a grand sight to see the immense nave of Notre Dame filled with men, old and young, who listened in rapt attention to the eloquent words of the preacher. The closing retreat in Holy Week, with the general Communion for men, was very edifying and inspiring."

A more minute account of his stay with the French Oratorians is given in the following letter:—

" L'ORATOIRE, PARIS,

" December, 1877.

" Who would have believed a year ago that I should be here and my *fidus Achates* with me, and yet it seems so natural to be a Catholic that I don't feel at all like a stranger, but quite *au fait* and to the manner born. I am perfectly happy, except in being so far away from home; still there is a great advantage in being out of the reach of controversy and free to become accustomed to one's position in peace and quiet, and in a country which is Catholic in so far as it is religious at all, for Protestantism has no hold here.

"We do not go out for lectures. I believe one learns more by studying than by hearing courses. One of the Fathers, a Doctor in Theology, superintends our studies and explains any difficulties we may meet with. We are treated with the greatest kindness by everyone. You should see us in the street in our clerical costume—great, low, broad-brimmed hats, caught up on each side; long coats, douillettes, black stockings and knee breeches, and me, minus my beard, which I regret only on account of the trouble of shaving.

"We went to a grand service at Notre Dame last Tuesday night. It was the close of the forty hours' adoration of the Blessed Sacrament. The adoration goes on uninterruptedly in the churches of Paris and the vicinity, opening in one as it is closed in another. The year is always begun at the Cathedral. On Tuesday evening there was a magnificent procession. The Host was carried by the Coadjutor, Archbishop Richard, followed by the Cardinal Archbishop, the Canons, numbers of clergy and acolytes, many choristers in red, and at least three thousand men, everyone in the procession carrying a lighted candle. Imagine the effect in Notre Dame at night, the high altar blazing with lights and the huge procession with its flickering tapers. Only men took part, with the exception of the St. Vincent de Paul Sisters who work in the parish, and who were permitted to join. To see all those men kneel down as their Lord passed by was a sight I shall never forget.

"We are still devoted to St. Roch's, where we feel very much at home, and where the singing is delightful. We generally go to the Jesuit Chapel in the Rue de Sèvres for Benediction on Sunday afternoon.

" I always think of Baby May when they have the ' *pain bénit* ' at Mass. It is a relic of a most ancient custom, the love-feast. In the churches of France, just before the consecration, a little procession goes up to the altar—a beadle, followed by a dear little girl like May, dressed in white and blue, with a lighted candle, then two boys in red, carrying on their shoulders a tray with a large round loaf of sweetened bread surrounded by candles. The bread is given by some parishioner and they generally send a little girl of the family to make the offering. After the bread has been blessed, the procession goes out in the same order, and later on in the service the boys hand round the bread in baskets. The custom is retained in France only, but is, I think, very beautiful."

His stay at the Oratory with the new manner of life it involved, seems not to have repressed his youthful gaiety or to have in any way affected his sense of humor. Thus he writes to one of his sisters:

" L'Oratoire, Paris.

" March 15, 1878.

" My Dear Bessie:

" You see I have yielded to your polite request and been photographed. Phema and I prefer the sitting pose, but the other is the favorite. How do you like the costume of an abbé? I am sorry I could not show my black stockings and shoe buckles, but when the "lady" in attendance at Le

150

Jeune's asked me what style I wished, and showed me samples, I suggested tentatively that perhaps full length would be 'un peu trop long.' She seemed entirely of my 'avis,' as there may be too much of a good person as well as too much of a good thing. I modestly tried to hide my hands but the 'poser' insisted upon their being visible, as he assured me they wouldn't look very badly; at any rate it would never do to be taken unarmed—but enough of myself.

"I have been, and am, reading Montalembert's St. Elizabeth. It is absurd and needless to comment upon it, as its reputation is world-wide. You must certainly read it and retract the accusation against her, who is known and ever was known in Catholic Germany, as 'die liebe heilige Elisabeth.' She is a most exquisite character, as you will readily acknowledge when you read her life. That little affair of the roses comes out most beautifully. Her husband was a most saintly young man; he died at twenty-seven. They were the most devoted couple imaginable. I advise you to find that little picture of *la chère sainte,* which I brought you two years ago, and you rejected. The preface gives a most interesting survey of the 13th Century, supposed by some people to be the Dark Ages. You will get quite another idea, I imagine. We went to Notre Dame on Sunday for the Conference. Monsabré is splendid; the nave was full of men, two or three thousand. We sat with the Archbishop and clergy and had excellent seats opposite the pulpit. The white frock and black coat of the Frère Prêcheur add greatly to the effect of the orator. He is very eloquent. The subject was the God-Man as proved by facts; the whole series is upon the Incarnation. It lasted an hour, but did not seem too long. His gestures are magnificent. He is middle-aged, rather fat, not handsome, perhaps a little too witty, as he made an occasional hit. The Dominicans are very strong in Paris and have a great many pulpits at their disposal. I know Père Chocarne and admire him very much. He is not, they say, *fort,* as a preacher, but a very spiritual man, with a beautiful expression. But I have to go out, so must close.

" Your affectionate brother,

" HENRY VAN RENSSELAER."

An interesting disclosure of Van Rensselaer's letters from Oxford is that of a longing on his part to lead the life of a religious. So great had been this desire that, had his belief in the Branch theory remained unshaken, he would in all likelihood have established in New York some religious brotherhood whose chief duty would be to labor among the poor in the congested districts of the lower East Side. It is not surprising, therefore, that after becoming a Catholic the thought of a religious vocation was still uppermost. Of his call to the priesthood he had never a doubt, but the further question of joining a religious community had to be decided. The experience with the Jesuit in Paris was not likely to lead him to become a member of the Society of Jesus. It was no easy matter for him to make up his mind as to what other religious order he would choose. The Oratorians in France, as well as in England, the Dominicans, the White Fathers of the African Mission, were all in their turn considered. These experiences should be told in his own words.

"My friend and I received some very wholesome but unpalatable advice from an American Bishop whom we visited during his stay in Paris. His keen and experienced eye detected the weak points in our religious composition. He told us, that in his judgment we needed to go through the mill, be ground fine, and made over. As his advice was unsought by us, it was decidedly unacceptable; we had quite a different opinion of ourselves at the time. After years made us see that his verdict was correct. In many respects the old leaven of Protestantism was still working in us, and time was required for the effect of the new leaven on the mass. I had long felt drawn to the religious life, even as a Protestant, but in what order was I to cast my lot? Of one thing I declared myself certain: a Jesuit I would never be. Anything else was possible, but to be a Jesuit—never. There I drew the line of demarcation. After hearing the celebrated Dominicans, Monsabré and Chocarne, I had a fancy for the Friar Preachers, especially after reading the fascinating life of Lacordaire by Chocarne. I even went so far as to call on Père Chocarne, who had a very attractive personality, and I arranged for a retreat. He candidly advised me to join the French Dominicans, as he said their studies were superior to those made by the American Friars. My sister and my friend would not hear of my joining the ranks of Frères Prêcheurs, and talked me out of the idea by ridiculing the possibility of my being a preacher. Next the missionary spirit took hold of me. I had been serving the Mass of one of the White Fathers, as the missionaries of the congregation founded by Cardinal Lavigerie for African Missions were called, and had become interested in the work. I had long talks with the Father in charge of the *bureau* in Paris; finally I confided to him my desire to devote my life to missions in Africa. He was a very prudent man and encouraged me in my intention to become a

missionary, but said, were he in my place, that he would
return to America and labor there, where, as an American
and a member of a well-known family, I should have more
influence in making converts, especially as I was a convert
myself. Besides that, he advocated my joining the Jesuits.
My sister and my friend had received my announcement of
my intention to go to Africa with decided opposition, so,
accepting the advice of the White Father, at least partially,
I abandoned the idea of Africa as the land of my future
work."

With the advice of Monsignor Rogerson, Van Rensselaer
next turned his thoughts to the Fathers of the Oratory,
founded by St. Philip Neri in the sixteenth century, and
having among its distinguished members in England such
men as Dr. Newman, Father Dalgairns and Father Faber.
But his stay at Brompton was a brief one. He writes:

"Our good friend Mgr. Rogerson had always intended
my friend and myself for Oratorians, but he did not care for
the French Congregation, preferring the English. He accordingly wrote to Father Morris, then Superior of the London Oratory at Brompton, and got an invitation for us to
visit there with a view to settling our vocation. To London
we went. Before presenting ourselves at the house, we in-
spected the church. It was the old one built by the saintly
Father Faber, which has since been replaced by the superb
Romanesque edifice.

"First impressions, in my case, seem to be prophetic for
me. As soon as we entered I said to my companion: 'This
is not the place of my abode.' We were most cordially received by the Fathers and allowed to take part in their community exercises. They were a very charming body of men,
several being converts. Although they are a congregation

not bound by vows, their internal discipline is rather severe. For instance, they seldom, if ever, preach outside of their own church. At recreation, so called, each has his own assigned seat which he must occupy. Everything was done in the Italian style, whether that style were worthy of imitation or reformation. Moreover there was an exaggerated devotion to St. Philip Neri, the great founder, which expressed itself in perpetual references to him in season and out of season. They smiled because St. Philip smiled, and laughed because St. Philip laughed, and so of other things."

CHAPTER X.

THE JESUIT NOVICE.

AS the life of the Oratorians was not to his liking, Van Rensselaer decided to return, for a time at least, to America, and, learning that Cardinal McCloskey was about to sail for New York, he embarked from Havre on the same steamer. The voyage was not without its influence upon his future. There were on board three Jesuits bound for the Rocky Mountains. One of them, Father Canestrelli, was a theologian of some note, and the successor of Cardinal Franzelin in the divinity chair of the Gregorian University in Rome. They were now travelling second class to an obscure mission among the Indians. They were bad travellers and were very sea-sick. Van Rensselaer saw a great deal of these men and administered to their wants as far as he was able. Their humility, poverty and self-sacrifice did much to counteract the prejudice he entertained after his disagreeable experience with the Jesuit in Paris, and brought about in him the first conscious attraction to the Society which formed such men.

Shortly after his arrival in New York, he made the acquaintance of the Rev. John Prendergast, S.J., then stationed at the Church of St. Francis Xavier, New York City. To mention Father Prendergast's name, is to call to the mind of those who knew him, one of the most remarkable of the New York priests of his time. A man of sterling character, he was fitted by his cast of mind and literary at-

REV. JOHN PRENDERGAST, S.J.

tainments to make a deep impression on the new convert. The acquaintance soon ripened into a friendship, and then into an intimacy which remained unbroken until death separated them a generation later. In scholarship Father Prendergast did not lose by comparison with any of the Oxford dons; in spiritual insight he easily surpassed them. What was of supreme importance, he could, like an elder brother, counsel and direct one who, as yet, was little better than a catechumen. He first suggested that Van Rensselaer should make a retreat, after the method laid down by St. Ignatius of Loyola in the book of Spiritual Exercises. Nay, more, Father Prendergast would himself act as his spiritual guide. Accordingly, towards the end of June, 1878, they withdrew to the Jesuit Novitiate at West Park on the Hudson, where Van Rensselaer went through the Spiritual Exercises under the guidance of his new director. At the end of the retreat, he applied for admission to the Society of Jesus, and was received by the Rev. Theophile Charaux, S.J., the Superior of the New York and Canada Mission.

Father Charaux wisely determined to send the earnest and devout applicant to Roehampton, England, for his novitiate, where he could receive a spiritual formation among candidates many of whom were converts like himself, and under superiors who had exceptional experience in training such men. After a few months passed with his family, he sailed on October 2, visiting Paris, Lourdes, and Paray-le-Monial, before he entered the Jesuit Novitiate on November 1, 1878. We are indebted to the family of Father Van Rensselaer for a series of letters sent from England during the following two years. They are written in an easy, familiar style; simple and utterly devoid of self-conscious-

157

ness, as all such letters should be, and reveal, not only the workings of his mind and heart, but the admirable preparation he was unconsciously making for his future apostolic career. The first two letters were written during the voyage.

" ON BOARD THE PEREIRE,

" October 2, 1878.

" Just one word before we are out of sight of land. This is an auspicious day for sailing, for it is dedicated to the Holy Guardian Angels, and these words were on my little French Almanac: ' C'est la voix de mon ange: Je suis ton ami et je te conduirai moi-même jusqu'au terme dans la voie où tu dois marcher.'

" It is always *au revoir*.

" HENRY."

" PEREIRE,

" October 11, 1878.

" We are not far from land. In a few hours we expect to pass the Scilly Islands and then it is a run of eighteen hours to Havre. It is quite calm and pleasant now, but we have had an awful time of it. Perhaps you saw by the papers that there had been a storm at sea; well, we had it in all its terror. For three days we were in danger, turned upside down every few minutes, huge waves breaking over the bulwarks and leaking down into the cabins; sleep was impossible. The smoking room was rendered useless; a wave broke the door and windows, and then the water rushed down into the ladies' saloon. Fortunately it was at night, when no one was there. It is all over now, *Dieu merci.*"

The following letter is the first he wrote from Roehampton :—

" MANRESA HOUSE, ROEHAMPTON,

" November 10, 1878.

" This place is beautiful; it was formerly the hunting lodge of the Earl of Bessborough, and adjoins Richmond Park. Our grounds are very extensive and we can take a long walk in them; but several times a week we go where we choose. Wimbledon Common is quite near, and a favorite walk is to the famous Star and Garter Inn at Richmond. The good walkers go as far as London, but it is a pretty long stretch, particularly for Americans, and I prefer steam legs to carry me. I was very kindly received, and put under the charge of General Sherman's son, who has been here since June. He made me feel at home at once, and we have a good many walks together. I have a fine view of Richmond Park from my window. It is like the open country, with splendid trees. The novices are a very jolly crowd, and we have many a laugh together; in most things we are congenial, a happy family in all senses of the word, and yet collected from many nations: English, Scotch, Irish, American, Belgian, German, French, Italian, Dalmatian, Syrian, Maltese; yet there is no national feeling, and the foreigners are usually the favorites. Americans are considered to have the power of adapting themselves to circumstances, perhaps because they travel so much. It seems to be a true reputation. We have an ancient novice who is half a Canadian, having lived much in Canada; his family has a large estate there, and he has crossed the Atlantic thirty times. The life is rather hard for an elderly person, but it is amusing to see what the things are to which different people attach importance. His greatest trial was having only one towel; he had always used six at a time."

Dating from his reception into the Church, Van Rensselaer had taken a deep interest in the work of the missions. The missionary spirit, so necessary for the apostolic man, took hold of him in the very cradle of his religious life and waxed stronger day by day as time went on. On January 22, 1879, he writes:—

" I am reading ' Marshall's Christian Missions.' It is intensely interesting. It is astonishing to find that there has been for three centuries, and still exists, a flourishing church in China, with thousands of martyrs and confessors. On the 31st of this month, a Jesuit Mission is to be begun in Central Africa, covering the discoveries of Livingston and Stanley. It belongs to this Province by courtesy to the discoverers, I suppose, for most of the Fathers who are to go are French or Belgian, the universal missionaries. These missions and their results are a most convincing proof of the truth of Catholicism. In all ages the preaching of the Gospel has been followed by precisely the same effects: perfect self-abnegation, marvellous supernatural courage, and miracles of healing, etc. To my mind, the greatest miracle is the supernatural strength given to young and old, women, and even children, to endure unheard-of tortures without denying their faith. The Chinese converts were begged by Mandarins simply to step upon the cross—they might believe what they chose if they would conform outwardly— but they scouted the suggestion and cheerfully suffered and died for Our Lord. Truly such faith puts us to the blush."

The following extracts from letters which were written at Roehampton give us a good insight into the work-a-day life of the Jesuit novice. Several hours a day are given to vocal and mental prayer, spiritual reading and self-examination. Of these duties Van Rensselaer says little, deeming them of slight interest even to his family, but dwells on the external occupations which afford more interesting matter for letter-writing.

"February 1, 1879.

"I am very busy this month as I have the office of First Refectorian, which is quite responsible. I have to direct all the work in the Refectory and attend to the proper serving of the meals. It requires management and common sense. You will say: 'What is the use of your doing such things?' Well, one reason is, that it rests our minds from studying; another very important one is, that it trains us to take supervision and direction and submit to bearing hardships, for it is not exactly a pleasure."

" July 13, 1879.

" I may not have another chance of writing for some time, as we are very busy hay-making. We have had rain every day for a month, but on Wednesday the weather seemed to change, so our grass was partly cut, and we were set to work to shake and turn it in order to get it dried as soon as possible. All our studies stop during the hay-making, and we are only allowed time for praying, eating and sleeping, the three necessities of our life. We even work after supper when there is danger of rain."

" August 1.

" We are still busy in the hay-field and are well sun-burned. I am sure it will do us a great deal of good to be so much in the open air and in such healthy exercise. The frequent showers doubled, or rather quadrupled, our exertions; it was necessary to do so much shaking to get the hay dried. However, we have got three-fourths secured in a stack, while the rest still demands our attention. We get through a great deal of work in the morning, when we do not talk, but in the afternoon our tongues do more than our hands. The weather has been unfavorable for fruit, but our strawberries have ripened, and very good ones they are. English people do not eat fruit as we do in America—half a dozen strawberries satisfy them. We have to gather fruit now for preserving—strawberries and black currants—so you see, we have a variety of work. I think, however, that I prefer the good old routine. It has fallen to my lot to arrange flowers for the Altar, so I am quite in my element. We have beautiful roses of all kinds."

162

"September 17, 1879.

"It is some time since I have written, as I have been very busy. First our week's Retreat; then for ten days I have been helping the cook, a very delightful occupation, as you may imagine, for the quondam fastidious H. V. R. However, I am getting on very well, notwithstanding the smells and the grease. It is hard work to stand over the steaming tubs, washing dishes and scouring pots and pans. As we have a large community, they reckon about seven hundred plates a day, but they are nothing compared to the greasy pots and pans. This work is supposed to be an antidote to pride, although one can be proud of being a good scullery man. This summer has been rather a contrast to previous ones, when I was decidedly an idler. Now, it is impossible to be idle, and I see that time is too precious to be wasted."

The Feast of All Saints, 1879, was the first anniversary of his entrance into the novitiate. No shadow of doubt of his being where God wished him to be ever crossed his mind. He was very happy, and wrote home assuring his family of his contentment.

"All Saints Day, 1879.

"To-day is my birthday in the Society of Jesus, and in one year more I hope to take my simple vows on this great feast. I am perfectly happy and very thankful for my vocation. I shall appreciate this year more than the last, for the foundation is not the most interesting part of the spiritual structure. I have passed through everything that

163

we have in the way of trials. Many will come again to my share, but they will be like old friends."

There was not much chance for letter-writing for a month or more, but the day after Christmas he wrote again :—

."December 26, 1879.

" I have been very busy for the past month as Refectorian; the long retreat is going on, and those who are making it do not help as usual. The lay-brother novice who was chief Refectorian went into retreat to prepare for taking his vows, and for five days I have had his place. To-day, however, my labors cease. In spite of all, I have had a very happy feast. We had a delightful Midnight Mass, preceded by the ' Adeste,' arranged by Novello for solo, duet, trio and chorus. I sang the bass solo. We had a High Mass in the public chapel, and in the afternoon we all went to Farm Street for Vespers. The fog was so thick that we almost lost our way in Waterloo Place. The Holy Innocents is our great day, and we hope to pay a visit to the Little Sisters of the Poor. On St. Stanislaus' Day three of us novices went to Nazareth House and were treated most cordially. The Mother General took us everywhere herself. She suggested that we ask for a holiday for her novices; so we did, only stipulating that they should say their beads for us. I have a great devotion to the Holy Innocents. This was a favorite devotion of St. Francis de Sales, who died invoking them. There is something grand not only in dying for Our Lord, like the martyrs, but in dying instead of Him, like these little Innocents. A very

Happy New Year. Each ought to be happier than the last, because it brings us nearer to Our Lord."

"Feast of the Epiphany, 1880.

"A great feast day, and many of the novices have gone to London to the different churches, but I thought I should like a quiet afternoon for writing. My little plan was interrupted by being called upon to help wash the dinner things, so I set it down as something to offer Our Lord on Epiphany; not much, it is true, but having given myself, I can only give what I can do in His service."

In the two letters that follow, his predilection for the missions again asserts itself :—

"Feast of Purification, 1880.

"I am trying to pick up a little Spanish and find it easy, knowing French well, and Latin, which is the mother tongue. I received an incentive from a letter Father W. wrote me from California. He had spent six weeks with a tribe of Indians, one hundred and fifty miles from Los Angeles. He taught them their prayers and did everything for them except burying them, as none of them would die just then. They fitted up a mud hut as a chapel and draped it tastefully with bright colored calicoes. It was really pretty, but weird looking, when filled with dusky men in skins, women in calicoes, and babies *au naturel,* He taught and preached in Spanish, and it must have been consoling to be able to do so much for those poor Indians.

It always fills me with enthusiasm to hear of real missionary work."

"February 27.

"Winter is coming to an end, bushes are budding, and the ground has thawed. I am not sorry, as my outdoor work is to break up earth for a new walk. Not an easy task to use a pickaxe on ground as hard as the nether mill-stone. I am translating from the French the Diary of Father Depelchin, one of our missionaries in South Africa. They have a great deal to contend with, especially the lack of water in crossing the deserts, and also of food, as the country is barren, and there are few animals. The poor missionaries have to live on a little rice or millet with small quantities of coffee to wash it down. Yet they write most contentedly and are grateful for the privilege of carrying the Gospel to the poor benighted savages. I enjoy translating it and feel as if I were helping them in a small way. You will be glad to hear that I get two hours a week practice on the harmonium, so I shall not forget the little that I know. Our voices, too, are well trained. We have a new choir-master, a novice who was the organist of St. Bartholomew's, Brighton. Three other novices, converts, came from that church. One was a curate, another superintendent of a Sunday-school, while the fourth, a lay brother, was a chorister. The singing has improved wonderfully under the régime of the Choir-master. We practise for an hour every morning. I can never have too much singing, as it is a great pleasure."

It was during these years that he wrote to his mother the following letters. In the matter of her son's conversion,

166

Mrs. Van Rensselaer remained unreconciled and unrecon-
cilable to the end. Later she declined to attend his ordination to the Priesthood, on the ground that she had once
seen him ordained a deacon in the Episcopal Church. The
letters display exquisite tact and delicacy in speaking to her
of his status as a novice and his desire to have her learn
something about the Catholic Church.

" LONDON,

" October 30, 1878.

" MY DEAREST MOTHER :

" As you see, I have left Paris. I only got here to-day, a
few hours ago, having had a very disagreeable crossing by
Dieppe and Newhaven. I was next door to being sick, but
escaped. I enjoyed my visit to Paris very much and should
have been sorry to leave, had it not been to enter upon my
life-work. Last week I was gone four days from Paris, as
I wanted to see Paray-le-Monial and Lourdes. The scenery
about Lourdes is beautiful; it is, you know, in the
Pyrenees, built partly upon a mountain and partly in the
valley through which the river runs. The church is exquisite and in very good taste, and full of magnificent banners
carried there by pilgrims and left as souvenirs of the pilgrimage. I noticed our flag hanging up. There are not
many people there now, as it is too late in the season and there
is apt to be a great deal of rain; besides, the holiday tours
are over, and people cannot leave home without some special
reason. Of course there are always some invalids there.
" I had quite a time getting to Lourdes, as I wanted to stop

at Paray-le-Monial. I left Paris on Tuesday at 8 :30 in the evening, and had to change cars at 3 A. M. and wait an hour. However, by the change I made the acquaintance of a young Belgian. He was such a swell-looking fellow that I hesitated at first about getting into the same carriage with him. I did, though, and found in him a fellow pilgrim. Although rather *mondain* looking, nevertheless he had resolved to fly the world and retire into a monastery, as he had been very worldly, he told me. He is only twenty-eight, handsome and rich, and his friends and family are *désolées,* but he has to follow his vocation. I liked him very much, and was pleased to find in real life what sounds very like a novel. On parting he gave me a very pretty illuminated parchment card with a motto, ' Pensons au Ciel et nous aurons le courage d'être fidèles à Dieu quoiqu'il en coûte.' Very appropriate for us both. I, strange to say, had a card with the likeness of St. Norbert, the founder of the Order of the Premonstratensians, which was the order my friend had chosen. His name was Van der Heyden.

I could only spend a few hours at Paray-le-Monial, but long enough to see the Chapel of the Visitation. I had hard work to get thence to Lourdes as it is all across country, and there were no through trains, and I was from 2 P. M. Wednesday until 7 P. M. Thursday *en route* and had to change six times. I made friends, though, so I did not mind it very much. I had nearly two days at Lourdes and got back to Paris on Sunday morning at 5 :30, as I wanted to be once more at the Sunday services at my old friends, the Paris Churches. . . .

" Your devoted son,

" HARRY."

JESUIT NOVITIATE, ROEHAMPTON, ENGLAND

THE JESUIT NOVICE.

" MANRESA HOUSE,

" ROEHAMPTON,

" November 17, 1878.

" MY DEAREST MOTHER :

" I have no news to write you from here, so I will tell you a little about my life at present. So, to begin. Imagine a very large room with three windows and six little cells partitioned off with curtains for doors ; the rest of the room is open, has bureaus and desks for each of us, with a pleasant fire burning in the grate. Each cell has an iron bed, with comfortable mattress, a washstand and a chair. There are very many such dormitories ; each has about six cells. Do not be alarmed at the word ' cell,' for it is in fact not at all alarming, but I can't think of any other word to suit. It is far more spacious than the prophet's chamber in the wall ; he certainly hadn't gas.

" It is night, and we are all sleeping the sleep of the righteous ; at a quarter past five in the morning a step is heard and a voice at each door calling out *Deo gratias* (Thanks be to God) ; everyone replies at once, *Deo gratias,* and jumps out of bed ; the fire is lighted and likewise the gas, and the work of washing and dressing begins. We have half an hour allowed us for it, then all go down to the Chapel, and the bell rings for the *Angelus,* which is so called because it is the memorial of the Incarnation of Our Lord, beginning with words ' Angelus Domini,' (the Angel of the Lord declared unto Mary, etc.), and ending with what you will find in the Prayer book as the Collect for the Annunciation of the B. V. M. Then all make a prayer called the ' morning oblation,' in which they offer up themselves, all their thoughts, words and actions, pains and sufferings of the day to Almighty God in union with those of Our Lord while on earth. It is very comprehensive, takes in everything, thanksgiving, intercession, confession of past faults, intentions for the future. There is no regular form for it, and ten minutes are allowed. Then we all return to our rooms and make a meditation on some text of scripture, events in Our Lord's life, or on some virtue or some vice etc., which one can choose at will. This lasts for an hour and is done kneeling for a quarter, standing for a quarter, sitting for a quarter, kneeling again for a quarter, during which resolutions for the day are made. Then all go to the Chapel for Mass; several times in the week we receive Holy Communion. At a quarter to eight we have breakfast, as much coffee, bread and butter as we can eat. At 8:25 we make our beds, doing it thoroughly, stripping them every day—this is *de rigueur*. At 8:35 we read Rodriguez on Christian perfection. Then we have an exhortation upon some duty, after which we do some work about the house, help in the refectory, or the sacristy, or the chapel, or the kitchen, or the library, for twenty minutes. This is followed in fine weather by some manual labor, raking leaves, digging in the garden, rolling the paths, drawing water for drinking, etc.

Of course the object of the work is to accustom us to help ourselves and to be ready for anything. It is good to have our hands going sometimes instead of our heads. The outdoor work lasts about half an hour. Then we study, and at 12:30 wash and get ready for dinner; at 12:45 we go into the chapel for what is called the *particular examen*, that is we renew in our minds all we have thought, done, said, or omitted since the morning, dwelling on the resolution made

in the morning's meditation to correct some fault or to practise some act of virtue. The Angelus bell rings at 1, and
when the prayer is said dinner begins. There is no talking at
meals, but instead there is reading, first a portion of Scripture, then some history or biography, ending with the list of
the martyrs and saints whose anniversaries occur on the following day. After every meal all go into the chapel for a
few moments of silent prayer. Recreation for an hour follows, with prayer for a quarter, reading of the Imitation of
Christ for another quarter, then work indoors and outdoors,
with some free time afterwards. Three times a week one of
us has to catechise the others as if they were children, in
order to get facility in questioning and explaining. Twice a
week we practise singing; and time is given for spiritual
reading, lives of saints, etc. At six there is half an hour's
meditation in the chapel, followed by prayers. Supper is at
7:35, with recreation for an hour. At 9 litanies are recited
in the chapel. After that we prepare points for the next
morning's meditation; at 9:30 make an examination of conscience about all we have done, thought, said during the
day; at a quarter to ten prepare for bed, and at ten lights out.

"So you see we lead quite an active and certainly a very
busy life; at the same time it is a very spiritual one. During
the day we speak only at recreation hours; at other times
whenever it is necessary, and then the language used must
be Latin if possible. After all we have plenty of time for
talking. On Wednesdays and Sundays we have long walks
in fine weather, and on Sundays do not work. We are a
very jolly set and very happy. Recreation hours are very
lively; there are no cares to weigh upon us and everything
to help us in our spiritual life. What more can we ask for?
Of course, this is only for a time. In time of peace prepare

171

for war, and this is our time of peace. The war time will come. We begin a month's retreat on the 24th, lasting until Christmas. During this I shall not be able to write any letters, but will make up for lost time when it is over, so do not be worried by not hearing from me, but write all the same. I have a commission for you. I want you to knit me a pair of hand muffs, also a pair of mittens. They will be useful for working and walking; black is the best color (excuse the bull), because it won't get soiled. I hope everybody thinks as often of me as I do of them.

" Ever your devoted son,

" HARRY."

" MANRESA HOUSE,

" ROEHAMPTON,

" Christmas Day, 1878.

" MY DEAREST MOTHER:

" It is quite strange to begin writing letters again after my long silence. My first letter is, of course, to you. You know well how much and lovingly I have had you in my mind to-day. We had Mass at midnight, beginning by singing " Adeste Fideles "; you may be sure that we sang it with all our might; one never tires of it, and it never seems hackneyed. Christmas would seem incomplete without it. At Holy Communion I thought particularly of you and all my family. When one thinks of the Holy Family, one's thoughts naturally turn to our own, and no wonder Christmas is the family festival.

" After the service we sang the Te Deum, which was very inspiring and solemn. We sang it to the old Gregorian, or rather Ambrosian music, and it added much to one's devotion to feel that those words and the music to which they were set had been in use fourteen hundred years in all countries, and in so many different nations, always the identical words, the evergreen Latin, ' Te Deum Laudamus.' After it was over we had some bouillon and bread, and then we went to bed, having had our first taste of Christmas, and the best part, too, I may say. We were up again for Mass at seven. Unfortunately, it was not a very pleasant day out doors, but rather foggy and snowy, and we were not tempted to go out except for a little walk. It is real typical Christmas weather, with plenty of cold and snow, in keeping with the season.

" I never saw anything more beautiful than it is here after a snow storm, when the sun comes out. We make ourselves useful, too, in shoveling or sweeping the snow from the walks, and as we can take more than a half-mile walk round part of the grounds, there is no lack of employment for our spare moments. It is very healthy and good exercise, and freshens up the mind and warms up the body. The house is kept very comfortable with open fires in all the rooms; some of them have great old-fashioned fire places with andirons.

" The decorations have been very tasteful and pretty. There was an abundance of material on the place—enormous hedges of laurel, great trees of holly, and no end of ivy. The hall ceiling is supported by columns, and round each is twined beautiful thick ivy vines, besides ropes of laurel and holly from column to column. You have no idea what a pretty effect of Bethlehem, and the cave, and the stable was made by means of brown paper and salt and greens, together with the figures of the Holy Family and the shepherds. Brown paper judiciously arranged makes splendid rocks, salt does for snow, greens for trees, etc. Really it is astonishing how realistic and pretty it is, and costs nothing but a little time and taste. It may sound childish, but notwithstanding it certainly does help one to realize the scene, and after all what is a picture, but canvas, paint, time and taste, or talent.

"Christmas being a great festival, we talked at table during dinner, which is very unusual. I am not quite sure that it is an improvement upon the reading aloud, but the change is pleasant occasionally.

"Saturday will be a great day for us—Holy Innocents' Day. We always have a great entertainment on that day, with a séance in the evening for our amsuement. We are spectators, the Juniors provide the performance. One of the features of the day is having an Innocent Beadle. You must know, that the Beadle is a very important person; he is a novice put in charge of the others, and has to make out all the notices, give all the orders for the different exercises of the day, ring the bells for beginning and ending every duty, answer all questions, give out whatever is wanted, pens, ink, soap, in fact do any and everything. You may imagine that it is not a sinecure; indeed, the man who is selected for this office must be a very holy and superior novice to exercise these duties with patience, and gentleness, and recollection. Well, on Holy Innocents' day his duties are suspended, and all of us draw for the Innocent beadle of the day; those who escape the doubtful honor amuse themselves by tormenting the unfortunate Innocent, who, however, can revenge himself by giving some unpleasant job to his tormentors. I hope it may not fall to my lot, although of course it is only fun and everything is done *con amore*.

"I must close with warmest Christmas greetings to everybody.

"Your devoted son,

"HARRY."

"MANRESA HOUSE,

"ROEHAMPTON,

"Feast of the Purification, 1879.

"MY DEAREST MOTHER:

"This is a good day on which to write a letter to you, the Feast when the Blessed Virgin, publicly in the Temple, offered her Divine Son to His Eternal Father. Up to this time all had taken place as it were in private, the birth in the stable, the circumcision in the house, the worship of the shepherds and the Magi, but to-day He was presented in the Temple and declared to be 'The Light to lighten the Gentiles and the Glory of His people Israel'—and Simeon could say, 'My eyes have seen the Salvation,' which was to be wrought by this wonderful child of promise.

"What a beautiful picture! The Holy Family, the Blessed Virgin, holding her Divine Son in her arms, St. Joseph carrying, probably, the modest offering of the doves, and the Priest who was to receive, as minister of the Most High God, God the Son Incarnate. Then Simeon and Anna, prophesying and thanking God for the signal favor they had received in being allowed to live long enough to see the

175

desire of Israel. At first sight we wonder why the Blessed
Virgin did not offer the lamb, and then we think that she
did indeed offer the Lamb of God, that taketh away the sins
of the world—the type would have been out of place in the
presence of the antitype. Then, too, she would set us an
example of humility and poverty. She, the princess of the
House of David, makes the offering of the poor, though
doubtless she had gold which had been presented by the
Magi. But she teaches us a deeper lesson of humility by
the very act of purification. She was not under the Law;
she, who had conceived by the power and the overshadowing
of the Holy Ghost, could not be held by the law made for
those who were mothers in the natural way. However, she
does not avail herself of her privileges, but consents to act in
obedience to the commandments of the Law.

" To any chance worshiper in the Temple this little party
may have appeared very ordinary, poor and unworthy of
attention, yet they were God the Son, His Mother, and His
foster-father and the protector of the Blessed Virgin Mary.
So it was all through Our Lord's earthly life. He did not
command the respect, and attention, and love of the people;
only a few chosen ones here and there could pierce the veil
and see beneath the human form the Divine Person. So on
Calvary, only the eye of Faith can recognize God, His
Mother and with her another protector, St. John, for St.
Joseph's work was ended, and he had gone to his rest in the
arms of Jesus and Mary. Did you ever wonder how you
would have acted had you been present in the Temple at the
time of the presentation? I am afraid most of us would have
turned away from such an humble party. We are so accustomed to think of Our Lord as God, that we fail to realize
His humanity and His humility. We are shocked at any-

thing poor and common, at least our feeling is one of compassion and condescension.   Well, as Our Lord's life on
earth was marvellous, so is it now in the Sacrament of
the Most Holy Eucharist.   As St. Thomas Aquinas says
in his hymn :—

> Sight and touch and taste,
>   May nought of Him discern,
> But the soul that hearkens,
>   Can the mystery learn.
> On the Cross Thy Godhead
>   Only was concealed,
> Here, not e'en Thy manhood,
>   Is to sight revealed.
> But in both believing
>   And confessing, Lord,
> Ask I what the dying
>   Thief of Thee implored.
> I do not, like Thomas,
>   See Thy wounds appear,
> But with him confess
>   My Lord and God is here.

What a wonderful gift faith is, and how impossible to
believe anything without it ; everything is so full of mystery,
yet it is not until we try to explain that we realize the
depths of mystery.   We really believe simply because we
start with the principle that God is omnipotent, and that
nothing that does not contradict His attributes is beyond
His power.   And so it is as easy for Him to manifest Himself under the veils of bread and wine as to manifest Himself in the body He took in the womb of the Blessed Virgin.
To say that it is impossible is to deny His omnipotence.

"I have written quite a dissertation, haven't I? but it is hard to think of Our Lord under one form without being carried away to the other, the one under which we now with eyes of faith see Him. It is a great privilege to know Our Lord now by the light of faith, to receive in Holy Communion Him whom we shall see face to face when faith shall become sight. In the meantime don't let us deceive ourselves by saying, I can't believe because I can't see. If we could see it would not be faith.

"We have had the last of the Feasts of the Incarnation now, and Lent will soon be coming with the new phase of Our Lord's life. Surely we ought to pray like Him when we have always His life set before us as an example to follow. But I must be closing now. I enjoy your letters very much, my dearest mother.   .   .   .

"Your devoted son,

"HARRY."

"MANRESA HOUSE,

"ROEHAMPTON,

"March 12, 1879.

"MY DEAREST MOTHER:

"It is quite a time since I wrote last, certainly not this month; but I have been kept so busy that I could not manage it. As I told you in my last, I have been Refectorian, and my offices lasted a month. For two weeks I was third as-

178

sistant and then promoted to first, which is much more responsible. I had no leisure at all to speak of; none for writing letters, for one always has certain odds and ends that can't be put off. Upon the whole, now that once more I am comparatively free, I rather enjoyed being in the refectory. It is a complete change, as one does not follow the ordinary exercises, but devotes all one's attention to the preparation for meals. But do not think by this that we spend all our time eating. There are only the ordinary three meals a day, with the addition of coffee at 5 o'clock to brighten us up a little for our meditation at 6. Meditations are never dispensed with; there is always the hour in the morning, the half-hour in the evening, and the usual quarter-hour at mid-day and at night for the examination of conscience to see what falls we have had and what progress we have made, and to make resolutions for the future. Every one has to allow full time to these, and to Mass in the morning and Litanies in the evening; so you see no matter what office one has, the most important spiritual duties are always insisted upon. Besides this, for half an hour before supper the first Refectorian reads aloud for the lay brothers in the kitchen from some life of a saint or chapters of the Imitation of Christ, while they are busy peeling apples, cutting toast, etc. It was always a very pleasant half hour. I used to get very much flurried at first in my office, but the last week I got quite accustomed to it. It is rather trying, as you have so many bothering you at the same time. For instance, in the morning about ten novices are sent down to help you, and you have to assign each a task and see that they do it properly. They only stay twenty minutes and do only part of the work, and then you and your regular assistants have to supply all deficiencies, which is sometimes more troublesome than if you did the

179

whole thing yourself. At meals I had to stand at a large table just outside the refectory door and give out all the dishes which came from the kitchen on a kind of turnstile, a one-storied dumb waiter; see that the servers got the right dishes and then pile up all the plates as they were brought out used, collecting the knives, forks and spoons, and putting them into partitions in a box to be washed and then sending the plates to the scullery. When sixty sit down to a meal, a good deal has to pass through your hands. But this is not all, for as soon as the first dinner is over, three minutes are allowed to prepare the tables for a second dinner of thirty people. This has to be done in an awful hurry-scurry, and then I sit down to this second meal. Such are the principal points of what I have been undergoing, and you can imagine that there is a good deal of anxiety lest something be forgotten, and it is quite a relief to be once more at the usual routine, in comparative quiet, and with some spare moments.

"I had a task given me directly after my time in the refectory, for my turn came to give *a tone* or short sermon before the novices. The text was, 'That no man overreach or circumvent his brother in business.' It is rather a difficult text, and I had only a short time to prepare, as the warning is given on Sunday morning to preach on Monday, with only the spare moments to prepare for the ordeal. It has to be extempore and I got very much confused and nervous, but I managed to scramble through with two awful pauses. But enough of myself; too much, I fear.

"Your devoted son,

"HARRY."

180

THE JESUIT NOVICE.

" MANRESA HOUSE,

" ROEHAMPTON,

" Feast of the Annunciation, 1879.

" MY DEAREST MOTHER:

".   .   . I am glad the cold weather is on the wane, as it is trying in Lent. They take great care of us, and do not allow any extravagances in fasting. Every one has to consult the doctor to see if he have strength; if not, only a little mortification of one's appetite, which couldn't hurt anyone, is permitted.

" This season has gone, so far, very quickly, and Holy Week will soon be here. I expect to enjoy it very much, as we shall have interesting services in our chapel and plenty of singing. I have been promoted to singing in the choir, which adds much to my pleasure, and we have been busily practising for some time for the Holy Week services. I should like you to hear them, for they are very well done. I am one of the basses, and it is interesting to sing a part and quite a novelty for me, as I have been accustomed to having it all my own way.

" What a beautiful feast to-day is, and yet, not coming on a Sunday, it does not receive as much attention as it deserves; for what is the festival of the Annunciation but the beginning of the Incarnation of Our Lord? We are apt to think of it as the time when the announcement was made to the Blessed Virgin, and to forget that when she gave her consent and said, ' Be it done unto me according to Thy word,' immediately the Holy Ghost overshadowed her,

181

and she conceived and became the Mother of God. I know that I myself never used to connect Our Lord's conception with the Annunciation; in fact I never used to think very much about it, and only contented myself with generalities and did not realize as much of the mystery as is possible for us and which we are bound to do. For what can be of greater importance and interest to Christians than all that is connected with the life of Our Lord on the earth, and His death and risen life? All these are mentioned in the beautiful collect of the feast, which is used by us three times a day at the *Angelus,* as I remember telling you, as the memorial of the Incarnation.

" I think I said in my last letter that I am no longer in the refectory, but have no office at present, taking things easy. The object, you know, of offices is not to get work out of us, but to teach us to be able to do anything useful, and to learn how to manage for oneself if in command, or how to obey if under another.

" Your devoted son,

" HARRY."

" MANRESA HOUSE,

" ROEHAMPTON,

" Easter Monday, April 13, 1879.

" MY DEAREST MOTHER:

" I will begin by wishing you all the Easter joys, and what joys can compare with them? Not even Christmas can equal

Easter, for it is the completion of what was begun at Christmas, and is the pledge of our own resurrection. Lent has passed rather quickly, the last week especially, because we were very busy preparing for the musical part of the services. Everything went off very successfully, the music was well rendered and was well chosen. On Wednesday, Thursday and Friday we had the *Tenebrae,* which consists of a beautiful selection of Psalms and Antiphons, together with lessons and the lamentations of Jeremiah, with appropriate responses. Everything was sung without accompaniment, the responses and antiphons in harmony, as well as the ' Benedictus ' and the ' Miserere.' At the close of the service the choir sang an anthem, ' Christ was made obedient unto death,' which was very touching. On Maundy Thursday we had a fine service in commemoration of the Institution of the Holy Eucharist. On Good Friday we went to our church in London for the Three Hours' service between 12 and 3. The time passed so quickly that I could scarcely believe that we had been really three hours in church. One reason was that there was a great deal of variety, and we were not kept long in any one position. The choir would sing an anthem, and then an address on one of the seven last words of Our Lord would follow, then some prayers, with responses by the people. It was very impressive and devotional. There were no drawbacks, everything went smoothly and we were most punctual, going in as the clock struck twelve and coming out exactly at three. There was an overflowing congregation, who were most attentive and stayed right through from beginning to end. Yesterday we went again to our church, in Farm Street, for Vespers, and had a beautiful service. One feels on Easter day inclined to shout for joy.

" We are taking things easy this week; at least we are

183

supposed to do so, but there is a great deal of walking, which sometimes is more tiring than anything else. I have come out from Lent in the best possible health, without a cold or an ache. The weather is cold and disagreeable for this season.   .   .   .

" It is a consolation that after all we can be so near in spirit and thought to those we love, as to imagine almost exactly what is taking place even three thousand miles away, for we can travel over space in the twinkling of an eye. Hereafter when we shall have glorified bodies at the resurrection, even our bodies will overcome all the obstacles that now keep us confined, just as Our Lord could pass through the sealed stone of the sepulchre or the closed doors of the upper chamber where the Apostles were assembled.   In the meanwhile it is a comfort to be able to be so near one another in spirit.

" With best love and Easter greetings to all,

" I am your devoted son,

" H. V. R."

" MANRESA HOUSE,

" ROEHAMPTON,

" London, S.W., May 7, 1879.

" MY DEAREST MOTHER :

".   .   .   I hope you have been more fortunate in weather than we have been, for May has not, so far, deserved its name at all, but is much more like March, altho'

184

we had our full share of March winds, too. The famous
east wind has been blowing pretty steadily even this month.
Everything in consequence is dreadfully backward; the trees
have only begun to bud this last week, but unfortunately
there have been little flurries of hail and snow which will
injure the blossoms of the fruit trees which have just struggled out. The cuckoo has been singing that springtime is
near, but this year he has been mistaken. We have a cuckoo
living close to the house; in fact, there are birds of all kinds
in the neighborhood and they furnish plenty of music. In
summer there are nightingales, they say, but they are such
late birds, and we such early ones, that I doubt if we ever
hear them. They don't begin to sing until ten, and about
that time we begin to snore. . . .

" Our life here is so regular that one week is very
like another unless some feast day happens to break the
monotony—monotony I mean in a good sense and not
tedium.

" I took a long walk on Sunday afternoon to hear Vespers at the Carmelite Church. It must have been nearly
twelve miles altogether, but it was a very pleasant day, warm
and sunny, and the road rather a pretty one, and I had a
chance to rest during the service. I feel at home in that
church particularly, because I know one of the Fathers, and
used to go there last year. They have a foreign congregation,
and a good many of the diplomats and others attend."

" May 9th.

" I had to stop and have not had a chance to finish until
now, when I have a few minutes. I have been busy preparing for a catechising which I had to give before the

185

novices and one of the Fathers. My subject was Confirmation, and I primed myself thoroughly so that I got through very well, only being criticized as being too learned and giving too many authorities. It is rather hard to treat as children grown men who know as much about the subject as you do yourself. And yet that is what we are supposed to do in order to get a facility in asking questions as simply as possible and to explain in short and easy words. Usually a story of some kind is told to enliven the young ones. We get another chance at story-telling every evening, for there is always a pious story with a good moral at our recreation and each one has his turn. I told one very apropos the other evening.

"We are all busy this month in preparing sermons, as each one has to preach before the community at supper time. As many of the novices seem to be trusting mainly to books, I selected an instance in St. Vincent Ferrer's life. He was a great Dominican preacher and missionary, and a very holy man. One day he was told that a distinguished nobleman was coming to hear him preach. The saint usually relied principally upon prayer for his sermons, but on this occasion, departing from his custom, he gave the time to extra study. The consequence was that he did not preach as well as usual, and the nobleman went home disappointed. However, he went another time unannounced and was delighted. This was told St. Vincent, who replied: 'No wonder, for the first time he heard Vincent preach, but this time it was Jesus Christ, Himself.' It is a pretty anecdote, is it not? But I must stop. With best love for everybody and most for yourself,

"Ever your devoted son,

"HARRY."

ELIZABETH RAY KING
MOTHER OF REV. HENRY VAN RENSSELAER

" Manresa House,

" Roehampton,

" August 17, 1879.

" My Dearest Mother:

" Many happy returns of your birthday; not such happiness as the world can give or appreciate, but true and solid, which can come from God alone, and which consists in growing in the deeper knowledge of Our Lord and of the end for which we were created—to serve, praise and reverence Him. Few people, when really brought face to face with this truth, will deny it, but at the same time they do practically deny or at least ignore it. Look at their lives, how perfectly aimless they seem, unless one can call that the aim of their life to which they devote most of their time, energy, attention and money. And what a waste of time it will seem to them when they are called upon to give an account of their lives. Vanity of vanities, indeed! Yet, with the best of intentions, how hard it is for us to keep really before our eyes the object of our being! We so crave after happiness that we practically do make it our aim, and so in the real sense it is happiness, but only that which comes from doing God's will as well as we can. What happiness, what satisfaction, when we can say and feel after something we have done, that our intention was purely God's glory! Too often some vanity, self-seeking or other motive has crept in to take away the merit of the action, or at least tarnish its lustre. The greater glory of God is our motto, this the object, the summing up of our lives. This will be the standard by which we shall be judged, and is it not a glorious one, too? The glory of God, who laid aside the glory which he had with His Father before the creation of the world. He abased Himself and we must exalt Him. He led the way and we must follow Him; the way of the cross is the only way that leads to true happiness. We may have the cross laid upon us or we may take it upon ourselves of our own accord. It is a great consolation for those whose lot lies in home duties, to think of Our Lord's life at Nazareth with His Mother and St. Joseph. What quiet and apparently uneventful lives they led for thirty years; to human eyes St. Joseph seemed only the carpenter; the Mother of God only his wife; and Our Lord Himself only the carpenter's son. Truly it matters very little what the world thinks of us, what opinion it passes upon us. We are living not for it and its judgment, nor can it appreciate pure motives. So it often happens that those who are considered unfortunate are very far from being so; for the trials they have undergone have been so many means of grace, means of bringing them nearer their Divine Model, who was the Man of Sorrows and acquainted with grief. Really, one's own experience tells one that frequently in penitential seasons of the church we have more true peace and comfort than at the greater festivals, which often bring with them dissipation of heart, and we do not feel as near Our Lord as when kneeling at the foot of the Cross. Then we throw ourselves, as it were, upon Him for support, for we feel our weakness and need His sympathy, and with such dispositions we can never fail to touch His Sacred Heart ever open to the sighs of His children.

" I wish that I could drop in upon you now and then to have a little chat. Letters are so unsatisfactory; one never says what one wants to, but very often does the reverse.

I hope I have not done so this time. At any rate you will understand me aright. You are always much in my thoughts. With best wishes, I am, my dearest mother,

" Your devoted son,

" HENRY VAN RENSSELAER."

" MANRESA HOUSE,

" ROEHAMPTON,

" November 16, 1879.

" MY DEAREST MOTHER:

" . . . Last Thursday was a great day with us—the feast of our Patron, St. Stanislaus Kostka. He is the patron saint of all novices, because he died a novice, when he was only eighteen years old. As the Church says of him in the collect for his day, Almighty God had bestowed on him in tender youth the grace of mature sanctity. He is the Patron of Poland, and one of the most popular of saints, especially among the young. I daresay you recollect seeing some frescoes representing scenes in his life in Our Church in Montreal.

" It was a day for long walks—sunny, though cold. Bro. Sherman and another and I thought we should spend our morning profitably by paying a visit to Nazareth House, a home for aged men and women and homeless children. It is under the care of Sisters very like the Little Sisters of the Poor. We were delighted with everything we saw, were very kindly received, and the Mother General of the Order showed us all over the establishment. Everything was in the most exquisite order. Each bed had a many-colored patch-work spread and looked comfortable and

189

cheery. The old people said that nothing could exceed the kindness of the Sisters, and there were some Protestants who told me the same. The Sisters, many of them of good family, do all the work themselves, and live entirely on what they get by alms. Their food consists of scraps which they beg. One cannot imagine happier, *more contented* and gayer people than these Sisters, who are brimful of charity and zeal. There were children either idiotic or nearly so, but I was glad to see them in such a home. We went away very much edified, and thankful that there are so many devoted people who were glad to leave the world and what it can give in the way of pleasures, and live a life of hard work and service for the bodies of others that they may save their souls. When we got back to Manresa House we had a panegyric of our Saint by one of the novices; then came Benediction and afterwards dinner with conversation. In the evening there was a séance in which the choir figured by singing several glees. Brother Sherman composed and read a very pretty poem on the bell which announces our duties. As he had the office of ringing it as beadle not long ago, he could speak feelingly. There were some other poems and readings, and altogether we enjoyed ourselves very much. The choir have been kept very busy of late getting ready the glees for the séance, and besides that we sing Vespers in our own chapel every Sunday afternoon; we have also to prepare new music for Christmas, which will be upon us before we know it.

"Love to everybody, much for yourself,

"Your devoted son,

"H. V. R."

" Manresa House,

" Roehampton, S. W.,

" April 22, 1880.

" My Dearest Mother:

" The weeks have been slipping by so quickly and uneventfully that I can hardly keep any track of my letters.
We are having most lovely weather now, for it is full spring.
The country is delightful. How thankful I am to be able to
enjoy it! With all the helps that the beauties of nature give,
one ought to live more in God's presence in the country than
in the city. Everything is so peaceful and fitted to raising
one's thoughts from earth to heaven, yet I doubt if country
people are as religious as the city people; perhaps the latter
feel more need of God's help than the others; still we cannot help feeling how weak man is when we see the changes
of nature. What can he do? Nothing; not even force a
blade of grass to grow; and so a lesson of humility is
preached by every blade of grass and every tiny flower. But
it is a lesson we do not heed, it is so contrary to our wishes
and inclinations. We make up our mind to praise and admire humility as a virtue; when, however, it is urged upon
us, we rebel. Why is it that so many thousands who call
themselves Christians, and profess to be followers of the
Crucified, cannot bear the sight of a picture which repre-
sents Our Lord crucified, much less a carved crucifix? It
is simply because it pictures to them too readily and vividly
what their Captain and Leader has done and suffered, and
what He expects of them. They are not prepared for any
such imitation of Christ as this. They do not object to

reading about it, but that is enough. You see how a blade of grass has carried me off. Still, we can never think enough about our own weakness and what should arise out of the consideration of it—what we should be, humble and ready to accept what Almighty God proposes to us.

" What a dreadful state of things in France! One must always hope for a turn of the scales, there are so many ups and downs in that changeable country. I am glad there is such a unity of action among all the religious orders and all the Bishops; they realize the truth that it is religion that is being attacked and not any one Order in the Church. It is certainly a strange Republic where there is no freedom. We have had some very good music lately, though I say it who shouldn't, being in the choir. We have been singing one of Gounod's Masses. We also had a séance in honor of the Provincial, who has been making his visitation. We sang " The Storm." To-day, the 23d, is St. George's Day, and is a holiday, which gives me a chance of writing. I have also a sermon on hand which I must preach on the 12th of May. My ideas do not flow as I should like. I wish you would get ' Christian Schools and Scholars.' It is a charming book, giving an excellent and pleasant picture of the early and middle age Christianity. It is not a controversial work at all, merely historical. They are really dark ages because most people know so little about them, but it is astonishing to find how bright the true light shone in those rude times. . . ."

" Ever your devoted son,

" HENRY VAN RENSSELAER."
192

Van Rensselaer's stay in England was drawing to a close. Under the strict discipline of the novitiate, he had become a new man with new ideals, new aspirations, new impulses, and new ways of thinking and acting. This mental and spiritual development, or rather transformation, is shown in a letter written while still a first year novice:—

"The time is slipping away, a time of much grace. The saying is, that the height of sanctity to which we aspire in the noviceship will be the highest to which we shall ever aspire in after life; so we must aim now at nothing short of being saints, however impossible that may now seem. After all, what *is* a saint but one who so fully corresponds to the grace given him that he merits more and more? It is simply acting up to our vocation and the abundant graces given to us. 'Pensons au ciel et nous aurons le courage d'être fidèles à Dieu quoiqu'il en coûte.' This motto was on a signet that a fellow-pilgrim to Paray-le-Monial gave me, and if we did but keep the end in view, all would seem very plain."

The progress he made in the knowledge and practice of spiritual things was such that he could now be entrusted with the guidance of other souls, and in the last letter from Roehampton, he writes enthusiastically of a work of this nature committed to his charge.

"May, 1880.

"I have a delightful task at present, to unfold the religious life to two lay-brother postulants; they are both converts of two years' standing, but totally unlike; both very

193

good, and earnest, and teachable. It is most humiliating to speak to them of high ideals and perfection, and then to realize how far short one is oneself. But it is most inspiriting to feel that one is really helping others. I have had a great increase of love for the Spiritual Exercises of St. Ignatius. I have been reading the life of Father de Ponlevoy, the author of de Ravignan's life, and his intimate friend. They were both men of the Exercises; everything they did or said was influenced by them. This is my aim, as it should be that of every Jesuit. Father Morris has been a great help to me. He has been away for two weeks giving a mission at Arundel. His place was taken by Father Purbrick, for many years Rector of Stonyhurst. He is a convert, an Oxford man, the most perfect gentleman I ever saw, most spiritual, most humble, most talented. There is a paragon. His short rule was a delightful one."

CHAPTER XI.

WOODSTOCK COLLEGE.

VAN RENSSELAER returned to America in the summer of 1880, with two other Americans, his fellow novices at Roehampton, Thomas Sherman, a son of Gen. William Tecumseh Sherman, and Thomas Kernan, a son of Senator Kernan of New York. After a brief stay at St. Francis Xavier's, New York City, Van Rensselaer, as he was still a novice, went on to the novitiate of the Maryland-New York Province, at Frederick, Md.

A few days after his arrival at the novitiate he wrote to his sister, Mrs. George Waddington:

" NOVITIATE,

" FREDERICK CITY, MD.

" August 1, 1880.

" MY DEAR BESSIE:

". . . I had a pleasant visit in New York, although I found the family very much scattered. I am convinced that it is unadvisable in religious questions to say anything aggressive. Try to let people know what the true religion is and then leave the rest to God. We, having the truth on our side, can always speak with authority, and this is peculiar to the Catholic Church. I found on the steamer that when one inquired into what people believed in their hearts, it

195

amounted to Universalism—that God is very good and merciful and will not condemn. They called themselves Presbyterians, and Episcopalians, and free thinkers; there was much they had in common, the rest they considered merely external forms. As I look back now on our trip, I think we wasted time; for several days we kept quite aloof until people began to question us, and even then we were rather on the defensive. Father Pardow, who was our leader, told me not to be shy in talking, but to improve my opportunities. so then I set to work, and having had experience in religious matters I discovered in myself a certain power. In the end I talked quite openly, though in the beginning everyone warned everyone else against us, and a third person invariably would come up to try to interfere. The captain regularly walked off with two ladies who wished to talk with me, and naturally I was at a disadvantage because I could not walk up and down the deck with ladies. In the end, however, I won over the captain; he and I became excellent friends, and he entered into a compact not to interfere. People respect you much more if you talk to them up and down without fear.   .   .   .

" I am delighted with the Jesuits I have met in America. They have overwhelmed us with kindness. I spent a few hours at Woodstock *en route,* and was charmed. I will tell you more about it when I go there in September. Frederick is a great contrast to Roehampton; there is something very gentle and sympathetic about the Fathers and novices here. Not that they were not good and kind in England, but John Bull has his peculiarities. It is pleasant to be in a religious habit, rosary and all. The Roehampton novices lose much by not wearing the habit. Here the novices are wonderfully edifying.

"I shall enjoy my month in this place immensely. The scenery in the neighborhood is beautiful, but best of all there is here a wonderful spirit of charity and gentleness; just what I need and hope to get, for my late experience on the ship tells me that what people yearn for is sympathy and kindness. . . .

"Ever your devoted brother,

"HENRY VAN RENSSELAER, S.J.

In the beginning of September he reported for his studies in philosophy at Woodstock, Md., where he was to spend three fruitful and happy years. On the approach of the Feast of All Saints, he returned to Frederick to take his first vows as a Jesuit Scholastic. The interruption was a brief one, for it was from Woodstock College that he wrote the following letter:

"WOODSTOCK,

"November 2, 1880.

"I have had the great happiness of taking the vows. I went down to Frederick on Saturday afternoon, spent Sunday in recollection and silence, and then on Monday in the domestic chapel, took my vows before the Community. Just think, I had about thirty Masses said for me that day, besides many receiving Holy Communion for my intention. There is such a beautiful feeling of charity in the Society. I like this quotation very much and it has made a great impression on me: 'Petit sacrifice, petit bonheur; grand sacrifice, grand bonheur; sacrifice complet, bonheur complet.'"

197

Most of the subjoined letters were addressed to his sister, who shortly after her conversion had been enrolled among the Daughters of Charity of St. Vincent de Paul. On the Feast of the Immaculate Conception, 1880, he writes:

" I do not know that I have ever spent a happier feast, except perhaps All Saints, and this was a breathing of the same air. We had our half-yearly renovation of vows. What the Society wishes is *homo in vita spirituali perfectus,* and for this, great talents are not necessary, thank God, else I might despair of attaining it, for I shall never shine as a learned man, nor do I regret it much. It has many dangers which I shall be spared. Let us desire better gifts, for desire paves the way."

The Christmas holidays brought with them welcome relaxation from the study of dialectics and abstruse metaphysics. He writes:—

" WOODSTOCK COLLEGE,

" December 27, 1880.

" What a delightful season this is! How one's heart overflows with love and gratitude to the God who cares so tenderly for His ungrateful creatures! This has been a very happy season for me; we are like a large, yet united family, rejoicing with holy simplicity in our little pleasures. We have had several entertainments, one most amusing, some acting Scrooge and Marley in Dickens' ' Christmas Story.' The parts were capitally taken, and we laughed ourselves hoarse. Last night we had a Christmas tree with a present drawn by lot for everybody, so that one got generally just the wrong thing—a non-smoker, for instance, would be sure to receive a pipe, etc. Some amusing things were said very apropos, and a clever local poem read. On Wednesday we are to have Father Ryan, the poet-priest, for our guest; he has a poem for the occasion, and there will be others from Ours, as we have several poets among us. The choir have several fine glees ready, so altogether we expect a pleasant evening. I have enjoyed singing in the Christmas choir and in the glees. It is my greatest amusement. You see by this that we are quite a lively set of people, in fact, the lightest-hearted in the world, I believe."

A month later his letter takes on a more sombre hue. It was probably written at the beginning of the Lenten season; the exact day of the month is not given.

" WOODSTOCK,

" February, 1881.

" How hard it is for us to make full use of our opportunities! There is not a moment in the day or night when we might not be meriting by a silent aspiration, a genuflection, even a smile, a pleasant word, a trifling act of forethought. These are the brilliants, tiny indeed, but they will add great lustre to our crowns. I remember Father Porter impressed upon us to make frequent acts of perfect charity. It might seem presumptuous at first sight, but he said it was not so, and we should tell Our Lord that we do love Him, or at least desire to love Him, as well as any creature can love Him, even the Seraphim and His Blessed

199

Mother herself. The desire comes from Him, so it must be most pleasing to Him, who is Perfect Charity. We must decide to make the recreation hour the most profitable of the day, and with this intention prepare for it by an act of perfect charity, either in the chapel or on our way to the recreation room. Our selfishness often hinders us from helping our companions; I speak from experience. There were certain novices in England with whom I was not much thrown, and I never sought them out when it was left free to choose. By accident, a few weeks before I left, I sat next one at recreation. He seemed downcast, and by some kindly questions I found that although within a few months of his vows, he had not grasped the idea of the religious life. He had all kinds of doubt as to his vocation. I tried to show him the serpent's trail, and pointed out the beauties of our life. To my surprise, I found that he had always felt drawn to me, although I had done nothing to deserve it. When I left he was one of the most affected and the last to bid farewell, as he stole away from the others and was at the lodge gate for a last good-bye. The other day I had a letter from him saying how happy he now was in his vocation. He had taken his vows, and his doubts had long since vanished. The moral may apologize for my speaking of this, and I was only the unworthy mouth-piece of the Holy Ghost."

Later he alludes feelingly to St. Joseph:—

" March, 1881.

" Let us have great confidence; this should be the dominant note of all our prayers; it will make them most pleasing to God. We should ask like children who feel they have a right to ask, and are sure of having their petition granted, because they cannot conceive the possibility of their Father being unable or unwilling to fulfil their desires. I think I owe a great deal to St. Joseph. I am convinced that he helped me to my vocation, as his month in Paris, our first month as Catholics, was a fruitful season to me, although I was then only groping in the dark and cold and could not tell whither Providence was leading me. Those are happy days to look back upon, but what a blessing to be settled in our proper place."

The winter of 1880-81 was unusually severe. Old-timers could recall nothing like it. All the more beautiful was it when the Spring came in all its freshness, and the scholastics could enjoy their long walks in the environs of Woodstock. How those days were spent and enjoyed by Mr. Van Rensselaer, we learn in the following letter :—

" May 12, 1881.

" Yesterday, the feast of St. Francis Jerome, Mr. X. and I made an excursion. We left at 7 A. M. and got back at a little after 6 in the evening. It was one of the pleasantest days of my life. Mr. X. is amiable, clever, intellectual and spiritual. We made our meditation on the way, pausing now and then, when it was concluded, to rest ourselves and pick wild flowers. Our chief object was to discuss the ' Fundamentum ' of the Spiritual Exercises, which we did from time to time, as the spirit moved us. The terminus of our walk was a mission church belonging to us, about ten miles away. We took a cold dinner with us and refreshed ourselves at midday in the shady woods by the bank of a stream. When we reached the church we played on the harmonium and sang hymns etc. to our heart's content, and then retraced our steps to Woodstock. It was a perfect day."

The following letters and extracts from letters, written at this time, show how, as a student, Van Rensselaer ever kept before him the high ideals of the novitiate.

" WOODSTOCK,

" May 22, 1881.

" MY DEAR SISTER:
" P. C.

" I must congratulate you upon having completed the two years successfully, and wish you perseverance not only until the vows, but until you are called to the reward of those who persevere until the end. Perhaps you may think the two years have not produced as much change in you as you expected and hoped, but we are poor judges in our own case, and I am sure that the progress has been real and great, although it may not seem so to you. One may safely admit in almost every case, that more might have been effected had there been a readier, and more generous, and more thorough correspondence with grace, and this must urge us on to greater activity, for active we must be if we would accomplish anything! This activity is shown largely in resisting, ' agendo contra,' as St. Ignatius puts it. How comparatively easy would the building process be if the foundations were solidly and surely laid, but with many of us our whole lives are liable to be spent in laying the foundation, beginning now with one corner, now with another, and then

202

changing our whole plan. The consequence is, at last we say we have spent time enough about the foundation and must see to the superstructure and often build on sand and not on the rock of solid virtues. So I confess it is with me in great measure. We would wish to grow to perfection without having practised the rudiments; we think of finishing touches before we have well drawn even the outline. The knowledge of our own weaknesses and follies may be turned into a source of strength if, knowing ourselves to be weak, we rely upon a higher power and throw ourselves upon His mercy and compassion. How can He be so forbearing with us? How hard we find it to be so with others! I think if we could conquer ourselves in this one point, victory would crown our efforts in all others. We are so exacting and rigid in regard to others, and how much we need to be borne with ourselves! They disgust us with some little gaucherie or want of bienséance, and we offend them, or at least should offend them had they not great charity, by our pride and overbearingness. Weighed in the scales, which would outweigh? There can be no question.

"Our lives must be apostolic and we must acquire the apostolic virtues and first of all charity, as St. Paul says, 'charitas Christi urget nos,' that is, charity should be the motive power of our lives, the cause of our words and actions. For why have we followed Him except for the love of Him? We must strive, then, to make this evident in act, for words without the acts make us laughable. Nor should we be downcast because we have made such failures in our attempts. We have failed, but that is past; success lies in the future, and strength in the present; the failures will at least teach us humility, and so we may draw good out of evil; constant effort will necessarily produce the effect which is in our power, but it must be a constant, persevering, undaunted effort—it shall be, that is our resolution.

"I sincerely trust that you may have the happiness of taking your vows in July; it gives stability of feeling. Have not the two years gone quickly? I can scarce believe that it is nearly a year since I left England. I often hear from Manresa; things are flourishing over there. I am struggling now really hard for the examination, and sometimes I am a little anxious about it lest I break down. However, I shall try to be prudent and then trust to Providence. We are reviewing all the philosophic matter of the year and, as you may imagine, it is not a small quantity, and being very abstruse is hard to remember. I shall have to finish this letter at once as time is up. Praying that the *Auxilium Christianorum* will obtain for you your heart's desire, as I doubt not she will, I am your devoted brother,

"HENRY VAN RENSSELAER, S.J."

"WOODSTOCK,

"Feast of Blessed Berchmans, 1882.

"MY DEAR SISTER:
"P. C.

"I am certain not to have time to finish this letter to-day, but I will at least begin to show that you are not out of mind on our Patron's feast. How far behind him we are in perfection! The comparison, even, seems absurd, yet why should it? He was of the very same nature as ourselves, and had the same passions to struggle against and flesh to mortify. Wherein, then, lies the difference? It must be in the steadiness of his resolutions. We resolve, but we so often fail in the execution through a want of constancy. We get weary in well-doing and yield to our inclination to indulge ourselves if it be only a harsh judgment or a cross word now and then. We cannot imagine our Blessed John ever giving way to such an indulgence of temper. By constant resistance of the inclination it will by degrees become so far weakened that at length it will die a natural death. We must not despair, though this consummation appears one of those things which, though indeed possible, does not seem probable. Why should we not aim at it with all our might, humbling ourselves under failure, but none the less persevering? The perseverance will finally be crowned. Do you not know from your own experience how changed you have become in a very few years, even in a year? Why, then, in another should we not make another stride on the thorny road of perfection? It is worth the attempt.

"You ask for some practical way of showing your devotion to the Sacred Heart. Is not the essence of a true devotion imitation of the object? If, then, we are really devout to the Sacred Heart, the effect should be in the words of the ejaculation to make our hearts like His Heart. It is, then, a most practical devotion; it is the making our hearts like His. Are they much alike at present? I fear we can find only too many points of dissimilarity; His Heart all love and charity and unselfishness; ours hard, cold and selfish. So every thought and word and act which will help increase the likeness will be an act of devotion; if we have the actual intention of its being so, so much the better.

At least we must have the virtual intention made in the morning when we offer up all that passes during the day. Reparation, of course, enters into the devotion, but it is the reparation which relates to ourselves. It is absurd to make reparation for others until we root out the bitterness in our own hearts. It will help to sweeten our endeavors to remember that we are practising the most wholesome and acceptable devotion to the Sacred Heart of our loving Lord. It will nerve us to know that by doing it we are proving our devotion to the Sacred Heart. How much He endured for love of us! Shall not we bravely and lovingly make a worthy return? And does not this tally well with the practice of making acts or ejaculations? If we have the words expressing our desire to become like Our Lord always on our lips, and mean what we say, must we not by the very fact become like Him? Will not the desire of our hearts at length become realized? Do not expect too much at first; be content with a few, but let those few be earnest and make up in intensity for their fewness. I do not mean to remain content with few, but add on by degrees and take an account of the reason you are unable to increase the number or even to reach the ordinary quota. But take heart and keep up your courage.

"We have a good Master. What comfort there is in the thought! When, after repeated failure, we are in a desperate state and tempted to give up in despair, then we should recall His tender love, His fatherly care and His untiring patience. They are really crucial moments for us. They test our motives. Are they unmixed with self-love or not? If self is there, then we feel hurt and sore and indisposed to make any further effort. If the intention is pure we may be sad, and justly too, because of our weakness and cowardice, but at the same time the thought of the loving help of God will make us ready and willing to take up our arms for another tussle with the enemy. Tussles they are, usually, and not a well-ordered campaign on the open field, the enemy in full view and his strength known and measured. Our enemy is always lurking around corners, ready to pounce upon us unawares and unprepared. Let us always be ready for him no matter when or how he attacks us. He is ever near us, within us. Our worst enemy is the irritable temper, the proud spirit, the hasty, ill-natured tongue. Our neighbors seem to be the cause of our irritation, but were we mild and meek and amiable, would they be? At all events not in the same degree as they now are with our domestic enemies unsubdued. .

"But you will be tired of my long-winded talk. I cannot honestly send you this without confessing that I myself am the most guilty of all. I had a little trial of patience, being kept in my room for two weeks after I came back from St. Inigoes with an abrasion of the skin, got by falling over a bench in the dark. Now, thank God, it is perfectly healed.

"I am so glad you liked Father Devitt. I thought you would, when I heard he was to give the retreat. Father Prendergast will be a help to you; perhaps you might have him to take Father Jerge's place, as the latter goes to Frederick for tertianship. You must remember me especially during my retreat; it begins on the 23d. Father Welch of Boston, a convert, gives it. I expect it to be very helpful. .

"I am your devoted brother,

"HENRY VAN RENSSELAER, S.J."
207

" WOODSTOCK,

" 1882.

" I had a delightful letter from Father Prendergast, written after he had finished the long retreat of the third year's probation. It was as good to me as a retreat; it filled me with love for the Spiritual Exercises of our Holy Father, St. Ignatius, or rather it stirred up the spirit of love and devotion I already bore them. They are our own special weapons and our greatest means of advancing the glory of God. I trust some day to be able to wield them powerfully.

" I am becoming quite an enthusiastic philosopher. Just now we are studying interesting matter, the soul; it enhances one's ideas of the dignity of man. I am studying as hard as my capacity allows; more would be worse than useless. I try not to worry too much over the examinations, and in spite of them am as happy as possible. All these things are of secondary importance after all, and if we keep before our minds the primary end, our perfection, they will not hinder, but even advance it. Every day the ideal before me seems to grow more tangible and real, and if we only corresponded more generously to abundant grace, the day might come when we should be worthy imitators of our saintly Fathers. Courage and confidence! Let us throw ourselves into that loving Heart where we shall find such power and zeal and burning charity, and come forth changed into new creatures. As of old, it will be said: ' Thou also wert with Jesus of Galilee, for thy speech betrayeth thee.'

" How much we may do or leave undone for Our Lord! It is the tiniest of insects that forms the great coral reefs and islands; so we, by adding act to act, tiny as they may be, shall raise a tower upon which we shall mount to Heaven.

We cannot imagine Our Lord to have been anything but affable, gentle and sympathetic even in trifling things. We ought to try to be the same, and we shall please him more and afford greater edification than by any amount of penance and mortification."

Here are some of his thoughts during the month of November :—

" I have been very much impressed this month, when meditating on the Holy Souls in Purgatory, with the mercy of God in giving this means of purification to those who have not, in their lives, availed themselves of their opportunities. We know that many die in a state only not bad enough for hell. Their love of God has been tepid, yet His overwhelming mercy finds a means to give them the joys of heaven, little as they would seem to deserve it. What would such a soul tell us if it could come back to earth? How it would exhort us to make use of every means of grace to the utmost, and to let no chance slip by unimproved to learn to love Him, who is to be hereafter our joy and our crown! We can help the Holy Souls and at the same time grow in the love of God by repeating frequently an indulgenced aspiration: ' Jesus, meek and humble of heart '; ' Sweet Heart of Mary, be my salvation.' We shall thus keep the thought of Jesus and Mary ever before our minds until they become the constant companions of our lives. Our lives should bear the character of reparation, for we are brands snatched from the burning. We might have been unbearable for pride, yet Almighty God saw the desires of our hearts and opened them to the light of Truth; more still, has chosen us to be His own particular companions, and yet more, apostles, to bring others to His feet. Let us keep this before our eyes, that the salvation of many depends upon our sanctification; that if we become saints, the glory of God will be advanced far beyond any conception that we can form.

" What peace and contentment it brings to have made the sacrifice of all things! I feel a growing love for poverty and never am happier than when I part with some of the few treasures I still have. To-day, for example, I have sent Francis my missal. I should like him to use it at his first Mass. We used to study it together in old times.

" What a blessed thing it would be to have such faith as to see God in everybody and in everything! How different, then, would be our lives, superiors and equals all invested with a halo of divinity because we see God in them as in a tabernacle! Then would our dealings with all become easy, for in them we should be obeying and serving Him whose least command is law, whose least service an honor. This was the practice of the Saints; this transforms earth into a Heaven where God goes in and out among us, and where we can constantly be advancing His glory. How much good we can find in everything if we only look for it, and instead of dwelling upon people's defects, dwell upon their good points and become ourselves amiable and lovable in proportion, and secure the Easter greeting of Christ: ' Peace be with you.' "

As Christmas approached, his thoughts took on the character of the festival, and a few days before its advent he wrote:—

" My Christmas greeting must be: ' That He may come and find prepared for Him a mansion worthy of Him.' The words of that prayer before Holy Communion have always had a peculiar fascination for me; in fact, I have an especial devotion to the season of Advent; there is something so touching, so pathetic in the words used by the Church in her antiphons and hymns; something of that longing after Him Who is to come, that it makes one homesick for the true home which awaits us when He shall come the second time to take us to Himself to be with Him forever. We might call our whole life an Advent-tide, for it should be one of expectation and preparation. We must live for the future, though in the present, and fulfil every little duty with a faith which pierces the clouds and sees them in the light of eternity."

The two following letters show that he was mindful of his sister on her patronal feast, that of the Seven Dolors of the Blessed Virgin.

" March 30, 1882.

" MY DEAR SISTER DOLORES:
" P. C.
" I might not have time to write to you on your feast day, so I will write now, that you may receive my letter perhaps to-morrow. You are blessed in having two fêtes a year; most people are satisfied with one. . . .
" I think we are rather inclined not to appreciate enough what it is to have had such a mother and father as ours. . . . We must work hard for mother now; what a pity that she should not have the comforts and consolations of the Church. But Our Lord has his own times of grace; perhaps her hour has not yet come; we must, as

211

of yore, try to get His Mother to use her influence to hasten it.

"We had our sermon here, too, preached by death. Our Father Minister, one morning last week did not go to the Sacristy at Mass time; they went to call him and found him stretched on the floor quite dead. It was a great shock to us; the first we knew of it was to hear the passing-bell ring towards the end of our hour of meditation. We knew of no one for whom to say the 'De Profundis,' as only one of the scholastics was sick, and he not dangerously. The mourning was general when we were told that it was the Father Minister; he was universally beloved and respected as a saint, although he had been among us at Woodstock only seven months. He was certainly well prepared by nearly thirty years of religious life of self-sacrifice. For seventeen years he was prefect of discipline in boarding colleges, and you may imagine what a life that is. Strange to say we found that the points of his meditation had been: 'The happiness a good religious would feel at the hour of his death, when he could look back upon a life of mortification and sacrifice.' Was it not a good proximate preparation for death? The cause was paralysis of the heart. He looked so natural and lifelike for two days that many declared that he was in a trance. Fortunately for our peace of mind, the unmistakable signs appeared on the third day, and there was no longer room for doubt. He is an immense loss to us. I was very fond of him and saw a good deal of him. It preaches a striking lesson to us to be ready. It seems often to be the lot of religious to die suddenly; certainly, with all our religious exercises, we ought to be prepared.

"It was a relief to hear from you after such a long silence. I imagined, however, that there was no real reason for your silence except want of time and energy, at least for writing. It does require a certain effort to put oneself down to write.

"Lent has passed very quickly and, as you may suppose, I have not been allowed to fast. However, one can gain much merit not only by the obedience under which one acts, but also by giving up little things at meals, nothing essential, but little extras, nor that regularly, but varying, first one and then another. In that way we can practise a good deal of mortification on a small scale without injuring our health or violating the intention of our Superiors in bidding us eat.

"I can scarcely realize that a whole year has passed since last Holy Week. When one is busy, time flies. If only our advance in perfection could keep pace with it; however, we must be content to go along slowly, provided it be surely, not losing any ground that we have gained, but steadily keeping in view the end for which we left the world, our own perfection and the good of others. But the first must always have the chief place in our endeavors, and we may be sure that the second will not suffer in consequence, since the ratio is a direct one.

"I find the use of ejaculatory prayers very helpful, such as 'Jesus meek and humble of heart, make my heart like unto Thine,' and 'Sweet Heart of Mary, be my salvation.' They are both indulgenced for three hundred days, so by repeating them we can help the Holy Souls, and at the same time form habits in our soul, acquire humility and gentleness, and thus avoid pride and harshness, besides keeping the thought of Jesus and Mary ever before our minds, until they become the constant companions of our lives, and associated with all our thoughts and works and words. Begin by making a determination to say a certain number, not

too many at first, before the midday, and again before the
night examen; then week after week try to advance the
number, and you will be surprised to find that your life seems
to be made up of ejaculations. This is by no means beyond
our reach, if we are faithful and zealous. Is not this the
life of recollection we want, and that which active saints
led? Nor will your work suffer in any way; on the contrary,
it will help to concentrate and spiritualize everything you
do, for is it not because we do not keep in mind the motive
of our actions that they are done in a purely material way?
As to one's success in meditation, remember, the criterion of
a good meditation is not sensible consolation and satisfaction, but the making of a resolution which will tell upon our
conduct during the day. We should accomplish much if
we only could grasp the idea of prayer, what it really is, the
communion of two, the outpouring of our desires and longings, the confession of our shortcomings and forebodings
into the ears of One whose delight is to be with the children
of men, frail and foolish as they are. Let us beseech Our
Lord more earnestly to teach us to pray simply, heartily,
and with unbounded confidence.

"As to devotion to our Lady, do not worry yourself
on that score; it is a thing which must be spontaneous
and cannot be forced. I am sure that you are a devout
client, and although you may consider things said and done
are sometimes not in good taste, yet in no way do you
derogate from her honor. If we think of her always as the
one whom Our Lord loved the most dearly of creatures,
we shall by degrees, as we become more Christlike, find that
we shall according to our measure love her as He did. I
find my devotion and confidence ever on the increase, and
if you take up the method of ejaculations which I spoke of,

you will find that the ' Sweet Heart of Mary ' will prove a
reality to you.

"Your devoted brother,

"Henry Van Rensselaer, S.J.'"

"Woodstock,

"Feast of Seven Dolors,

"1883.

"My Dear Sister Dolores:

"P. C.

"I do not know which of the two feasts of the Dolors of
Our Lady is your favorite. This one, it seems to me, should
be. In consequence of its being so near the Passiontide of
her Divine Son, we can realize better what her sufferings
were in the chief of her dolors, as she stood at the foot of
the cross. That, too, must be our station, if we would be
true followers of the Crucified. Not like the faithless, or
rather weak in faith, Apostle, standing afar off, viewing the
cross and the suffering, but without faith and confidence
enough to draw near and claim a share; but like our Blessed
Lady and her generous companions, not ashamed to face the
shame nor too weak to bear the pain. That little band is
a cause of reproach to manhood and of glory to womanhood,
for there were four to one—the weaker sex showing itself
stronger than the strong. Is it not hard with our proud na-
tures to try to practise what we admit readily enough in
theory? Crucified to the world we should be, dead to self-
love and self-pleasing. This is only our plain duty, as it
seems so clearly to us in meditation and prayer; we take our

resolution to act upon it, we rise from our knees feeling quite heroic, go to the chapel perhaps for Mass; one of our neighbors has some habit very disagreeable to us, away goes our heroism, irritation sets in and has full sway; we forget what is going on, we are inattentive to the action of the sacrifice, we are unstrung and nervous. We excuse ourselves, saying: 'How can one help being put out under the circumstances? It is all because of my nerves. I was not myself. It is a defect of my nature for which I cannot be held accountable—my misfortune not my fault.' So ingenious self-love rattles on, providing out of its treasures reason after reason, some of them specious enough to deceive the very elect if not on their guard. And where is the root of the evil? It lies within us; the external incident, whatever be its nature, did but serve as a match to set fire to a lot of combustible material that we imprudently keep within us. What will quench this fire? What will render this dangerous fuel beyond danger of a spark? Only a continual supply of 'that water that springeth up unto everlasting life.' That water flows from the riven side of Our Lord, and near the sacred fount must we be continually; nor is there anything to hinder it. No great exertion is required on our part, only a living in the presence of God, only a constant union with Him; corporally, when it is allowed us in Holy Communion; spiritually, when not our privilege. If we had that thirst after justice we should have, we would of our own accord turn to the Fountain of Justice. 'As the hart panteth after the waterbrooks, so longeth my soul after Thee, O God.' Such would be our desire, such indeed it is, I am sure, my dearest sister, but we must not rest in desires, but use the means of putting them into action.

"Struggle on with your aspirations, they may not come spontaneously now, come they will in time. Do not be discouraged and do not be satisfied with what you do. We must ever cry, 'More, O Lord, more grace': and with the grace let there be hereafter a greater faithfulness. St. Peter of Alcantara says: 'Let us aim at the highest, and by the grace of God, we shall be able to accomplish something for His greater glory, who has been so bountiful in His best and perfect gifts to us.' Those gifts have been given with a purpose; we shall frustrate it, unless we make ourselves fit instruments in the hands of the Heavenly Workman. Unfit we shall be, unless we extract all those roots of bitterness that lie deep down in our hearts, poisoning all the sweet water of our lives. That overweening love of self which makes itself a very tyrant, the end and measure of all that we do or is done to us. Drag it up by the roots we must, for it is useless to lop off the upper growth. It has sent out feelers and offshoots in all directions and twined itself by them closely around our hearts, and strengthened itself in all those years we have allowed it to live and flourish. It can be rooted up—it must be, and when? Why let it live a day longer? Let us begin at once, and a long pull and a strong pull and a pull that will be repeated day after day until it yields. We can do it and we will. I feel what I say, otherwise I would never have the assurance to write it. I am trying to practise what I preach or I could never have the face to preach it. I know only too well by experience all that special pleading of which I have spoken. Nature is responsible in a measure for our character, but we, too, are responsible for the way in which we have yielded to our weaknesses instead of fighting against them; we have enervated ourselves and then we blame our nerves as if they were the sole cause of our troubles. No, it is our soft self-indulgence. If we have violent tempers and strong passions it is because persons with such temperaments can by their very disposition do greater things and endure more than those who are more softly and gently disposed. We may use these passions as instruments of advancement, but not until we have them fully under our control. We shall get them under the curb only by constant watchfulness and self-restraint, stopping an ebullition ere it has gone too far. Doing this, we shall eventually get the mastery. Let us make up our minds not to excuse ourselves, but courageously admit our past faithlessness and resolve to make up by generous wakefulness, ever on the alert to foresee a coming storm and to be ready for it. This is a rather incoherent sort of a letter, but you will take it for what it is worth. . . . Thank the kind Sisters for the Agnus Dei, and recommend me warmly to them.

" Ever your devoted brother,

" HENRY VAN RENSSELAER, S.J."

What his thoughts were during Holy Week may be seen in a letter he wrote to his sister a week later.

" WOODSTOCK,

" MAUNDY-THURSDAY,

" March 22, 1883.

" MY DEAR SISTER DOLORES:

" For my greetings to reach you on Easter Day, I must write now. To-day we commemorate that greatest of bless-

218

ings bestowed by Our Lord, the institution of the Blessed Sacrament of His Holy Body and Blood, to be the soul's food in this journey through the wilderness, when nothing but the Heavenly Manna can be found to sustain and strengthen it. It is a day of days indeed, telling of the height of treason and of fidelity, of the depths of human depravity and of Divine mercy and forgiveness; how Judas betrayed and sold, how Christ forgave and would have saved. Did human nature ever look meaner than in the person of the traitor, or nobler than in the Betrayed. The whole history of the Passion is full of antithesis,—the Apostles dreaming of an earthly kingdom and its pomp and show, undesirous of shame and ignominy, as yet far from being spiritual-minded; their Master, the King of Kings, whose kingdom was not of this world, who thirsted for affronts and obloquy, and whose mind was set on things above, not on the things of the earth. Can anything be more pathetic than the contrast between the Master and the Disciples? He looked for some one to comfort Him, to sympathize with Him. He looked in vain; they could neither appreciate nor enter into His sentiments. Yet they had been under His training and influence for three years. What reason had He ever given them for such expectations as they counted upon? None; He had fled at the time when the people, full of enthusiasm on account of the miracle of the feeding of the multitude, would have taken Him and made Him king. He had a throne which He would one day ascend amidst the shouts of the bystanders; that throne was the cross, the acclamations, jeers of derision and scorn. It is easy for us to wonder at the stupidity and blindness of the Jews, for the defects of others are always apparent enough; our own escape our attention, so much are we engrossed with others. I often ask myself on which side I should have been had I been present on Calvary. It is hard to be on the losing side, and did ever a side look more hopeless than that of the Crucified? Hear the testimony of the very Disciples: ' We hoped,' they said, ' that it was He that should have redeemed Israel.' They hoped until the death on the cross put an end to hope. What strength of faith was requisite to see in that Man of Sorrows the Messiah, the Son of David of the royal race! What faith, to rise superior to the opinion of the rulers of society! It demanded a higher faith than the chosen band had, at least practically. They lacked, indeed, not the virtue of faith, but the will to exert the act.

"Can we not well understand the case? Does not our everyday life give some faint image of like conduct? Scarcely a day passes but human respect nips some virtuous action in the bud; I speak feelingly, for it is my own history. We call this truckling by euphonious names when we try to apologize for it to ourselves. It sometimes wears the garb of humility. We, in our lowliness, do not wish to attract attention, we wish to be like the rest. At other times we like to think the chance inopportune. No doubt St. Peter thought the question of the maid-servant so. That wasted opportunity brought on another and another, and the three combined gave him cause for life-long penance and sorrow. But, dearest sister, you need rather encouragement than anything else, for I remember well, even in Protestant days, how you braved the ridicule of the family and eyed your plate for dear life. It was modesty, as you understood it then, severe, repelling, but well meaning. What you could do in those days in such matters with less spiritual help, you can now do with more ease and edification. Perhaps you tell me that prayer seemed easier then than now; it may be so, but that proves nothing at all. God's criterion is not the ease with which we work, but rather the difficulties we surmount, such as a half hour spent in battling against temptations to impatience on account of the heat or ventilation, or the seeming barrenness or want of interest of the points given, or the manner in which they are given—all small things, surely, in themselves, but gigantic when they play upon the imagination. We begin to wonder at the stupidity and indiscrimination of those in power. We could give them a valuable hint or two, self-love whispers, forgetting that we have come into religion not to have our own way but to submit to crosses and contradictions for the love of God. *Sursum Corda!*

"Let this Easter-tide be a resurrection for us. We have been bound down by earthly things long enough. We have been looking too much through colored glasses, the coloring matter self-love. We will break them and see things in the pure white light of truth. We must make some generous resolutions, and what is more, we should begin without delay to put them into execution, expecting indeed not great victories at first, but cheerfully bearing up under occasional defeats.

"I am almost tempted to put all this into the fire, it sounds so trite and commonplace. Our Provincial, Father Fulton, is making his visitation. I had a very satisfactory talk with him, although I have but little chance of going on to theology without some teaching, there is such a demand for professors in the colleges, and so many scholastics who have finished their five years' term. Justice demands that they should have first chance for theology. It will be a new experience for me, and were it not for delaying ordination I have really a wish for it. However, whatever the decision, I am perfectly content. I shall expect the worst. . . .

> " Your devoted brother,
>
> " HENRY VAN RENSSELAER."

The Woodstock community of which Mr. Van Rensselaer was a member until the summer of 1883, was not only very large, but cosmopolitan as well; in it were Belgians and Germans, Italians and Frenchmen, Spaniards and Canadians, with sons of the Emerald Isle and Englishmen, though of course the German and Irish-American element predominated. With all these Mr. Van Rensselaer was a general favorite. He was a model of strict observance, never obtruding himself or his personal history or his opinions on others, and, strange to say, a close friend of men of the most antagonistic qualities. Affable towards all, he showed, perhaps, a preference for associating with men of other provinces or nationalities, and exercised without effort and without pretense a remarkable influence among his companions, many of whom were younger than himself, and on that account lacking in experience.

For philosophical studies and the abstruse generally, he had no special aptitude, though his common-sense way of viewing knotty problems caused him to be sought after by those less favored with natural gifts. He was always ready to lend a helping hand. He was a rapid penman and could take down, almost verbatim, the lectures of the professors. In consequence his notes were in great demand by his classmates, but no matter how often he was appealed to or how ill-timed the appeal, he was ever ready and obliging.

222

CHAPTER XII.

The Class-Room.

THE three years devoted to the study of philosophy were now drawing to a close, and in the summer of 1883 Mr. Van Rensselaer was to take the next step in the training of a young Jesuit, and assume the responsibilities of a teacher in the class-room. His first assignment was to St. John's College, Fordham, where he remained from September, 1883, until the following June. His interest in young men began to manifest itself at once. To him was assigned the charge of the Students' Sodality of the Blessed Virgin, a task than which no other more to his liking could have been selected.

It has frequently been observed that men who have influence over students of maturer years are often unable to manage the callow youths just entering upon their teens. The boy was a riddle which Mr. Van Rensselaer, not only when he was in charge as a professor, but all through the years of his ministry, could never solve. Not that he was not a favorite with the lads with whom he had to deal, but he was too kind-hearted and too good-natured to exercise the necessary control.

It was quite otherwise with the more advanced students who formed the College Sodality. The place of meeting was the Community Chapel, which he made attractive by the addition of bright frescoes, a handsome new altar, and elaborate chapel furniture. He would aid their devotion, but he would also provide for their comfort. In the sanctuary was placed a quaint little bell of exquisite workmanship. He had found it somewhere in Germany and it bore the following inscription :—

> " Die Kaiserglocke heiss' ich;
> Des Kaisers Ehren preis' ich;
> Auf heilger Warte steh' ich,
> Dem deutschen Reich erfleh' ich
> Dass Fried' und Wehr
> Ihm Gott bescheer."

Which may be rendered :—

> " The Kaiser's bell am I;
> And Kaiser praise on high;
> From belfry 'gainst the sky,
> For German land I cry:
> O God, her peace defend.
> O God, her might extend."

Once a week during the school year there was a meeting, and every fortnight an instruction, in the preparation of which Mr. Van Rensselaer put forth his best efforts and gave early proof of his deep interest in young men. It is not too much to say that the zealous activity of these college days was but the apprenticeship for his more extended, though not more valuable, work in the ministry. Among his papers is a blank-book of over a hundred pages containing a series of " Sermonettes " delivered at these regular meetings of the Sodality. They are neatly written and give evidence of exceptional care in their preparation. The character of these instructions may be learned from a glance at the index :—

1st.   On the dignity of a Sodalist.
2nd.   Aim of the Sodality.
3rd.   Self Sanctification.
4th.   Self Examination.
5th.   Advantages of Frequent Communion.
6th.   On Purity.   (Feast of the Purity B. V. M.)
7th.   On the Presence of God.
8th.   Idea of a Saint.   (All Saints.)
9th.   Souls in Purgatory.
10th. Vocation.
11th. On Duty of Thanksgiving.   (Thanksgiving Day Tide.)
12th. Preparation for the Coming of Christ.   (First Sunday of Advent.)
13th. Spirit of Joy.
14th. The Constituents of a Happy New Year. (Jan. 6.)
15th. Duty and Inclination.
16th. The Use of a Sodality Badge.
17th. Purification of B. V. M.
18th. Character.
19th. Formation of Character.
20th. Jesus Christ, Our Ideal.
21st. Devotion.
22nd. Christian Enthusiasm.   F. Ozanam.
23rd. Humility.

His second and last year as a teacher was spent at Loyola College, Baltimore.   No doubt it was a sacrifice to be taken away from Fordham and from the young men in whom, with the fervor of his new work upon him, he had taken so lively an interest. There may have been some feeling of disappointment at that, or of discouragement that he should be sent from New York, where his family and friends were within easy reach, and that he should be called upon to resume the uncongenial work of teaching. If there was any such feeling he gave no indication of it whatever, but struggled heroically through the ordeal.

Van Rensselaer had the true idea of the duty of the Jesuit professor towards the boys or young men under his charge. The interest in them begun in the class-room is not to end there, but to follow the young man after he leaves college, and to become one of his most valuable assets during his whole life. In Baltimore, as at Fordham, he won the hearts of his pupils and became their life-long friend.

It was in Baltimore that his literary activities may be said to have begun. As shown by his autobiographical sketch, he had not only a facile pen, but a keen literary instinct. His style is distinctive and even characteristic. His memoirs exhibit a vigorous, graphic way of putting things, a hatred for hypocrisy and cant, a bitterness, at times, toward those who differed with him, and an expression of his feelings which might be termed playfully sarcastic. His first venture in print was the composition of an historical drama, in collaboration with a confrère of the professorial staff. The full title ran, "King Alfred, an Historical Drama in Five Acts." It was printed for the occasion, and appeared again in a second edition in 1893. The choice of King Alfred was a happy one, as it proved an excellent subject for the college stage, enabling the young actors to venture upon something more serious and profitable than the farce or " adapted " comedy, which generally forms part of the public entertainments in schools. It was produced in the fall of 1884, and met with great success, notwithstanding the fact that in the battle scene, duly represented on the college stage, *all* the participants managed to be slain in the sanguinary encounter. The book received from the London *Month* a very flattering notice, which we reproduce here :—

" The historical drama of King Alfred, which has just been produced by two American writers, is an excellent version of the well-known story. It takes some liberties with the actual sequence of events, but here the authors have the precedent of other historical plays to justify them. They have introduced the legendary incidents of the King's hiding in the swineherd's hut, the burning of the cakes, the visit in disguise to the Danish camp, and the rest. The play is full of incident, the comic element has not been forgotten, and there are songs for which music has been provided, to give scope for the vocal powers of the performer. With the exception of some humorous passages, the play is in blank verse, and it contains not a few really beautiful lines."

As the Christmas season drew nigh, his pen was ready with another drama which, as befitting the occasion, was more religious and devotional. It was the legend of good King Wenceslaus, and was acted by the students on Christmas Eve, as an academic exercise before their departure for the holidays. The theme was the charity of the King to the poor; the time, the eve of Christmas, and the moral obvious even to the untutored.

As Van Rensselaer was still a scholastic, and free from the work of the ministry, he employed his leisure in these and similar literary pursuits, helping, at least indirectly, the whole student body, and fostering a college spirit among them.

He wrote still another drama, "Felician," portraying the life of the early Christians, which reads like a dramatized chapter or two of Wiseman's "Fabiola." Then came a lecture in February, still in MS., on Early Phases of Christian Art, which formed one of a series delivered by members of the College Faculty. Another interesting fragment from a never finished drama of "Clerical Life," furnishes an additional proof that his pen was not idle.

About this time his interest in missionary work was renewed, and he wrote several valuable papers on the Indian question, including a "Sketch of the Catholic Church in Montana," "The Apostle of Alaska, Archbishop Seghers," both of which appeared in the *American Catholic Quarterly,* and a "Plea for the Indians," in the *Catholic World* for March, 1886. To appreciate the motive of his writing on these subjects it may be well to state that, while teaching at Loyola, he had made up his mind to offer himself for the Indian Missions. The reasons which induced him to take this step were manifold. He was aware that he was not a success in the class-room, and in the missionary field there was plenty of other work in which he might prove more successful. A thought which particularly appealed to him was, that the Indians had a claim upon the descendants of those who held their lands, and at that time his family was still in possession of such lands. Then, too, Americans, he fancied, could, in the far West labor more effectively than foreigners; they might understand better the character of the settlers with whom the Indians come in contact, and they could better represent to the Government officials, both high and low, the grievances of the aborigines and defend them by voice and pen against the encroachments or the injustices of the whites; and why, he added, should Americans sit still and deplore the great lack of missionaries, and yet not volunteer to make good the deficiency? In the Maryland-New York province there seemed to be no dearth of laborers, but it was not an easy matter to find recruits for the Rocky Mountains.

The spiritual aspect of this self-immolation commended itself above aught else, for he was convinced that this greater sacrifice on his part would be fruitful even for those of his family who were still Protestants, and, after all, was he not but following up the first inclination he had as a Catholic, to be a missionary in Africa. These reasons, and the dislike he had for a life of comparative ease, urged him to make the sacrifice. Accordingly, he laid the matter before his superiors and with their approval wrote to the General at Rome asking to be transferred to the Mission of the Rocky Mountains. It speaks well for his missionary zeal, for his spirit of detachment from places and persons, that he was not only willing to offer, but actually offered himself for this arduous missionary work, and had no feeling but one of joy at the prospect.

It is interesting to know that his petition was granted, and the transfer was made. His name was dropped from the Province roll and duly entered among the members of the Rocky Mountain Mission. On the Feast of the Immaculate Conception, 1884, at the foot of Our Lady's Altar, he made the following vow:—

LOYOLA COLLEGE, BALTIMORE, MD.

Feast of the Immaculate Conception, 1884.

I, Henry Van Rensselaer, Scholastic of the Society of Jesus, do, on this day, the Patronal Feast
of the Church in the United States, solemnly offer
and devote myself forever to the Apostolate of the
Indian Mission in the Rocky Mountains, so help me
God, Our Lady, Our Holy Father Ignatius and St.
Francis Xavier, Apostle of the Indies.
    Amen.
      HENRY VAN RENSSELAER, S.J.
    L. D. S.

It is easy for us to look back and admire God's way of
dealing with this noble soul. Had this change been effected, the Far West would have gained another missionary, but New York would have lost an apostle. The
" divinity that shapes our ends, rough-hew them how we
will," was preparing his soul for the work of converting
the sinner by re-casting his character in the heroic mould of
self-sacrifice. He might never reach the object of his desires, but the ambition to be worthy of it and to fit himself
for it, was the secret alembic that transformed him into an
apostle. The great St. Francis Xavier yearned for the conversion of China, and died before he touched the shores.
Yet he is the Apostle of China, in intent and purpose, and to
his brilliant coronal of triumphs he has added new lustre
through his longing to add to the Kingdom of Christ the
vast multitudes of the Celestial Empire.

Henry Van Rensselaer's hopes of laboring among the

Indians, for whose salvation he had solemnly pledged his life, were never realized, but who will be bold enough to say that the glory of his apostolic life among the sick and the poor is not enhanced before God by the act of generosity which prompted him to offer the best that was in him for the salvation of the ill-treated and neglected red-man?

We have at our disposal only one letter coming from Baltimore. It was written to Sister Dolores and is a beautiful expression of the thoughts which refreshed his spirit. In it we get a glimpse of a very tender devotion to the Blessed Virgin.

" LOYOLA COLLEGE,

" Baltimore, 1885.

" A happy coincidence of Our Lady's feast with one of the most glorious of the year, and appropriate, too, for how was she the help of Christians except by being the Spouse of the Holy Ghost? The devotion to the Holy Ghost has always been one of my favorites; it does not necessarily require practices that would occupy much time, an occasional ' Gloria ' during the day in thanksgiving for all his benefits. We do not thank God enough; the Psalmist says: " His praise shall be ever in my mouth." Nothing is so gracious as thanksgiving. The Holy Ghost is the author and inspirer of grace. On His motion do we depend for every meritorious thought, word and action. To Him we owe all the Sacraments and all His seven-fold gifts. Are not these motives for special devotion? We shall never know until we see her face to face what Our Lady has been to us. Just as one never realizes how much one's own mother is to one

231

until separation proves how quietly, unobtrusively, lovingly, she has been rendering us continual services. In Mary's case we shall never find out by separation, but in the light of the Beatific Vision all will be made plain to us. I attribute my vocation to her, remembering what an impression the title ' Queen of the Society of Jesus ' made upon me when I first heard it at West Park.

" It drew me to desire to be her special subject in this, her kingdom. I came across a saying in a book relating to the Christian life: ' Si on est moins qu'un héros, on devient moins qu'un homme '; it seemed to me that we might put it in this way: ' Si on est moins qu'un saint, on devient moins qu'un religieux.' To avoid this we must set to work in earnest to become saints. Let us run a race—I challenge you. This year of college life has been given me by Our Lord for a time of reparation."

CHAPTER XIII.

Ordained a Priest.

I N the fall of 1885, Van Rensselaer began his theological studies at Woodstock preparatory to ordination. The fact that he had now the Rocky Mountains Mission to look forward to filled him with enthusiasm, and his pen was active in behalf of the Indians. Soon after his arrival he wrote to his sister:

"Woodstock College,

"September 19, 1885.

"I am glad to be once more settled and at work. I have got the one thing I needed to add to my means of perfecting myself, and that is the missionary vocation. I am now as light-hearted and merry as a boy. There are several aspirants to the mission here, and Alaska is to some the land of promise, desired because of its privations—the spirit of St. Ignatius still breathing in his children. Do you see the 'Fervorinos' on the Indians and Alaska in the Catholic Review? Perhaps you recognize the hand?"

The following letters, addressed likewise to Sister Dolores, display not only an intense desire to advance steadily in the pathway of sanctification, but an anxiety to have her also profit by the experiences in the spiritual life which he was daily undergoing. Apart from the help they furnish towards a better understanding of the process by which his character was moulded, they may be found useful for those

233

in the cloister or outside of it who would be guided by supernatural principles in the ordinary affairs of life.

" WOODSTOCK,

" Feast of Immac. Conc., 1885.

" MY DEAR SISTER DOLORES:
                    P. C.

" It seems to me a very long time since I wrote to you last. Why I have been so remiss, I cannot say. The best thing is to repair the omission. We have finished a triduum before the semi-annual renovation of our vows. It was a treat, for we had Father Maguire to give it. There is something magnetic about him. All that he says is very simple, but very impressive, owing to the way in which he says it. The real force is, I think, his personal holiness. That makes the apostle; that wins souls and stirs up the lukewarm into a glow. That is something by which you too can be an apostle, for it is common to all those devoted to God. What other reason had we for becoming religious than to become holy? It was that which God willed for us when in His mysterious wisdom He chose and called us, to draw us nearer to Himself, to be among His own immediate familiar friends, close to His own Person, to shower upon us constant proofs of His love and friendship. 'This is the will of God, even our sanctification.' Is it our will too? Is it an efficacious will which directs the use of means to gain that end? Oh, how comparatively easy it is to acquire holiness! We have only to use the means within our reach. No heights of meditation and contemplation are required, no macerations

234

of the body absolutely needful, no extraordinary works to be wrought. We have only to live in union with Jesus Christ and His Blessed Mother, only to fulfil each little insignificant duty as it presents itself for His sake; in a word, only to correspond with the grace and inspiration He gives us, only to obey Him in our superiors. Not a hard task, it may seem, but still it is; the very easiness of it makes it hard, strange as that sounds. We could force ourselves to do great and out-of-the-way things more easily perhaps than small, commonplace things. We find an hour's or a half-hour's meditation a hard and irksome work perhaps, yet we may delude ourselves by imagining ourselves capable of a life of contemplation. We offer ourselves as victims for ignominy and insult, yet we turn pale and are indignant if anyone seems to treat us with less than ordinary respect. We would perform wonderful feats of fasting; we cannot even put up with the food set before us without grumbling at least in our hearts. Yet God asks really so little of us. '*Age quod agis!*' Whatever you do, do it with all your heart. That makes the saint. That made the sanctity of good Father Sadlier,* for I believe that he was a saint, ever forgetful of himself, ever mindful of others, self-sacrificing to a fault. Devout, but without ostentation, a piety that charmed and won affection. I had the happiness of spending three weeks at the Boston Villa with him, and there I discovered his virtues and rejoice to have known him, for he was a true son of Ignatius, ripe for Heaven, and so we lost him. . . ."

*Francis Xavier Sadlier, S.J., mentioned in this letter, was the son of Mrs. James Sadlier, the well-known writer. He died at Holy Cross College, Worcester, Mass, on the fourteenth of November, 1885, with a great repute for holiness.

" . . . One thought seemed to run through the whole of our retreat this year which may be useful to you. Conformity to the will of God is the touchstone which turns all to gold. Nature rebels at something said or ordered, something unpleasant. It is the will of God. Why should I rebel against it? It is unpleasant only because I put myself in opposition to it. How much the imagination has to do with our judgments! It should not be so; but still it is so. God wants it of me. Is not this sufficient motive to make sweet anything bitter? But, one will say, I don't like it. Don't like what God wishes? Let him make an act of faith, and, by the help of God, he will like it. The battle is over, the struggle is at an end. It seemed to me that this one thought would, if made a constant companion to be consulted on all occasions, make us saints in a very short time. It has done so in times past, why not then in ours?

" Try this receipt and tell me if you do not find it palatable. I am so glad to have the chance of assisting at a Benediction in your beautiful chapel. In two years, D. V., I hope to give it myself. Oh, how holy one should be to be entrusted with such an office!

" Pray then for me, and commend me to your good sisters in religion. . . .

" Ever your affectionate brother,

" HENRY VAN RENSSELAER, S.J."

" January 31, 1886.

" MY DEAR SISTER DOLORES:

" P. C.

" I don't think that I have written to you this year, so I had better begin before the first month has passed. I was

236

quite shocked at ———'s death, coming as it did so suddenly. I hope it found him well prepared. It must be a great trial to his wife.

"I sent her a most consoling account of the death of the celebrated Father Hermann's mother. You remember he was the wonderful musician, pupil of Liszt, a friend of Georges Sand, Mario, and others—a Jew, miraculously converted by the Blessed Sacrament. He afterwards became a Carmelite, was distinguished for his sanctity, and died a martyr of charity attending the soldiers in the Franco-Prussian war. Well, the aim of his life was the conversion of his family, and especially of his mother. In spite of all his efforts she died a Jewess apparently, to his intense grief. He spoke of it to the Curé d'Ars, who told him that six years later, on the feast of the Immaculate Conception, he would have good news. The six years passed, and on the day named Father Hermann received a letter through a Jesuit Father from a lady, who, after edifying the world by her piety and by the devotional books she wrote, died in the odor of sanctity. To make a long story short she received a revelation in which the whole scene of Father Hermann's mother's death was shown to her. After the last breath, or at least when it seemed that she had lost consciousness and had ceased to breathe, Our Blessed Lady threw herself before the throne of her Son and begged as a special favor to her, the soul of the mother of her servant Hermann, who had so faithfully served her and had committed to her keeping the soul of his mother a thousand times. She implored Our Lord not to allow this precious soul to be lost, and the petition was granted, for straightway a mighty grace was given to the dying Jewess; in a flash she saw the whole truth and cried out interiorly:

' O Jesus! God of the Christians, the God whom my son adores, I believe in Thee, I hope in Thee, have pity on me,' and she was saved. The lady was bidden by Our Lord to communicate this to Father Hermann for his consolation, and as a proof of the power of Our Blessed Lady over the Sacred Heart of her Divine Son. Did you ever hear anything more consoling and strengthening than this? It has given me a new impulse in the spiritual life, a strong determination to show myself, as St. Ignatius says, remarkable in God's service.

" The whole life of Father Hermann is very striking and has had a wonderful effect on me, showing me how ungrateful I am, I, who like him, have received so many extraordinary graces, and yet am so backward in perfection after seven years of religious life. Let it animate us both to greater efforts. Is it not shameful that we should be such ordinary religious, yielding to so many pettinesses and weaknesses, and scarcely ashamed of them, excusing them as common to our nature? Common, indeed, they are, but we, who are vessels of election, should triumph over them. We haven't confidence enough in God, we haven't the idea ever before our minds that God expects more of those to whom he has given more. We don't dare attempt great things, and what are great things? prolonged prayer, and fasting, etc.? Not necessarily, but the greatest thing is self-immolation, self-conquest, to which we can turn every action of our lives, every word we speak. We shall never be truly and solidly at peace and full of joy until we rest not in self, but in God alone. Never happy until our thoughts turn naturally to God without our bidding, until all we do is done for Him; if done for Him, everything will become sweet in the doing, everything will be well done, for we are not servants, but sons of His love. Pray much for my advancement; it is so easy to grow weary and work by fits and starts, in which case we accomplish nothing.

"Ever your devoted brother,

"HENRY VAN RENSSELAER, S.J."

"April 23, 1886.

"MY DEAR SISTER DOLORES:

"P. C.

"I want these few lines of greeting to reach you by Easter, and therefore I write to-day. I hope that you have been able to take part in some of the Holy Week services. Ours have been, so far, very devotional. I am always fortunate in being in the choir, so that I have an active part. Besides this I painted a beautiful Paschal candle. I tried my hand last year with a certain amount of success, and I felt encouraged to offer to paint one for the Chapel this year. It is very elaborate. I put on some brilliant crimson bands, relieved with tracery of black and gold, and in the first division I placed the cross, where the blessed grains of incense go, filled out in bright blue and gold. In the panel above are two palms crossed, representing victory over death and hell; above comes a butterfly, emblem of the resurrection, then the monogram of the first two letters in the Greek name of Christ X. P. (Chi, Rho) and above all the crown.

"A thought that has made a deep impression on me these last few days, especially yesterday (Maundy Thursday), is the necessity of practical charity in our thoughts. I say

239

practical, because we have it in abundance theoretically; what we need is the practice.   .   ."

As the day of his ordination to the priesthood approached, his happiness increased. No wonder; it would mark the end of long years of preparation and the consummation of the longings of a lifetime. He would shortly appear in a new rôle as the representative of the Good Shepherd seeking the lost sheep within and without the fold, and dispensing the Divine mercies to the sons of men. No one could act the part well who had not studied the character he was to portray and imbued himself with the spirit of the Divine Master.

In April, 1886, he wrote:—

" I have never felt better than during this Lent; so you see theology agrees with me. I am not sorry, though, that a year out of the course is nearly gone; a year nearer the end. Next year at this time I hope to be practising the ceremonies of the Mass. Pray that I may become more self-sacrificing and unselfish. It is so necessary in a priest, above all in a Jesuit, and most of all in a missionary. I take the greatest comfort and delight in the thought of the missions. What a debt we have to pay the Indians! "

In the month of May he dwells upon a thought from one of his meditations.

" We had our triduum last week and the Renovation on Sunday. A thought that came to me most forcibly was the ' Quid ad te? Tu sequere me.' Why do we lose our peace of mind? Very often by worrying and meddling about others. *Quid ad te?* What business is it of mine? I came into religion to sanctify myself primarily. If others have this or that defect, *quid ad te?* Attend to yourself, and you will have more than enough to do in following Christ. How can we keep step with Him if we are perpetually turning aside to follow others? *Sequere me*—that is our work, to follow Christ, and that demands all our attention. We shall accomplish most for others by closely following Him, for did He not go about doing good. Living charity is the most powerful preacher, and example does more than eloquent words. Our Blessed Lady will be as she has always been, our Auxilium."

Six months later, on the Feast of the Immaculate Conception, he speaks of a renewed and strengthened purpose to become holy.

"Our triduum is over and has brought me great peace of mind and a strong determination to make a new start. Rather a shameful confession that, after eight years of religious life.

"But were not these very renewals of our vows intended for this very purpose. It is a great grace not to be discouraged at one's failures. Disgusted with ourselves we may be, but the grace of God is so strong, the intercession of our Mother so powerful, the prayers of our saints so fruitful, that we must say, 'I can do all in Him Who strengtheneth me.' Courage, then, and confidence, and we shall see what Christmas will bring us."

When the day set for his ordination was announced his joy knew no bounds, as is attested by the brief extracts from his correspondence here given:—

241

" Woodstock,

" March 28, 1887.

" On Friday, the Feast of the Compassion of the most Holy Virgin, I shall begin an eight days' retreat to prepare for the crowning happiness of my life, my priesthood. I have permission to be ordained in New York on the eve of Trinity Sunday. It all seems too good to be true, and I almost dread at times that it is a dream—only two months more. I have the loftiest ideal of what I should be, but oh, how far off from it I am! This Holy Week must be the turning point in my life and the beginning of a risen life of unselfish devotion."

" Easter Eve,

" April 9, 1887.

" I never had two happier days than those on which I received the two steps to the altar. Bishop Curtis pontificated, and it added much to my joy to have him. I have just finished acting as deacon at this morning's ceremonies, in which I sang the ' Exultet ' and that beautiful ' Ite missa est, alleluia.' "

The Eve of Trinity Sunday, 1887, saw Father Van Rensselaer raised to the dignity of the priesthood. The ceremony took place in St. Patrick's Cathedral, New York, with Archbishop Corrigan officiating. The next day the newly ordained priest said his Mass with much fervor in the Church of St. Francis Xavier, and a day or two later returned to Woodstock to complete his studies in theology and prepare as he thought for the Indian Missions.

The life he was now entering upon was altogether new —the life of a priest. Hitherto his uppermost thought and endeavor had been his own sanctification; henceforth he was to blend with that the sanctification of his neighbor. He felt, though he did not express it in words, that a new spirit had come over him, that with special significance might be applied to him the words of Scripture: ' The Spirit of the Lord is upon me wherefore He hath anointed me; to preach the Gospel to the poor He hath sent me, to heal the contrite of heart'; and with the graces of his ordination imparting this new life, he began that silent apostolate for which he was to become so noted later. We are not left altogether in the dark as to his first works of zeal, nor are we surprised to find that he began on the most unpromising material, the tramps. The following letter came from Woodstock some time in the spring of 1888:—

" The hour of the Holy Sacrifice is the happiest one of the day for me, and Holy Week will indeed be one of penance, when we shall have to forego the Offering for three days.

" I have had great consolations lately with my tramps; one, well educated and well connected, a Protestant, came three weeks ago. I took an interest in his case and brought him into the parlor, encouraged him and tried to restore his self-respect. I gave him a Catholic book to read while I was in class and explained some Catechism to him. When he left me after a few hours, he had learned to make the Sign of the Cross and the Hail Mary, and had formed a firm resolution to become a Catholic. I recommended him to invoke St. Joseph for a position. He did so, and has now a place in the best dry-goods house in Baltimore with a salary of eighteen dollars a week. Is not that a triumph of the Sacred Heart? He said: 'I never knew what prayer was before.'

"There are many other instances, too; one, a Jew of twenty-five, who had passed himself off as a Catholic, so that a companion, a real Catholic, always believed him to be one. I exhorted both to confession and put before them clearly the end for which they were created. They had their supper and went off to a hay-rick, where my transient boarders lodge. There the Jew confessed the truth to his companion, but said he wanted to become a Catholic, and the other resolved, after many years, to square his accounts. The next morning they came to breakfast and begged to remain another day. The Jew had learned the Our Father, Hail Mary, Creed and Act of Contrition, and insisted on being baptized. I put him off with an evasive answer and made him study Catechism all that day. In the meantime I consulted Father Rector, and he said: 'If he knows sufficient Catechism and what he is doing, he might, under the circumstances, be baptized.' So, after Mass the next day—it was a holiday, the 22d of February—I went through the whole Christian doctrine with him and then baptized him. Happily one of the workmen left that day, and Father Minister told me I might keep both men. They have been here a month and give great edification in every way; another triumph of the Sacred Heart. I think I have found my vocation in the Society, the waifs and wanderers. 'The poor have the gospel preached to them.' Not that I have given up the Indians, far from it, but there are hosts of neglected men in the Far West, waiting for some one to stretch out a hand to them."

On Christmas day, he wrote: "As you see, I am at home this year. We had Midnight Mass, at which I assisted, then rested till five when I began my three Masses. I had everything beautiful about me, the decorated chapel, handsome vestments, and rich sacred vessels, but no congregation to assist. Next year I hope I shall be in the Mountains with a crowd of faithful Indians, or cowboys, or whites, it does not matter much, provided there are souls to be helped. It is hard for me to hold myself in. I have had such an abundance of zeal, which will, I hope, have an outlet in about three months. After all, what is the greatest work in the sight of God? Our sanctification. This is the thing to be kept in view. God wants me to be a saint; if I am faithful He will work great things for His glory through me. How? That is for Him to determine."

CHAPTER XIV.

Work in the Ministry.

I N the Spring of 1889, Father Van Rensselaer began his zealous labors in New York City. For four years he had looked forward to a life among the Indians of the North-West, but at the last moment a new Provincial of the Maryland-New York Province used his influence to keep him in the East. This Superior felt that the good to be accomplished among the Indians by the newly ordained priest was largely problematical, while the province over which he presided could ill afford to lose the services of so valuable a man. Submissively, Father Van Rensselaer accepted the transfer to his former status in the Maryland-New York Province and was soon after detailed for duty at St. Francis Xavier's, West Sixteenth street, New York.

It would be no easy task to give even a succinct account of the various works of zeal that filled up the seventeen years of his ministry in the metropolis. A large share of the parish work fell to his lot, yet he never seemed to grow weary, and no matter how numerous his activities, he was always ready to undertake more. Sick calls, Masses at inconvenient hours, service in hospitals, visits to the poor, sermons and lectures, retreats, triduums, sodalities of men and boys, class for converts, St. Vincent de Paul Society, Xavier Club, Deaf Mutes, Ancient Order of Hibernians, Knights of Columbus, daily visits to the Xavier Club and the Nazareth Day Nursery, confessions, baptisms, marriages, pledges to the intemperate, employment for the needy, visits to the prisons; all these represent in a general way the round of occupations that kept him busy from dawn till far into the night. The bare enumeration of these works of mercy and love sounds like a litany of his good deeds in the vineyard of his Father. With all this he never murmured nor gave the impression of being overworked. He went about each duty as if that were his only concern in life. It is only when all his zealous labors are catalogued and viewed in retrospect that the list causes one to inquire in astonishment how he was able to accomplish so much. Would you believe that he found time, moreover, to write plays of an amusing character for his young men, and that he took charge of the rehearsals himself?

He had a predilection for singing High Mass on Sundays, and no church service, however long or fatiguing—and there were many in the course of the year at St. Francis Xavier's—caused him to utter a word of complaint. "The Three Hours' Agony" on Good Friday he claimed for himself. Except upon one occasion, when he gave the discourses upon the Seven Words from the Cross, he always led the exercises, the fervent unction with which he recited the prayers never failing to move the hearts of the people and to contribute largely to the beauty and dignity of the devotion.

He had little love for preaching, and the most enthusiastic admirer would hardly have called him an orator. Still he occasionally surpassed himself and discoursed with genuine eloquence. His last sermon at High Mass was delivered at St. Francis Xavier's, in October, 1906, and those who heard him on that occasion will recall the original way in which he handled a trite subject. The gospel of the day was the parable of the unmerciful servant. The preacher unfolded the narrative after his own fashion, and then made an application to existing conditions of human society. He called the parable a drama in three acts. In the first act, there is the debtor of ten thousand talents, or, say, a million dollars. The King is the magnate, the captain of industry, the multi-millionaire. The servant who owes a million dollars is his right-hand man, or agent, or chargé d'affaires. But in modern parlance he is " a plunger " and has been risking his master's money and speculating in stocks, counting, of course, on the sure thing. Then comes the unexpected slump in the market, followed by the usual catastrophe, and the dishonest speculator loses everything, even that which he could never have claimed as his own. There is no way out of his embarrassment except to throw himself on the mercy of his employer. He admits his crookedness, pleads for extension of time, and gets his family and friends to intercede for him. The magnate relents and freely forgives him. The gratitude of the rehabilitated servant is profound. Act two: Transformation.—The suppliant becomes the throttler. The humble petitioner is transformed into the relentless creditor. Before the week is out he demands the payment of an hundred pence, say one hundred dollars, from his clerk. He himself has been forgiven a debt of a million dollars, and he exacts the payment of one hundred from his fellow servant. The poor fellow pleads for mercy. In extenuation he urges that his wages are but ten dollars a week, and he has appropriated only one hundred in the course of the year. He admits his guilt, but offers in excuse that at home there is an invalid widowed mother. There was an impending eviction of the family, now happily averted. On his shoulders falls the care of younger brothers and sisters, who would starve if they depended solely upon his meagre allowance. But his pleadings are in vain. He is summarily ejected and given over to the officers of the law. Act three. The tables are turned. The master treats the heard-hearted wretch as he treated his clerk, and exacts the full penalty. Here the preacher proceeded rapidly to an enlargement of his theme and spoke on Christian forgiveness. Christ, he held up as the model who taught the lesson of forgiveness by word and example from the cradle to the grave. " By this shall all men know that you are my disciples, if you have love one for another." This is the victory over the pagan world. As was said in the early days of Christianity, " See how the Christians love one another." Christ taught the lesson of forgiveness from the cross. Then he instanced St. Stephen praying for his murderers, Blessed Fisher and St. Thomas More, St. Jane Frances de Chantal, St. Monica condoning the faults of husband and son, in contrast with the conduct of fathers and mothers generally. He alluded to a case that had come under his notice, of a father who had disinherited his son for some boyish escapade. On his death-bed his heart was still hardened. He would not forgive even his own flesh and blood, and unforgiving he went before the awful judgment seat. The measure of our forgiveness will be the measure of God's mercy. " As we forgive those who trespass against us." The trifling offence of our fellow man he set over against the infinite offence of sin, infinite in its effects, for it entails the loss of heaven. God forgives, gives preventing grace, that is, He is the first to make the advance. He goes to meet the sinner, grants pardon for the asking, and forgets the offence; considers repentance a personal favor, a cause of congratulation. " There shall be joy in heaven." He concluded with an appeal for self-examination and forgiveness if we hope to be forgiven.

249

This is only a brief outline of the sermon, but it will serve to show how very original in conception, how practical and direct were his discourses to the people. Though he always gave careful preparation to his sermons and addresses, he never wrote them out in full. One reason for this was that he could never trust his memory to retain a carefully conned and polished composition. His voice was somewhat against him, but, with his earnestness and fervor of delivery, his wealth of thought and illustration, he always made a deep impression upon his hearers.

There is an enormous amount of written matter left among his notes; skeleton sermons for every Sunday in the year—sometimes half a dozen for the same Sunday—sketches of discourses for festivals, for special occasions, for the different societies with which he was connected, all of them attesting his unflagging zeal and the high idea he entertained of the work of a priest in the pulpit and on the platform.

The Spiritual Exercises of St. Ignatius he made a profound and life-long study. He had for his use a printed copy of one of Father Roothan's editions, over two hundred and fifty pages, octavo, which is literally covered with annotations and suggestions, written so closely between the lines and on the margins as to be almost undecipherable. Besides this annotated copy of the Book of the Exercises, there are drafts by the score of meditations and instructions for triduums and retreats, adapted to various classes of men and women, proof of the elaborate care he bestowed upon this important branch of a Jesuit priest's work. Over and above the ordinary retreats to religious communities and the laity which fall to the lot of every Jesuit, Father Van Rensselaer was called upon to give an occasional one to the clergy. These retreats, by reason of the far-reaching good resulting therefrom, are without doubt the most important charge which can be entrusted to a priest. That he conducted them successfully, is the testimony of those who made them under his direction, and is borne out by the following tribute from a diocesan newspaper. It is headed " A Knickerbocker Jesuit."

" The priests of the diocese are very grateful to the distinguished Jesuit Father, the Rev. Henry Van Rensselaer, for the delightful way in which he conducted the spiritual exercises of their retreat last week.

"It is true, of course, that, humanly speaking, the fruit of a spiritual retreat must always depend on oneself. Yet, the personality of him who conducts the exercises, and the vigor and freshness with which he puts things, has not a little to do with the success of a retreat.

" These Father Van Rensselaer possesses in a striking degree. To begin with, he is a man of knightly presence, without fear, without reproach, who speaks as God's ambassador. One easily perceives, too, that he is endowed with a noble soul, who despises everything low or mean. He is, moreover, a gentleman of distinguished family, reared in luxury, with large patrimony, and on whose future the radiant sky sweetly smiled. Brought up an alien to the Church, his eyes, like Paul's, were mercifully opened to the light of faith; and further favored by a divine call to a life of perfection, he left all the glittering world had in store for him to follow the Master.

" Trained in the military school of Loyola, this scion of New York's Four Hundred is a soldier of the Cross. To pierce the sinful hearts of men with the power and mystery

251

of the Cross is his one grand passion. He has, moreover, the art of putting things with striking force. And as one gazes on his handsome face, and listens to the music of his voice—enhanced by the unmistakable New York accent— the old truths have a new meaning and fascinate the heart as never before.

" This is God's way of using human gifts and advantages for His greater honor and glory and the salvation of souls."

In 1896, Father Van Rensselaer was invited to preach at St. Mary's Cathedral, Ogdensburg, which may be regarded as his native city, Woodford, the family estate, being only half a mile to the west. The local press treated his coming as an event of unusual interest. One daily paper devoted two columns to a description of Woodford, with a picture in half-tone of the old Van Rensselaer residence, " from the porch of which, with its massive Corinthian columns, one looked through vistas of the intercepting foliage, across broad meadows to the majestic flow of the St. Lawrence." In this account there is a brief reference to Henry Van Rensselaer, Inspector General of the Army, and former owner of Woodford, another to the visit of his eldest son Stephen, also a soldier, who won his spurs at Gettysburg, and then the article concludes : " Some decades of years passed, and a new generation had almost forgotten the associations with Woodford, when the youngest living son and namesake of its former owner, came among his townspeople. He, too, had enlisted, but for spiritual warfare under the leadership of the great Captain, St. Ignatius Loyola, in the Company of Jesus, and his mission is the peaceful one of winning souls to Christ."

The sermon at Ogdensburg was largely an account of his

CHURCH OF ST. FRANCIS XAVIER,
NEW YORK CITY

conversion to the Church and, indirectly, of the development of the Protestant Episcopal Church in America from the time of the American Revolution. The portion of the sermon which gave the story of the development of the American Episcopal Church was substantially the same as the introduction he wrote to his autobiography and is as follows:—

" I was born of very religious parents of the strong Protestant type. My father was of Dutch Reformed origin, while my mother was a Protestant Episcopalian. Fifty years ago the distinction between those sects was comparatively unimportant. They were all Protestants and were proud of it. The good old dominies of those days would scarcely recognize the transformed sects of to-day. The name Catholic was a by-word. The term priest was not yet usurped by ministers, with the exception of a few who were eyed askance as dangerous characters, secret allies of the Scarlet Woman and in her pay. The evolution of the Episcopal Church into a so-called branch of the Catholic Church is interesting.

" Originally an off-shoot of the Established Protestant Church of England, this American branch was cut off by the Declaration of Independence and had to assume a new corporate existence and title. The staunch Protestants of those days were proud of their Protestantism and asserted it in their new name. But they had bishops, so-called, and therefore they were Episcopalians. So their sect was thenceforth to be known as the Protestant Episcopal Church, a name which suited it admirably. They were on friendly terms with other Protestant denominations, and their Protestantism connoted the supposed errors of Rome.

" The Oxford movement, strong in England, had only a comparatively slight effect in the United States. But the example of Newman and the galaxy of great men who followed him to Rome could not fail to make an impression on some of the earnest-minded ministers of the day. The vivifying breath of the Holy Spirit was about to infuse life into the dry bones of Protestantism. The true concept of a living Church, with power to teach the truth, was dawning. The vision of the eternal priesthood according to the order of Melchisedech, with its visible representatives offering sacrifice, rose up before them and fascinated them. The five sacraments that had been discarded so contemptuously by the prime movers of the great revolt against the Church, seemed in the new light no longer ' old women's fables or corrupt following of the Apostles,' but channels of divine grace instituted by Christ Himself. The glorious Communion of Saints appeared, as it is in very truth, the realization of the close relations that exist between the members of the Church militant on earth and of the Church triumphant in heaven. It was no longer an empty expression in the creed, repeated thousands of times without even an inkling of its meaning. It was, indeed, the ever-presence of the ' cloud of witnesses and the spirits of the just made perfect.' The great fact of the Incarnation stood out in its magnificent proportions, and in consequence the essential part played by the Virgin Mother forced itself on the acceptance of all honest minds. Even the unique privilege of St. Peter as the Rock upon which Christ built His Church, as the receiver from Him of the Keys of the Kingdom of Heaven, as the feeder of His sheep and lambs, His own representative as the Good Shepherd of the flock, seemed less impossible of belief.

" Such a growth in the acceptance of Catholic doctrines was gradual and met with many obstacles. The prejudices of over three centuries died hard, if they died at all. The journey to the true Jerusalem, the City of God on earth, was up-hill and laborious. It demanded courage and perseverance. In many cases it was a bloodless martyrdom.

" Perhaps the most striking way to show this growth is to follow the evolution of the eucharistic service, for this was the axis on which the movement turned. In good old-fashioned Episcopal churches there was a chancel and in the chancel a communion table—a veritable table with four legs, and when in use, once a month, it was covered with a regulation linen table-cloth. Being a table for the Lord's Supper, as it was then commonly called, there was ordinarily nothing on it. Then an ornamental cover was placed over it, and this became later a frontal. The empty space between the legs was filled in, and it took on the semblance of an altar. Next a shelf made its appearance at the back of the table. On the shelf a cross of flowers was introduced on a feast-day—Christmas or Easter. The flowers withered and were removed, but the wooden cross remained. Next, two candlesticks with candles, for light in the early morning only, flanked the cross. As it was no longer a receptacle for flowers, two vases were substituted. By this time the old-fashioned Communion table had blossomed into a simple type of altar. The large flagon of wine, the capacious cup, and the plate of bread were no more visible on the table. A credence, or side, table was provided. The elements, as they were called, were covered with a veil, and the bread was in the form of wafers. The ministers, and they were not ashamed of the name, of old stood at either

255

end of the table, so that the congregation could witness all
their actions. This was technically termed the northward
position, although north and south would have been more
correct. But the eastward position (the altar end of the
church theoretically was supposed to face east) became
prevalent, and the minister stood with his back to the people,
giving him a chance for various ritualistic practices
which he interpolated unknown to the congregation.
But the dress of the embryo-priest had to keep pace with the
development of the altar. First he donned a cassock reaching to his feet, with a moderately long surplice. The broad
black scarf, worn on all occasions, gave way on great feasts
to a white one. This done and accepted, the other colors
were soon adopted. But the surplice was not an eucharistic
vestment. A sort of combination chasuble and surplice
served as a go-between, until the regular chasuble was no
longer an object of suspicion. For a while the material was
linen, sometimes handsomely embroidered; silk soon replaced
the linen, and a set of silk vestments of all the liturgical
colors became a part of every ritualistic establishment. The
evolution was well nigh complete; the chancel had become
the sanctuary; the table, the altar, and all its appurtenances
were there. The cross had received its figure and was a
crucifix. The step on which it had stood had grown tall and
evolved into a tabernacle. Candles blazed on the altar even
in broad daylight. Not one sanctuary lamp burned before
the altar, but seven, as being more scriptural. The Communion service, or the Lord's Supper, by dint of omissions
and additions, might pass for the Mass, and was with great
ostentation announced as such. True, the language was
English, but it was so mumbled that it could be mistaken for
Latin, or some unknown tongue. Stations of the cross were

erected; statues of the saints graced the sanctuary or side altars; confessionals were provided, and holy water stoups enhanced the semblance of Catholicity.

"With all this external growth, doctrinal teaching had been in the lead. The 'faithful' were forbidden to call themselves Protestants and were Catholics or Anglo-Catholics; whereas Catholics must be contemptuously called Romanists, for, according to the new Gospel, Romanists were only a sect, originating in Italy, while the Anglican Church was *the* Church, pure and undefiled, conformable to primitive Christianity.

"Of course the ritualists proper were, and still are, a very small minority in the Protestant Episcopal Church. But they had a certain influence in leavening the Protestant lump, and in raising portions of it in doctrines and practices. But by far the more influential party is that known as the Broad Church, which, in reality, is so rationalistic that it rejects such fundamental truths as the Divinity of Christ, and consequently the Trinity, and perforce the two commonly accepted sacraments as real means of grace, and denies the inspiration of the Scriptures. The Low Church party contains the old conservative Protestants, and might be characterized as Evangelical or Bible Christians, respectable, but unreasoning. Then come the High Churchmen, holding various attitudes of belief, the greater part being High and Dry, and so considered very safe, with no danger of reaching the height whence a fall Romeward would be likely."

The Ogdensburg *Courier,* in its résumé of the discourse, states that "the speaker made an elaborate argument in support of his present religious belief, and closed the lecture, saying: 'I thank God I am what I am.'"

In November, 1897, the venerable Clarence Walworth celebrated the hundredth anniversary of the laying of the corner-stone of the first St. Mary's Church, Albany, N. Y., of which he had been pastor for over thirty years. Father Van Rensselaer was an old-time friend, and the family affiliations with the early history of Albany suggested him as one of the speakers for the celebration. The occasion was inspiring. Albany, the old Fort Orange, was once the home of the patroons and for generations the centre of their influence throughout the State. In the history of the trading post, and its development into the capital of the Empire State, the Van Rensselaer family had played a conspicuous part. On the other hand, the Jesuit Mission sites were not far away, and if we include the land bordering on the St. Lawrence as far as Ogdensburg, they were actually situated in Van Rensselaer property. The first of the Mohawk Castles, the historic Auriesville, where Jogues, and Bressani, and their fellows toiled and suffered for the faith, was only forty miles distant. There was a fitness, then, in the selection of Father Van Rensselaer, a descendant of the old patroons, and a brother in religion of those heroic missionaries, to tell the story of the Church's growth in a land endeared to him by so many ties. There is no record preserved of the discourse delivered on that occasion, though he doubtless made it the object of special preparation. In a chronicle of the event it is referred to as an eloquent sermon on the text, " This is none other than the house of God; this is the gate of Heaven."

In the " Life Sketches of Father Walworth," published in 1907, there is a pen picture of the preacher as he appeared in the pulpit of historic St. Mary's:—

" Tall and dark amid the resplendent glory of the ceremony, stood the Jesuit in dear old St. Mary's oaken pulpit. He stood there in the heyday of manly beauty, a lineal descendant of the first Albany patroon, and all the while a crucifix glimmered at his girdle. He was every inch a black-gown, a devoted missionary, a devoted son of Loyola, and so, too, was the one of whom he spoke, Isaac Jogues, discoverer of Lake George, a friend of Megapolensis at Fort Orange, and martyr of the Mohawk Mission. The vigor and graces of a noble orator were his, and who could say that Father Van Rensselaer was not the right man in the right place for that occasion?"

CHAPTER XV.

Tertianship and Messenger of the Sacred Heart.

UPON the completion of his studies, every Jesuit is sent back to the novitiate to spend a year in the humble employments and spiritual duties which helped to lay the foundation of his religious life. This year is usually called the third year of probation, or, to distinguish it from the novitiate, the tertianship. In Father Van Rensselaer's case, however, it was only after some years of the ministry that he was sent to Frederick, Md., to complete his spiritual training, and it was while there that he wrote the following interesting letter to his mother:

" Novitiate,

" Frederick City, Md.,

" September 20, 1893.

" My Dearest Mother:

" I suppose you are anxious to know how I am settled in my new quarters. There could not be a greater contrast than between New York and Frederick. The latter is the dullest little town possible. No hustle, but withal noisy, as everybody speaks out loud in the street, to the great annoyance of those inside the house. The inevitable small boy makes it lively, too. Moreover, it is enlivened by church bells. There is quite a rivalry. We, however, always have the lead, as we begin at 5 A. M., but the others make up for it later on. I do not think that I have sat as much in four years as I have the last eighteen days since I have been here. In fact the last thirteen years seem like a dream, for I have gone back again to my novice days. This illusion is kept up in a way by having many of my early friends in religion here with me, so we feel very much at home. The Rector is an old friend of mine, formerly a fellow-student at Woodstock.

"The neighborhood is beautiful. Frederick Valley is very fertile, and the mountains that shut it in make a fine background on every side. The town is more like an old European one than its sister Americans. There is little or no progress. The people are comfortable; in fact Frederick is said to be the richest town of its population in the country —9000 inhabitants and eleven banks with $3,000,000 deposits. The people, descendants of the hireling Hessians, are not very attractive, but of a hard, repulsive type. I like the darkies, who abound and have good manners. A good many battles were fought in the vicinity, and the graveyard has a long row of headstones of soldiers. Our house was used as a hospital. But enough of the place.

"We begin our thirty days' retreat next Thursday, and it will be over on the 30th of October. Fortunately we have a very interesting Father to give it, Father Villiger, who has just returned from a visit to the Holy Land, so that his descriptions of the sacred places will be graphic and authentic. As a great deal of the time will be spent in meditating upon the life of Our Lord, it will make the scenes more real. Take good care of yourself.   .   .   .

"Ever your devoted son,

"HENRY VAN RENSSELAER, S.J.

261

After his tertianship Father Van Rensselaer was sent to Philadelphia as one of the Assistant Directors of the Apostleship of Prayer. The assignment was the very reverse of acceptable to him, for he had been always hoping to be employed exclusively in the external work of the ministry. But, like a submissive religious, he swallowed his disappointment, and set himself to what was to him a very irksome task, that of revising manuals, reviewing little books of devotion, devising decorations for banners or badges, with occasional preaching in parishes where the League of the Sacred Heart had to be organized or needed reviving. His very fine literary taste, however, which he had never ceased to exercise, was of great service in whatever writing was assigned to him, and not a few contributions appear over his signature in the volumes of the *Messenger of the Sacred Heart* between the years 1894 and 1898.

He had a happy knack of verse-making, a result of long practice, and he frequently pressed it into service in explaining the various devotions and practices of the League. It will be sufficient to cite one which has found its way into the League Manual. It is entitled:—

THE PROMOTER'S CROSS.

'Tis the King's own sacred sign
  Setting us apart
For a mission all divine,
  Of His Sacred Heart.
Let our Cross our ensign be,
Leading us to victory.

Not the metal value we,
　Though 'twere precious gold;
Its indulgenced dowry
　Has a wealth untold.
Let our Cross our ensign be,
Leading us to victory.

Whose the image 'graved on it?
　Jesus' Heart aflame.
Whose the superscription writ?
　Jesus' Holy name.
Let our Cross our ensign be,
Leading us to victory.

Let our Cross be full in view,
　Proud that men should know
We are to our mission true
　Whereso'er we go.
So our Cross our ensign be,
Leading us to victory.

There are others on the League motto: "Thy Kingdom Come"; the "Quid Retribuam?" etc.

When the Central Bureau of the Apostleship of Prayer was transferred to New York in September, 1894, Father Van Rensselaer found himself face to face with the Men's Clubs and Associations with which his whole life was to be subsequently identified. His occupations in the Apostleship, however, prevented him from having anything to do with their direction and organization; but at last, after repeated solicitations with superiors, his connection with the Apostleship and the *Messenger of the Sacred Heart* came to an end.

CHAPTER XVI.

Xavier Club and Kindred Bodies

EVERY St. Patrick's Day, for some years past, the crowds that lined Fifth Avenue in New York, were treated to a surprise, and the surprise came regularly. Mounted on a spirited horse, which he managed superbly no matter how it capered, sat smiling and serene, a black-coated, Roman-collared Chaplain, who was clearly a popular favorite. He was, as every one saw, not a Celt, and yet there he was at the head of the Second Division of the Ancient Order of Hibernians. It was "Father Van," and his appearance was a signal for applause and clapping of hands, waving of hats and flags and handkerchiefs. What right had he to be there? Not much in the way of a racial claim, it is true, though there were Pattersons in his family, and they were Irish, and that, besides his own personality, was enough to give him a passport to his rather anomalous position as Chaplain of the A. O. H., and to be one of the notable figures in the St. Patrick's Day parade.

Of course it was by some commented upon, criticised, and condemned. Was it not mere posturing and pretense, and a bid for notice and popularity? His friends often told him that such things were being said of him, and those who were not friendly let him know of it sometimes in unkindly ways. But Father Van Rensselaer was singularly impervious to uncharitable remarks, or even to harsh disapproval or denunciation, when the censors were self-appointed, if he knew he was right. He would smile at them gently, perhaps his lip would threaten to curl a bit, but usually he would not reply.

He knew that his Hibernians not only believed in him, but were fond of him, so he kept right on his course.

We find an expression of this esteem in a notice taken from a local Irish paper on the occasion of his funeral, and which, therefore, cannot be suspected of flattery. It is perfervid at times as becomes the Celt, but it is all the better for that.

" Father Van Rensselaer was a remarkable figure, which once seen would not easily be forgotten. Standing over six feet, handsome and broad-shouldered, he was distinguished looking in any gathering. He was descended from one of the oldest of the Knickerbocker families of the Empire State, yet he had a strain of Irish blood of which he was justly proud. He became converted to the Catholic faith and joined the Society of Jesus many years ago, and during all the time of his ministry he never wearied of doing the Master's work—assisting the needy, lifting up the fallen, consoling the afflicted and admonishing the wrongdoers. Those who were in sorrow or distress never sought his help in vain, and many a man to-day prosperous and happy owes his present condition to the kindly sympathy and assistance received from this truly humble follower of Him who hath commanded : ' Do unto others as you would that they should do unto you.'

" For many years he was an active member of the Ancient Order of Hibernians, and always took a deep interest in the welfare of the Order. As Chaplain of Division No. 2 of New York, he was unceasing in his efforts to increase the membership, and it was his greatest delight to say that it was the largest and most prosperous Division in New York County. Although connected with many organizations, he loved the Hibernians best of all, and never missed an opportunity of praising the Irish character. While he had many a kind word or excuse for any little failing we might possess, he was always happy to be with the boys, and on last St. Patrick's Day, mounted on a handsome horse, he rode up Fifth avenue at the head of Division 2, the proudest man in that great parade, and the only chaplain who braved the fatigue of that long ride, to show by his example that we should not be ashamed nor afraid to turn out on the 17th of March to do honor to the memory of Ireland's Patron Saint.

"And never was such an ovation accorded to any man as came from the hundreds of thousands who thronged that mighty thoroughfare when the word was passed along the line, 'Here comes Father Van.' Then, as his name was shouted from lusty throats, the scene beggars description, but will long live in the memory of those who were present that day. The true-hearted sons and daughters of Erin were proud of him, and he was with his own people, for he was more Irish than the Irish themselves.

"Little did we, who marched with him on that occasion, imagine that before the year had run its course he would be called to receive the reward of the just for having 'fought the good fight,' and having kept the faith; he is now numbered amongst God's chosen ones. With him has passed away one of the grandest characters of the Catholic priesthood in this country. He was the embodiment of all that was noblest and best, and a living illustration of the sublime maxim of our grand and noble order, 'Friendship, Unity and Christian Charity,' in its broadest significance."

Perhaps the most remarkable appearance that "Father Van" ever made on his prancing steed, was in the memorable Columbus parade, when the first of the Catholic societies swung into line at midday, and the last man passed the grandstand at one o'clock in the morning. It was night when Father Van Rensselaer, at the head of the Xavier Club, his Deaf Mute Societies, and others which he had founded or was active in promoting, came into sight. The transparencies, the torches, the Roman candles, the paraphernalia of the various associations made it a notable section of the procession, while the shouts and the cheers that greeted the leader gave ample proof of the popularity he enjoyed. The men in line responded. There was a detachment carrying a banner with the legend that they were the Xavier Deaf Mutes. Behind them, not separated by a sufficient interval, were some more Xavier marchers. "Look at the poor deaf and dumb boys," exclaimed an old lady; and just then the regulars burst out with their club yell, "Hurrah! Hurrah! X-A-V-I-E-R !"—"Poor things," she continued, "its the only consolation the deaf mutes have, to hear themselves shout like that."

In the parade on that occasion the Xavier Club had more young men in line than any other single organization, and the fine showing made by them and their co-religionists drew forth at the time, the following spirited editorial from the New York *Sun:*—

"The Roman Catholic Parade on Tuesday night was a demonstration of great interest and significance. It is not remarkable that many thousands of those devoted to that faith were in the long line, and that Fifth avenue was crowded with applauding spectators, for the Roman Church comprises in its fold the great majority of the Christian believers of New York. The impressiveness and the deep significance of the parade came from the fact that nearly all those who took part in it were young men.

"At this period it is assumed in many quarters that religious skepticism is prevalent, among the younger generation more especially, whether Catholic or Protestant. The sons are said to be falling away from the faith of the fathers, and feminine devotion is described as chiefly active in keeping alive the flame of religious belief. The descendants of Roman Catholic immigrants are supposed to have shaken off their ancient faith in a large measure, to have become comparatively indifferent to it, and to have passed beyond the power of priestly control.

"To some extent, doubtless, this is true. The Roman Catholic Church needs to make strenuous and persistent efforts to keep its hold on the children of its spiritual household who come hither from Europe. But that the diversion from its ranks was not important was demonstrated by this remarkable parade of many thousands of young men. The recent Christian Endeavor Convention showed that among young Protestants also, the incursions of skepticism have not been as serious as they seemed superficially.

"The circumstance that these Roman Catholic youth and young men came out in numbers so vast, proudly proclaiming their faith to the world, proved the ardor and intensity of their loyalty to the Church. They glory in being Roman Catholics and bearing banners and wearing insignia which make known to the multitude that they are unquestioning in their religious allegiance and aggressive in behalf of the doctrines of the Church of Rome. 'Church and Country,' was the motto borne aloft by one of the societies, and it is

the motto of them all and their inspiring watchword. First
and foremost they count their spiritual citizenship; but that
their patriotic allegiance is enthusiastic also, they showed
by bearing and wearing the national colors as loyal citizens
of the republic.

" When young men are thus eager to turn out in multitudes to manifest their fidelity to the Roman Catholic
Church and their subjection to its spiritual sway, one of the
secrets of its increasing power in this country is revealed.
The parade of Tuesday evening showed how deep the faith
of its followers is, and how ardent is their devotion to it,
though it makes no compromise with the modern spirit of
unbelief, but adheres the more stoutly and inflexibly to the
ancient dogmas rejected by the contemporary skepticism,
which denies all supernatural religion whatsoever.

" The religious sentiment is still the dominant force in the
world, and never in all history was it more passionate than
to-day."

The Xavier Club was one of Father Van Rensselaer's
pet enterprises. Its dominating element was athletics. It
had no religious obligations connected with its membership,
and for that he was frequently taken to task, but in this, as
in other matters, the censors did not sway him. He had an
idea which he followed persistently: that his personal influence would be powerful enough to induce his gymnasts
and runners and bowlers to perform their religious duties,
which, perhaps, they would balk at if they had to acquit
themselves of their obligations in company with others, and
with a certain amount of parade. After all, men are not
all made alike, and what will suit one will be distasteful to
another. But there is no doubt that their zealous Director

did not let them choose their own gait or go as they pleased. He followed them persistently, to bring them back if they strayed, or to keep them in the right path if they were faithful. He knew as well as any one else that much may be said on both sides of the question of such clubs; that they are not Church associations, that they are detrimental to family life, and the like; but, on the other hand, that they exist by scores outside the Church and in surroundings that are professedly antagonistic; wherefore he proposed to take conditions as he found them and try to get what good might be obtained by such aggregations. Men, and especially young men, cannot be prevented from entering them, and so he took them at their weak point.

The Club's quarters were at first west of the church, on Sixteenth street, but the building was demolished to make way for the Greenwich Savings Bank. Two houses opposite the College were then fitted up, and finally a suitable place on West Fourteenth street was procured, which the Club still holds. It grew rapidly in point of numbers, and had its difficult times in the beginning with schism and even incipient riot, but the tact of Father Van Rensselaer succeeded in aiding it to weather the storms. Its name figures extensively and always at the top of the list in the great athletic meets of the country. Possibly in these days, when the Holy Father has athletic societies show their prowess in his presence, such instrumentalities may receive a new impetus.

The casual observer would not have imagined that Father Van Rensselaer was the kind of a person that men of all classes would take to. He was tall, handsome, refined, well-built, well set up; a most presentable man in many ways, indeed, but there was nothing of the hail-fellow well-met in him. He was not expansive, hearty, jovial, witty, and he lacked many of the qualities that make for companionship and sociability. Indeed he was rather feminine in his general ways and manner of approach, but he was undeniably a favorite. His refusal to undertake the direction of women, his evident desire to win men to the practice of religion, and his unsparing labor in pursuit of that end always assured him a welcome, and made success a foregone conclusion. His boldness in accosting men of all conditions of life, even total strangers, wherever and whenever he met them, on the street, in the cars, on steamboats, in stores, in social gatherings, was at times startling, and one would fancy exposed him to insults and rebuke for what might seem his meddlesome officiousness; but he does not seem to have met with any such rebuffs. Perhaps his very boldness in inquiring so abruptly and so audaciously about a man's spiritual condition or religious belief, took from the individual he addressed the power of making what would have been thought the natural reply. Some one has said that it was not safe for a sinner to be three minutes in his company. An instance or two may illustrate this.

On one occasion he was assisting at a mission in the parish of a distinguished and zealous pastor who was conspicuous in the attention that both he and his curates gave to their flock. One morning the barber came to the house for the usual exercise of his skill. Father Van Rensselaer took his turn in the chair, and before the operation was finished he found that the man with the razor and brush was a lapsed Catholic who had been some years away from his duty. Getting him to confession was, of course, easy, and to the astonishment of the worthy pastor, who tells the story himself, the man who had been so close to him for so long a time, and whose spiritual condition he never even suspected, was made suddenly, by an outsider, a devout member of the parish.

Another example may be quoted as illustrative of this rapidity of apostolic work. Standing at the grave of the father of one of his devoted friends, he said something or other to the husbands of two of the mourners, and discovered what he had not known before, that they were not Catholics. Possibly the earth falling on the coffin gave point to his words, but at all events, there in the cemetery, before the homeward procession left the gates, the conversion of the two men began, and to the delight of every one they were shortly afterwards baptized, and have ever since proved excellent Catholics. What gives point to the incident is that there was a priest in the family, a close relative of the two men who were so expeditiously transferred to the Lord's household.

It was this pursuit of souls that prompted him, although already connected with other associations, to accept the office of Chaplain to the Knights of Columbus. We have no means of knowing much of his relations with them, though we find in his papers sketches of some of the discourses he delivered at their meetings in his capacity of spiritual guide. There is, for instance, a very elaborate study of the great Centre Party of Germany, that lifted Catholicity in the Empire out of the " slough of despond," and made it a pillar of strength for law and order. There is one on King David, and another on the Crusaders, and another which is an affectionate and minute study of the great Catholic leader, Windthorst, and so on. Such models held up to the Knights must have been potent influences in helping them to realize their ideals.

In the Resolution of the New York Chapter of the

Knights of Columbus on the occasion of his death they speak of him as "this noble man, this good, sincere friend, this enthusiastic worker, this pious and loving priest whose memory we revere." They express their "sincere sorrow for the death of this worthy priest whose sole aim in life was to carry on the work of Our Lord and Saviour. His life was an exemplification of true Christian manhood, and the highest type of membership in our honored Order." As a memorial of their esteem they proposed the founding of a scholarship under his name in St. Francis Xavier's College.

CHAPTER XVII.

Various Works of Zeal.

THE motive that actuated Father Van Rensselaer in establishing the Xavier Club, naturally led him to be an ardent supporter of the movement endorsed by the St. Vincent de Paul Society to form Boys' and Girls' Clubs. Here again the old objection was made: " Why not keep these boys and girls at home?" The answer was, they were not at home, they were on the street; and besides, that wealthy Protestant churches of the city were sweeping them in by thousands, amusing them, instructing them, getting them situations, and weaning them from the Church. Perhaps by showing an interest in them they might be drawn away from proselytizing influences, and ultimately induced to spend their evenings at home, though the tenement house conditions of New York made that a difficult proposition to deal with. The front stoops and entries have their drawbacks as well as club rooms, and so he gave the movement his hearty support. His first Girls' Club was placed under the direction of the Religious of the Sacred Heart and their associates, " The Children of Mary." Nobody, it was felt, could object to the influence that would be exerted in the walls of a convent. The girls were secure there at least. But the convent was torn down, and the Religious removed to the Bronx, and Father Van Rensselaer had to set about begging for something else. He kept at it until he secured another house which he soon put in perfect order. The Sisters of Charity look after it now.

It is almost like a contradiction to find this unwearied apostle of men interested in babies. Connected as he was with the St. Vincent de Paul Society, he knew the needs of the poor, and saw the advantage of a Day Nursery where poor mothers who had to go out to work could leave their little ones to be cared for. He therefore induced some of his wealthy acquaintances to pay the expenses of a few trained nurses, and then he went around begging for house-furnishings and food. One friend promised a daily supply of milk, another of bread, another of sugar; and though that is seven years ago, for the Day Nursery was started in 1901, the supplies have continued uninterruptedly till this day. A store of drugs was also contributed to be used by the sick poor. The nursery finally passed into the hands of the Sisters of Charity, and one of Father Van Rensselaer's last works was to secure a house next to the convent to give a permanent abiding place for the benevolent work.

In one instance of which we have been told, and doubtless it is but one of many, the Father went himself to take the children of a sick woman to the Nursery, that they might have the happiness of going to the country with other little ones for a two weeks' holiday. He carried the little baby in his arms, and tenderly led the two others who could scarcely walk without his helping hand. At the end of the two weeks, he restored the children to their sick mother.

Father Van Rensselaer was one of the first to take up the work of the Catholic Seamen. He had Promoters of the League of the Sacred Heart on the different liners that came into port, and they were so zealous in their work that it was not an unusual thing, when a vessel was docked, to find

"Father Van's" spiritual auxiliary, the Promoter, leading to St. Francis Xavier's Church as many as fifty oilers, stokers and sailors to go to confession and receive Holy Communion. This went on until the Diocese took up the work and appointed a permanent Chaplain to look after the seamen.

We have before us the list of Promoters which he carefully kept, dating back to 1896, the year in which the Seamen's Reading Room was established. There is a letter written on the S.S. Campania, November 30, 1896, and signed by four seamen, three of whom are found on Father Van Rensselaer's list. They are thanking Father McCormick, their new Director, for the efforts made in their behalf, but they do not forget their old friend. It is worth giving in full:

"S.S. Campania,

"November 30, 1896.

"Rev. Father McCormick:

"We, the undersigned, acting on behalf of the Greasers, Firemen, and Trimmers on the above steamer, fully realize the endeavor made by the Committee of the Catholic Reading Room to make our stay in New York as comfortable as possible, both spiritually and socially, and ask you to convey to them our sincere thanks, accompanied by the enclosed amount, being the result of a collection, of nine pounds, fourteen shillings, and to assure them of our love, respect and gratitude. We also desire to thank Rev. Father Van Rensselaer for the kindness he has always shown towards us. Trusting, Rev. Father, that you will accept this as a

LITTLE ONES OF NAZARETH DAY NURSERY

sincere token of the love and the reverence we feel towards
yourself and the Committee, we are, Rev. Father,
"Sincerely yours,
"JOSEPH HARRINGTON.
" JOHN DIXON.
" JAMES ASHE.
" JOHN ROCHE.
"Signed in behalf of the Greasers, Firemen, and Trimmers."

The Fathers of St. Francis Xavier's in New York have
for many years carried on a mission among the Deaf Mutes.
Father Costin, as early as 1869, had learned the language
in the Deaf Mute Institute at Fordham; Father Freeman
succeeded him and went regularly to the city to teach the
silent brethren, whom he had contrived to gather together,
in the college hall; and so it went on from year to year,
several of the Fathers being able to converse in the sign
language.   On any Sunday at the present time you may see
a group of sign-makers engaged in active conversation outside the College door after the congregation is dismissed.
Besides the union for strictly apostolic work, various
literary, benevolent, and dramatic associations had also been
organized among them. The dramatic element asserted itself
frequently, and every year theatrical representations of
gorgeously costumed five-act dramas were given before
large audiences which talked incessantly across the hall to
people in the opposite seats without, however, causing any
audible disturbance. The acting was, of course, all panto-
mime, but most artistically performed, affording continual
pleasure to the eye. Some one behind the scenes interpreted
meantime for the afflicted part of the audience who could
hear, but could not understand.

This dramatic association and most of the others had for one reason or another been disrupted, and the deaf-mutes were held together only by the bond of their religious necessities. But the good Samaritan came in the person of Father Van Rensselaer. He did not know a word of the sign language, but in some mysterious way he succeeded in binding up the wounds of the various organizations, set them on their feet again, gave them the wine and oil of his advice, and all are now rejoicing in their former vigor. The glory of this resurrection is accorded by the present Director of the deaf-mutes to Father Van Rensselaer. Indeed the various societies themselves convened after his death and framed a set of resolutions which they published in all the local Catholic papers.

Such was the character of his work. He never waited to be approached. He was out hunting for souls and always acting in obedience to the command: *Compelle intrare.* He was called long distances to visit the sick beds of the timid or obdurate, and it was a common thing for sinners who were not sick to be sent to him, " for he was easy with men." One poor fellow had been induced by his friends to go down to see him, and so one night while " Father Van " was seated in his confessional he saw the newcomer nervously going about studying the names on the confessionals. He was on the point of giving up, not finding the one for which he was looking. His spiritual agitation had driven it out of his mind. Father Van Rensselaer came out to help him: " Are you looking for anybody in particular? " " I am," said the other. " Well, what is his name? " " I don't know; I've forgotten it. Maybe it was Kelleher or Kinsella, or something like that." As Kelleher and Kinsella were near enough to Rensselaer, he had evidently found his man, or his man had found him, and it took but a short time to put the best robe on the poor shamefaced prodigal.

It was not, however, for the ordinary sinner that he felt an attraction. He sought the most abandoned ones, visited them in prisons, and stood with them on the scaffold, although his almost feminine aversion for anything shocking or ghastly prompted him to avoid that kind of work. He was a constant visitor to the cell of Carlyle Harris at Sing Sing, and succeeded in making him a Catholic before he was executed.

Were a visitor at the College of St. Francis Xavier to glance at one of the parlors on any Wednesday night, he would see it crowded with men of all conditions. In the midst of them sat Father Van Rensselaer. He was preparing them for baptism. He kept up the work year in and year out; new groups taking the place of the old ones. How many men he thus brought to the faith we have no means of determining at the present moment, but the persistency with which he continued the exacting labor, even when suffering from the ailment which finally carried him off, is worthy of all praise. Of course his work lives after him, and this class of instruction for converts is continued after the methods which he adopted.

CHAPTER XVIII.

With the Fire-Laddies and the "Finest."

IN the popular mind Father Van Rensselaer is especially associated with the firemen of New York. He was never Chaplain, though he would have been delighted to have enjoyed that distinction, but he performed as a free lance the work of many regular officials. He pursued the "smoke-eaters" continually; in the street, in their homes, and in the engine houses. The work was an extensive one, for there are many Catholics in the Department; but the Protestants appear to have always accorded him a ready welcome. It was all done in such a light-hearted manner that the straightening-out of consciences lost its terrors. The "boys" all liked him and were not averse to playing many a prank at his expense, knowing perfectly well he would not take it amiss. Thus on one occasion, we are told, when Father Van Rensselaer was climbing the stairs to catch the men in their beds, the officer below touched the electric button and the whole company slid down the pole to the ground floor, so that when his Reverence reached the top floor he found himself solitary and alone. He enjoyed the joke as much as the perpetrators did. He had to continue the hunt, of course, and he descended, but not by the pole.

One of the favorites of the Department was Chief Gicquel, a man conspicuous for the many acts of heroism performed in the discharge of his duty. Gicquel died and was buried from St. Francis Xavier's. Father Van Rensselaer sang the Mass and preached at the funeral. We have a sketch of what he said on that occasion, and it appears that the Chief had made a bargain with him. "If ever you hear that I am sick or injured, come to me wherever you are." The compact was kept, happily not amid the ruins of a fire, but in the peaceful surroundings of the Chief's home.

The men as well as the officers were faithful to him, and whenever he was ill, which was of frequent occurence towards the end of his life, it was a common and almost expected thing to see the fire-laddies making their way to his room for confession.

His foible for the Fire Department pursued him when away from New York, and we find him in Boston making his way around to the engine houses to see "the boys." He evidently caught them, for we find affectionate letters from them among his papers. They even went to the Fire Commissioners and asked for some testimonial to show what they thought of him. The Commissioner gave him a badge, which, one of the firemen said, "The Commissioner would not have given to his own son."

We append an account of this incident taken from one of the Boston papers:—

"The Rev. Henry Van Rensselaer, S.J., of New York, made a brief visit to Boston recently. During his stay, Father Van Rensselaer, who is the Chaplain of the Fire Department of New York, visited a large number of firemen and heard their confessions. Some of the men had not been to confession previously for years, their neglect being partially due to their long hours of service.

"Father Van Rensselaer won a warm place in the hearts of the firemen of Boston, because of his kind labors for their spiritual good. Wishing to give him a testimonial of their regard, they chose one of their number to wait on Fire Commissioner Russell, to get his permission to present the Reverend gentleman with a fireman's badge, as it was intimated that such a gift would please him better than money or anything else. Mr. Russell did a very courteous and kindly act in answer to the request, not only readily giving his consent that Father Van Rensselaer should be thus honored, but he would also have presented him a solid gold badge, at his own expense, had not the rules of the Jesuits forbidden its acceptance. The good priest was given a regulation fireman's badge, with his name and the date of its presentation inscribed on its back. Father Van Rensselaer is the only man outside the members of the Department to be honored with the regulation badge."

The following is the letter of the Fire Commissioner, which seems to be an answer to one of Father Van Rensselaer, acknowledging the receipt of the fireman's badge:

" Fire Commissioner.

" Bristol Street, Boston.

" My Dear Sir:

" I am very glad to get your thoughtful note. It is needless to say that my remembrance of my uncle, Father Coolidge Shaw, draws me tenderly towards those of his Order. Certainly Father Finnegan is a trump.

" That simple badge, not of silver, is a slight recognition of the feeling you have inspired among the men who know you.

" Very truly yours.

(Signed)   H. S. Russell.

" May 14, 1898."

Of course the policemen were "held up" on their beats by this spiritual roundsman, nor were the station houses immune from his investigations as to whether officers and men had been faithful to duty. Like the firemen, they responded, and it was a common thing to see them at Mass, or dropping into the church for a visit, or climbing the stairs to see him when he was ill. Like the firemen also, they were well represented around his coffin before the remains were carried to their resting place at Fordham. There some of them stood at the grave and murmured the last prayer as the coffin was lowered, and the clay was heaped over the body of their devoted friend.

Such was, in general, the work that Father Van Rensselaer chiefly devoted himself to for many years. His methods were his own, and were spoken of with disparagement at times; but it is to his glory that he brought back many a stray sheep who but for him would have been lost, and went far afield in search of those who had never known the faith and almost compelled them to enter the True Fold of the Divine Shepherd. Had it not been for his aggressiveness they would have remained outside.

CHAPTER XIX.

Last Illness and Death.

ON Sunday, June 2, 1907, appeared the first symptoms of the malady which in a few months was to carry him off. That day he had sung High Mass at St. Francis Xavier's, and after a light repast started out to attend an afternoon meeting of the Knights of Columbus. He got as far as Union Square and was in the act of boarding a car when he fell in a faint to the pavement. He was hurried to the New York Hospital, where he presently revived, but for the next ten days was given absolute rest and allowed to see only the doctors and hospital attendants. In falling he received a severe scalp wound which also needed attention. Meanwhile the news of the mishap had gone the rounds of the newspapers and was received everywhere with expressions of deep regret. During his stay in the hospital no hour of the day was without its stream of sympathetic visitors representing rich and poor, Protestants and Catholics alike, who made anxious inquiries about the patient and gave expression to their deep personal regret that anything untoward should have happened to good " Father Van." His ailment was diagnosed as vertigo. In reality it was much more serious. For years he had suffered periodic attacks of gout and rheumatism, which for months at a time had kept him confined to his room or in the hospital. After his seeming recovery, he made light of the mishap and would have resumed his usual duties in the parish, but the physicians prescribed an extended rest, and by their advice he repaired for a time to South Norwalk, Conn., where there in a country house for the Jesuit Scholastics of the Maryland-New York Province. In the early part of July another change was made to the Shrine of Our Lady of Martyrs, Auriesville, N. Y., where he remained until the second week in September.

Though relieved during the latter period from regular duties, his life was not altogether inactive. Even this isolated spot in the country was to yield abundant opportunities for doing good. Within a few weeks his spiritual influence spread out among the farm hands, the scattered groups of workmen on the new canal along the Mohawk, and the men of the neighboring villages. As a result, several old-time sinners were reclaimed, and in one instance an alliance that for years had caused great scandal was broken up.

Among the day-laborers on the canal he discovered a young Frenchman, a graduate of a Jesuit college abroad, who, in spite of his education and evident refinement, could get no employment befitting his station in life, but was compelled to earn a living by digging in the trenches side by side with the most uncongenial associates. To him Father Van Rensselaer's coming was a godsend. In the evening they would sit on the porch of the little bungalow that served the Fathers of the Shrine as a shelter during the summer months, and the happy youth would forget, for the time being, the toil and heat of the day in the sympathy and companionship of his priestly friend. Father Van Rensselaer made strenuous efforts to have him appointed to some lighter grade of work, such as that of timekeeper or accountant, and, though unsuccessful, his interest was as sincere as it was commendable.

During his life Father Van Rensselaer had carried on a large correspondence with all classes of persons, exercising thereby an apostolate which was the more to his liking as it never came to the surface and was seen by God alone. The number of these letters that are still extant must run into the thousands; but notwithstanding a public appeal, only a few brief notes from his pen were communicated to aid in the preparation of his biography. The fact speaks volumes for the value set upon them by their fortunate possessors. On the other hand, the letters of which he was the recipient, being largely confidential, were scrupulously destroyed. Only a few, comparatively, which were received at Auriesville, escaped the fate which befell all the others.

A summary of these few will enable us to judge of the general character of his correspondence, and of the opportunities it afforded him, and which he accepted, of working in many directions and of extending his power for good beyond parochial or even city limits. Among these letters is one from a penitent of his who had gone to California. The man gives a good account of himself, for " he had made the mission and is working steadily," but would like a letter of reference. He concludes thanking God that " his hand is fine," alluding evidently to some accident which he had met with while in New York, and owing to which he had fallen in with " Father Van."

There is a letter from the Department of Parks, New York, granting permission " for the members of the Xavier Club to make a satisfactory use of their permit." In another a mother writing from New Jersey seeks his advice about sending her daughter to a convent school. A Californian pleads in an eight-page letter for his active interest in the spiritual welfare of a younger brother, a Protestant, living in New York, " who is going through a heavy strain on mind and body." A French teacher, addressing him in French, bewails her physical ailments, which she enumerates, and entreats his help in obtaining pupils.

Another post brings a note from a man who is looking for a position and has to " get a letter from a well-known priest to Mr. ——, the head of the firm. One from your Reverence, if you would be so kind, would, I think, suit the purpose. Anxiously awaiting an answer, etc."

This is followed by a request from abroad respecting the " whereabouts of a poor friendless woman, who may have fallen into the hands of unscrupulous men or women anxious to possess themselves of her savings."

A pastor in a rural district writes in the interest of a penniless and homeless woman who had " lost one of her limbs," and has sought in vain for admission to a city hospital. Would Father Van Rensselaer use his kindly influence for the poor unfortunate?

Then all the way from Tennessee comes an odd petition from a poor fellow whose foot had been cut off in a railroad accident, that Father Van Rensselaer would " see the St. Vincent de Paul Society in regards to an artificial foot " and then, supposing his petition is granted, would " Father Van " work for his admission into some religious order " like the Trappists " or any " Catholic Order," for, even with a cork foot, he could " earn a living and prove a useful member of the community."

In a letter written in French from Boulogne, a mother thanks him for the interest taken in her son. " My mind is at rest since I've learned that Joseph is in your hands; he, too, tells me how happy he is, and speaks of you, mon Père, in all his letters."

Then one whose husband has ceased to support her entreats him for a letter to a certain wealthy citizen, that he may be induced to lend her a thousand dollars to buy at once a desirable house in a select neighborhood.

From Chicago, a woman writes for information about two students at the College twenty years ago, and inquires for their residence at that time.

A member of the Boston Fire Department is on his way to New York and wishes to introduce to his old friend " Father Van " another fire laddie from the Hub, a convert.

A young lawyer bespeaks his aid in securing an appointment in the Lawyers' Land Titles Office.

The acting Police Commissioner answers an application of Father Van Rensselaer for the reinstatement of a patrolman recently dismissed.

A young man in Buffalo, who signs himself " Your affectionate son " and is seemingly a convert of Father Van, congratulates him on his reported recovery, and asks the address of his god-father.

There is another letter from a young Frenchman seeking employment. The same day his influence is solicited to get the writer a position in a printing establishment in New York. A young man who thinks he has a call to the priesthood seeks an appointment to talk the matter over. He hopes that Father Van Rensselaer will remember him as the person he once called " Little Jimmie."

A lawyer expresses the hope that " we may soon see you home again listening sympathetically to the troubles of all New York," and endeavors to enlist his co-operation in a real estate deal. " I think a letter from you," he says, " would expedite matters."

And so the correspondence runs on and on, as if "Father

Van " were synonymous with a Bureau of Vital Statistics, or an information or employment agency. But the initiated know that he was but a zealous priest who was " all things to all men that he might win all to Christ."

Nearly two months passed at Auriesville, and on the whole the patient seemed to have improved. There was certainly no indication that the end was drawing near. He went about as usual, was most attentive to his religious duties, the Mass, the divine office, the daily meditation, the examination of conscience, and the rest. He also heard confessions, preached a short sermon every Sunday, and gave Holy Communion to the throngs on the pilgrimages. One day towards noon—it was the 20th of August—as he was reading composedly on the porch, he was seized with a violent spasm and would have fallen forthwith had not a companion caught him as he collapsed. Though he soon revived, his weakness thereafter assumed a more serious aspect. He tried not to lose heart, but he could no longer conceal from himself the gravity of the situation. A week later he wrote the following to a friend :

" The Shrine, Auriesville.

" August 28, 1907.

" . . . I am sorry to say that I have had a set-back. A week ago I had another attack. It was induced probably by a long walk of seven miles, the result of a drive and a breakdown of the wagon. It is discouraging, for I was beginning to consider myself on the cured list. I have had a very useless existence this summer, chiefly vegetating. There is really nothing to be done here except enjoy the fine scenery and air. I am anxious to get back to work. . . . Give my love to all the family and ask their prayers.

" Sincerely,

" H. VAN RENSSELAER, S.J."

On the same day he wrote to the Father Provincial for permission to return to New York and take up again his duties in the parish, thinking, no doubt, that, while the repose of a secluded spot in the country could not effect a permanent cure, he might as well fight it out in the midst of occupations which had become to him as his very life. The Provincial wrote back encouragingly:

" NEW YORK,

" August 30, 1907.

" DEAR FATHER VAN RENSSELAER:

" P. C.

" I received yours of the 28th. I sympathize with you on account of your temporary set-back; I cannot think of it as anything but temporary. Be not discouraged. The doctor will take good care of you, and I only ask you to follow strictly his injunctions. The Lord knows best, in whose cause we are spending our energy and our life. I expect to be at Auriesville for September 8th; shall then see you and talk matters over. In the meantime take your leisure and do not worry about work here. I am not forgetting you in my prayers.

" Devotedly in Christ,

" JOSEPH F. HANSELMAN, S.J."

290

There was nothing for him to do but await the coming of the Provincial. So sure had he been of his recall to New York, that he had packed his valise and was ready to start by the first train. He tore open the envelope in nervous haste, read the letter without changing countenance and, looking up at his companion, smiled sweetly and said: " Father Provincial advises me to wait." He took the advice with as much composure and apparent contentment as if he had been expecting to remain. The habit of obedience, strengthened by thirty years of unquestioning submission, is not apt to be ruffled by a trifle.

He left Auriesville with his mind made up to prepare for the inevitable. He felt that the hand of death was upon him. On the last day at the Shrine, a friend who was under the impression that Father Van Rensselaer had already left for New York, entered his room abruptly and found him on his knees in rapt prayer. He was not very hopeful, and said that he believed he had only a short time to live. The sequel proved that he was right. A day or two after his return to New York, Dr. Delafield, his brother-in-law, called on him, and that distinguished physician saw at a glance the terrible inroads which the malady had made in a few short weeks. He must go to the hospital at once.

It may be said that Father Van Rensselaer's last moments were in keeping with the whole tenor of his life. During the three weeks he spent in the hospital he was loath to be treated as a sick man. He would not lie down except at night, nor part with his cassock, which he wore constantly in preference to a garb which would be more comfortable. With his accustomed fervor he offered the Holy Sacrifice of the Mass almost to the very end, and clung with childlike faith to his beads and his crucifix. Love for his crucified Lord had been

291

a characteristic devotion of his life, and a love which through all the years of the scholasticate led him to make the Way of the Cross daily, was necessarily bound up with a tender devotion to the Mother of the Crucified.

When he made his First Communion in Paris, his sister Euphemia, who became later Sister Dolores, was at his side and received Communion with him. The same devoted sister had the sad consolation of ministering to him through his last illness and of remaining with him to the end. No more touching scene could be witnessed than his reception of the Holy Viaticum. He lay there in the stillness of the early morning, quite alone, save for the nurse, Sister Dolores again, and the Jesuit Father who brought the Blessed Sacrament. Father Van Rensselaer held the altar card unassisted, and when the Holy Viaticum had been administered to him, Sister Dolores, kneeling by his side, received Holy Communion, too. She had been with him at his first Holy Communion, and was now with him at his last. The priest left them alone to make their thanksgiving together.

As the end drew near, a fellow Jesuit, a familiar friend of his for nearly thirty years, whispered: " And so, Father Van, you are going to leave us; you are going to Heaven." Unable to speak, he nodded and smiled. There was no sorrow in his heart, since the bitterness of the chalice he was about to drain was sweetened with the hope of a blessed immortality. With St. Paul, he could truly say: " I have fought the good fight; I have finished my course; I have kept the faith. As to the rest, there is laid up for me a crown of justice which the Lord, the just judge, will render to me."

He expired peacefully on the 3rd of October, the eve of the first Friday. His remains were removed to the Church of St. Francis Xavier, where, following the custom of the

Society, a low Mass of Requiem was said on Saturday morning by the Provincial, the Rev. Father Hanselman. There was no sermon or eulogy. The services were rendered more than usually impressive by the presence of His Grace, the Most Rev. John M. Farley, accompanied by his three Vicars General, besides several other Monsignori of the Archdiocese of New York and of the Diocese of Brooklyn, a large number of clergy, secular and regular, Christian Brothers and Sisters of Charity. Fully three thousand persons were crowded into the sacred edifice. The Xavier Club was represented by nearly its entire membership, and there were large delegations from the New York Chapter of the Knights of Columbus, from the Ancient Order of Hibernians, and from among the firemen, policemen and letter-carriers of the metropolis. The Archbishop gave the absolution after the Mass. The body was then conveyed to St. John's, Fordham, and laid to rest in the little cemetery already hallowed by the dust of many of his religious brethren.